W9-BVC-143

Succeeding at Social Enterprise

HARD-WON LESSONS FOR NONPROFITS AND SOCIAL ENTREPRENEURS

Social Enterprise Alliance

JOSSEY-BASS
A Wiley Imprint
www.josseybass.com

Copyright © 2010 by Social Enterprise Alliance. All rights reserved.

Published by Jossey-Bass
A Wiley Imprint
989 Market Street, San Francisco, CA 94103-1741—www.josseybass.com

No part of this publication may be reproduced, stored in a retrieval system, or transmitted in any form or by any means, electronic, mechanical, photocopying, recording, scanning, or otherwise, except as permitted under Section 107 or 108 of the 1976 United States Copyright Act, without either the prior written permission of the publisher, or authorization through payment of the appropriate per-copy fee to the Copyright Clearance Center, Inc., 222 Rosewood Drive, Danvers, MA 01923, 978-750-8400, fax 978-646-8600, or on the Web at www.copyright.com. Requests to the publisher for permission should be addressed to the Permissions Department, John Wiley & Sons, Inc., 111 River Street, Hoboken, NJ 07030, 201-748-6011, fax 201-748-6008, or online at www.wiley.com/go/permissions.

Readers should be aware that Internet Web sites offered as citations and/or sources for further information may have changed or disappeared between the time this was written and when it is read.

Limit of Liability/Disclaimer of Warranty: While the publisher and author have used their best efforts in preparing this book, they make no representations or warranties with respect to the accuracy or completeness of the contents of this book and specifically disclaim any implied warranties of merchantability or fitness for a particular purpose. No warranty may be created or extended by sales representatives or written sales materials. The advice and strategies contained herein may not be suitable for your situation. You should consult with a professional where appropriate. Neither the publisher nor author shall be liable for any loss of profit or any other commercial damages, including but not limited to special, incidental, consequential, or other damages.

Jossey-Bass books and products are available through most bookstores. To contact Jossey-Bass directly call our Customer Care Department within the U.S. at 800-956-7739, outside the U.S. at 317-572-3986, or fax 317-572-4002.

Jossey-Bass also publishes its books in a variety of electronic formats. Some content that appears in print may not be available in electronic books.

Library of Congress Cataloging-in-Publication Data
Succeeding at social enterprise : hard-won lessons for nonprofits and social entrepreneurs / Social Enterprise Alliance.—1st ed.
        p. cm.
    Includes index.
    ISBN 978-0-470-40532-1 (pbk.)
    1. Nonprofit organizations. 2. Nonprofit organizations–Management. I. Social Enterprise Alliance.
    HD62.6.S83 2010
    658′.048—dc22

                                                                                    2009054088

Printed in the United States of America
FIRST EDITION

HB Printing   10 9 8 7 6 5 4 3 2 1

ACC LIBRARY SERVICES
AUSTIN, TX

Praise for *Succeeding at Social Enterprise*

"This is a must read for anyone starting or growing a social enterprise. The lessons learned offer valuable, practical and real insights from pioneers in the field. The frameworks and tools presented can be implemented immediately to help drive success and expand your social impact."

—Kriss Deiglmeier, Executive Director, Center for Social Innovation, Stanford Graduate School of Business

"By successfully weaving together the best thinking and advice from a diverse set of our field's leading experts and practitioners, *Succeeding at Social Enterprise* will be the new 'must have' handbook for Social Enterprise."

—Jed Emerson, www.BlendedValue.org

"This is a timely book needed for a movement that's taking off. The leading thinkers and top practitioners in this book make today's pressing issues clear to both the novice and the experienced social entrepreneur."

—Kevin Jones, Founding Principal, Good Capital

"Written by the nation's leading experts on starting, building and leading a successful social venture, this book is a profoundly important contribution to the growing body of literature on social entrepreneurship. No other book brings to bear this kind of business experience, practical advice and wisdom on the challenges of creating and sustaining a social enterprise."

—David Roll, Founder, Lex Mundi Pro Bono Foundation

Succeeding at Social Enterprise

Join Us at
Josseybass.com
▼

JOSSEY-BASS™
An Imprint of
WILEY

Register at **www.josseybass.com/email**
for more information on our publications,
authors, and to receive special offers.

CONTENTS

Foreword   xiii
  Robert Egger
Introduction   xxi
Preface   xxxi
  Kris Prendergast

PART ONE Start-Up and Structure   1

ONE Aligning Mission and a Social Venture   3

Keith B. Artin

Case Study: From $18,000 to $10 Million in Fifteen Years   4
Criteria for Aligning Mission with Business Ideas   12
Conclusion   14

TWO Doing Good Versus Doing Well   17

Kevin Lynch and Julius Walls, Jr.

Guiding Principles   19
Practicalities Beyond Principles   22
Mission Leverage   23

THREE Business Planning for Enduring Social Impact 27

Andrew Wolk

ITN*America*—Using Business Planning to Help Replicate
   a Flagship Program 29
The Process of Business Planning 30
Conclusion: Business Planning Accelerates Social Impact 44

FOUR Aligning Staff and Board Around a Venture 47

Wendy K. Baumann and Julann Jatczak

Running with an Idea 48
Lessons Learned 50
Have Fun 63

FIVE The Life Cycle of Social Enterprise Financing 67

Jeannine Jacokes and Jennifer Pryce

Conclusion 83

PART TWO Methods 85

SIX Product or Service Development 87

Mark J. Loranger

What's Different About Planning a Social Enterprise? 88
Case Study: Growing a Green Business 89
Lesson Learned: Follow a Structured Process 91
Let Mission Drive Enterprise 97

SEVEN Image, Advertising, and Communications 99

Martin Schwartz

An Image Must Be Grounded in Reality 100

Lessons Learned: Learn Advertising by Trial and Error 101

Image Building Never Stops 108

EIGHT Generating Sales Through Great Customer Service 111

Martin Schwartz

Building a Business on Exemplary Service 112

Two Customer Service Lessons 118

Sales Make the World Go Round 120

NINE Advocacy and Social Enterprise 123

Charles King

Social Enterprise Advocacy: More Than a Funding Stream 132

TEN Innovation and Technology Strategies 135

Sean Milliken, Clam Lorenz, Oktay Dogramaci, and Nancy Chen

Lesson 1: Don't Go It Alone 136

Lesson 2: Make Your Service Convenient and Relevant 139

Lesson 3: Focus on "What," Not "How" 140

Lesson 4: Ask Your Customers What They Want 142

Lesson 5: Trust the Data—And Make the Change! 144

Conclusion 146

ELEVEN Building a Performance Measurement System: Using Data to Accelerate Social Impact 149

Andrew Wolk

Case Study: How Performance Measurement Increased Social Impact 151

The Role of the Performance Measurement System 152

Making a Commitment: What to Consider Before Starting
to Measure 153

Five-Step Process to Build a Performance Measurement System 154

Report Cards: Making an External Commitment
   to Self-Improvement   167
Conclusion: Performance Measurement as an Essential Tool
   for Accelerating Social Impact   167

TWELVE Value Versus Waste   169
Kevin Lynch and Julius Walls, Jr.

Enter Lean   171
The Lean Tool Belt   175
The Lean Social Enterprise   180

PART THREE Leadership   **185**

THIRTEEN Good Board Governance Is a Good Business Practice   187
Sonia Pouyat

A Cautionary Tale   189
A Tale of Recovery and Success   193
Board Effectiveness Adds Value   195
Good Governance and Social Enterprise   197

FOURTEEN Leading Change   201
Deborah Alvarez-Rodriguez

Case Study: Converting Costs to Profits   202
Lessons Learned   205
Leading Change from the Inside Out   210

FIFTEEN Leadership Succession   213
Jim Schorr

Case Study: Leadership Succession at Juma Ventures   214

Lessons Learned   218
Conclusion   224

SIXTEEN Scaling Back or Shutting Down the Venture   227
Gerry Higgins and James Finnie

Case Study: Closing a Respected Social Enterprise   228
Conclusion   240

Index   243

MAKING CHANGE THE PRODUCT YOU SELL

I remember it as if it were yesterday.

I'm sure my father thought it was going to be a Hallmark moment— where he, a Marine Corps officer and jet pilot, offered sage advice to me, his wayward son. His tone contained the perfect mix of concern, sincerity, and love. His arms were dutifully draped over my shoulders. Our eyes connected as he delivered his message . . . no doubt intended to help me avoid the disappointment of the dead-end he assumed that pursuing my "life's dream" would lead.

It didn't quite work out that way.

That father-son moment took place at one of the crucial junctures of modern American life—the day before I was to graduate from high school. In my heart, I knew the old man was trying to guide me, but at that moment, in May of 1976, as I balanced between being a pseudo-hippie and a proto-punk, his comment stung like the first line of a hurtful haiku.

"Son, you should be a salesman."

My response was instantaneous, and as if completing the poem, I retorted;

"Old man, are you nuts?
I'm going to change the world!"

You see, changing the world had been my life's ambition since I was twelve, when my mother and I watched the movie *Casablanca* together. From the moment I first saw Rick's American Café, it was ordained—I told everyone who would listen that I was going to open the greatest nightclub in the world.

What my father didn't understand was that I was not interested in selling liquor for my keep or clumsily challenging authority with dangerously loud rock and roll music: my vision was to build a stage, and then use that stage to produce shows that would act like a beacon and guide my prodigal peers to the Promised Land.

This idea may have crystallized when I saw Rick's, but the vision had been percolating during the course of growing up in the 1960s.

I had turned ten in June of 1968, just a week before Bobby Kennedy was murdered and just two months after an assassin's bullet had taken Dr. King's life in Memphis. In the weeks and months that followed, I watched as those terribly turbulent times were tempered by the power of music. I witnessed how Kennedy and King's shared dream of an America unencumbered by racial, generational, or gender divides was made manifest, briefly, yet gloriously . . . at high school gym dances, on TV shows like *American Bandstand* and *Soul Train*, and in my own home.

Through the music of the Beatles, the Temptations, Marvin Gaye, the Jackson 5, and the Rolling Stones, I found common ground with my classmates and my parents as we, for the first time, began to share a musical culture. From the rollicking, reckless abandon of Little Richard, which my father, a Vietnam vet adored, to the powerful life stories that Johnny Cash, the Man in Black, sang to men locked up in San Quentin, to Simon and Garfunkel . . . music would help my family, and millions of others, come together and cross that bridge over the decade's troubled waters.

Six years later, following that conversation with my father, I lay in bed and dreamed of how a purposeful nightclub in the nation's capital might use the medicinal power of music to reexplore those ideals and guide people to important conversations that seemed to have been left behind in the 1960s.

The next day, my formal education ended and my life's work began.

Soon afterward, I got my first job in the "biz" and I followed my nightclub dream for over ten years, learning everything I could about how to run a business that I would use to stage shows that would integrate music, theater, satire, and dance with subtle, yet powerful social messages of equality, opportunity, and unity. I worked from one side of the coin to the other, from sweaty, seedy punk clubs and sophisticated, swanky supper clubs . . . and during that run, I was lucky enough to meet some of music's greatest performers. From the Ramones to Mel Tormé, from Prince to Sarah Vaughn, I saw all the rebellious heroes of my youth as well as the giants of jazz. All the while, I was fashioning a business plan that would show that you could connect music with mission, merge profit and purpose, and change the world by the way you ran a business. I wanted my nightclub to prove a point and counter the canard that my generation had to choose between two seemingly divergent career paths—either making money or making a difference. I wanted both.

Then I made a fateful mistake: I volunteered one night to serve on a truck that served meals to the homeless on the streets of Washington.

I'll be honest with you . . . I didn't really want to do it. I was in fact, quite the hypocrite. I could sure talk a pretty good game about peace, love, and understanding . . . but in truth, I had to be dragged kicking and screaming to do something in my own backyard . . . and in doing so, my life was changed.

Not in that I looked into the eyes of a homeless person that night and, like the biblical Paul, had to heed a spiritual call to abandon the wanton life. Rather, I made the mistake of asking how the group managed the business of "feeding the poor."

I found that the group I was reluctantly volunteering with had purchased all the food they served that night from one of D.C.'s priciest grocery stores. That got me thinking about the food-service industry I had grown up in, and how we collectively threw out countless tons of good food each night . . . not out of avarice, but for the lack of a health-code-approved alternative.

But what really caught my attention was when we pulled up to our first stop that night, across the street from the State Department, and I saw a line of men and women standing in the rain, waiting for us to arrive.

As we took to the task, my initial fears were quickly mitigated and I felt the warm sensation volunteers get when they try to help. But something else happened. As we served the line, I kept hearing the refrain "see you tomorrow night" repeated over and over to men and women who then faded into the mist of our Capitol City, juggling the sandwiches, fruits, and cookies we had handed them. Although feeding folks was right, I realized that we hadn't done anything to help them off the streets and out of the rain. It was at that moment that I became aware that we had, with love in our hearts, set these men and women upon an endless loop. This model was designed to redeem us, the givers, not liberate the receivers. Therefore, nobody was truly being served. We had *all* become stuck in a cycle that would be repeated the next night and the next night, and the next.

That's when I felt compelled to be part of changing that system.

By the time my wife, Claudia, and I had arrived home that night, I had the rudiments of a business plan worked out. And as crazy as this might sound, my idea was pretty darn simple—to use the same business model as FedEx, only use it for food.

The only problem was selling the idea.

A week or so later, I called together the very groups that had been taking turns buying food, cooking, and serving it, and I proposed my idea—if they collected food from the restaurants, hotels, and caterers and brought it to a central kitchen, then they could feed more people better food for less money. But more important, if you offered the same people being served a chance to enter a culinary training program, the line could be shortened by the very way the food was prepared and served while also "repaying" the food donors with access to qualified, entry-level employees. Everybody wins. BINGO.

To be honest, I kind of half expected to be offered the "Volunteer of the Year" award. But to my surprise, the very people who I'd assumed would flock to my idea actively tried to shoot it down.

"It's illegal for restaurants to donate food—the health department won't allow it," one said. It wasn't—they would.

"Even if it isn't illegal, restaurants or hotels won't do it," chimed another. I already had thirty high-profile food businesses signed up.

Then I heard the kicker.

"We know you mean well, but you can't train the homeless."

I was shocked. And when the shock wore off, I got angry. Then I decided to do something about it.

As if triple-dog-dared, I set my nightclub dream aside temporarily to show them that not only could this idea work, but it could work in a way that would challenge and ultimately change the entire way we thought about serving our community.

And it did. I used every trick I had learned from running nightclubs and applied it to feeding the "homeless." Little did I know that what I had learned about staging shows could be applied to the nonprofit sector, so much so, in fact, that when I launched my budding social enterprise, I never looked back.

For the past twenty years, the DC Central Kitchen has safely collected tons of diverse food donations each and every day, which is brought back to our kitchen (in the basement of the biggest homeless shelter in America), where we produce and then distribute forty-five hundred balanced meals to partner agencies. Men and women out of prison, addiction programs, or homeless shelters, who are enrolled in our twelve-week culinary arts training program, do the cooking while also managing volunteers. Since we opened on Inauguration Day in 1989 (George Bush Sr. was our first donor), we have distributed twenty-two million meals (which have saved partner agencies and the city tens of millions of dollars) and helped over seven hundred men and women find full-time work (where they have contributed millions in taxes). More importantly, close to twelve thousand people volunteer at the Kitchen annually, and then take our mantra that "Waste is wrong, whether it be people, food, or money" out the door with them and back home, where they can reinterpret it in their own communities. Now there are community kitchens like ours in cities across America, multiplying its effect and boldly challenging the status quo.

But that is only 49 percent of what we do. Our real job—how we spend 51 percent of our time—we want to sell an even bigger theory: one that defies recessions and could even help restore our ailing country's economy.

We want to challenge the very concept of charity in America. We want to usher in a new economic era. We want Capitalism 2.0.

Which brings me back to my father.

Turns out the old man was right. I am a salesman. In fact, I am one of the best.

For twenty years, I have used the Kitchen as a front for my real work—to sell people a higher level of freedom.

Sure, it is about freedom from hunger and unemployment . . . but why stop there? I wanted to take that notion even higher and propose a way in which we could free ourselves from the need for traditional charity—to make charity an antiquated concept.

To do that we have launched numerous social enterprises—from frozen meals we sell in grocery stores, to a full-service catering company, to a sustainable produce distribution business, to street food carts. These businesses take our message outside of our four walls. And whether they are frequented by loyal friends or visiting tourists, or profiled on Oprah or in the *Financial Times,* they are showing people, in the simplest terms, that in the smallest forms of commerce, lie the keys to economic freedom.

Take our newest social venture: Capital Carts. When you buy one of our signature sandwiches down at the corner of Ninth and F Streets, right across from the Spy Museum, you are affecting change in five powerful ways. You support a new gradate who is working toward owning the cart. You support other graduates who work at Fresh Start, our catering company, where employees prep the food sold on the cart and start at $13 an hour with full benefits. Any profit that Fresh Start makes goes back into the very training programs that prepare millions of meals while helping the next class of trainees get the skills they need to own their own futures. And because we purchase most of our ingredients locally, you also support local farmers. And all you had to do was buy a delicious, healthy, affordable lunch!!!

But here's the catch . . . our version of success isn't more carts, although that would be cool. No, we use this strategically located cart to generate press, which elevates that five-star idea and model for change. THAT is the goal. We want people to read about this effort or see it on the news and say to themselves, "Wow, can a nonprofit do that . . . and if they can, how can I help . . . and if this keeps a person out of jail and paying taxes, there should be more . . . and if I can get results like that by buying lunch, why can't ALL my purchases do the same thing?!?"

And that offers intellectual freedom, which is what I really seek to sell. I want to break down the barriers people have, so that they see powerful new ideas, and realize the role they can play in making them a reality.

To cut to the chase—my Pop was right about me, but there is a huge difference between a salesperson and a social entrepreneur.

When I go to work, I'm not selling the Kitchen, even though I think it rocks.

When I ask for money, my goal isn't to build a bigger Kitchen, even though it could be a nice alternative to the cramped quarters we've long called home.

Nor is my goal in attaining media attention to take the Kitchen "to scale," even though we've helped those other cities develop a similar model.

No, I'm a social entrepreneur. I'm not selling the Kitchen. I'm selling an idea. I'm selling freedom. I'm selling the future. The Kitchen is but one example of a business model that can take us there.

Some of you who bought this book are like me, born entrepreneurs. Some will have already opened one or more social enterprises. Others may have recently retired from a life of running traditional businesses, and may be considering opening a social enterprise as an encore career. Others will just be entering the workforce, looking for a way to make money, while not only doing no harm, but making your community, our country, this shared world a better place. Right ON. That's a powerful, game-changing idea. Follow it with audacity, innovation, and passion.

But what I hope you will take from this book is the knowledge you will need to help create a moment in the collective conscious of our communities, this country—and indeed the world—a moment when people clamor not for a few successful products, but when they realize that the most sustainable and effective philanthropy of all will be in how they choose spend their money every day. This is the 14K gold lining of our movement—the alchemy happens when pennies become power, and money and meaning generate sustainable social change.

Mahatma Gandhi, Dr. King, and César Chávez showed, through the **boycott**, that mere pennies had power. They offered conclusive proof that if the *poorest people* didn't buy salt in India, ride the bus in Montgomery, or buy table grapes in stores—the power, no matter how big in outward appearance, would shift.

Social enterprise takes that idea a step further, creating, if you will, a twenty-first-century alternative—the **boycott**—which rewards businesses that put community interest above individual gain, and incentivizes others to follow suit.

If your social enterprise can show everyday people, from the richest to the poorest, that every purchase has the power to liberate, then you will join the ranks of those great leaders who dared us to dream.

People will tell you it can't be done. It can. Others will say it's naive to try to change the world. Believe that you can. Step up to the plate. Be bold. Spread the word. We need you. The time is NOW.

Robert Egger
President, DC Central Kitchen/V3 Campaign
November 2009

INTRODUCTION

Social enterprises may seem like a new beast, but they aren't. From Goodwill Industries to newspapers written, printed, and sold by homeless people, to vocational services for people with disabilities, the notion that one can produce a social benefit, produce good products, and earn some income is not new. What *is* new is a systematic body of literature to help nonprofits explore and develop social ventures. *Succeeding at Social Enterprise: Hard-Won Lessons for Nonprofits and Social Entrepreneurs* is an important step in that direction. Some twenty authors contributed to this book—all of them social entrepreneurs willing to reflect on their successes and failures, extract lessons learned, and share those with you in the hope that you might benefit from their experience, gaining from the good and the bad. It's yet another contribution to social good produced by their generous hard work.

Social enterprises are at least partly businesses, and one would think that standard business practices would help them succeed. In some cases that is true. Yet social enterprises are most often hybrid animals. Some use volunteers. Some are accountable to volunteer boards whose members bring diverse business acumen—from zero experience to Fortune 500 experience. Social enterprises push themselves to operate in an entrepreneurial fashion while accomplishing the charitable goals of the organizations that house them. They are embedded in organizational cultures born of a covenant to deliver a public benefit, often at personal sacrifice. These dynamic tensions make social enterprises wily beasts that require special care. The authors who contributed to this book have deep and lengthy experience in tending these unpredictable beasts; more than one author here has been bitten and has the scars to show for it!

The chapters in this book move gradually from the issues surrounding the start-up and structuring of a nonprofit social venture, through the techniques of creating, marketing, and selling services and products, to some of the managerial issues such as technology and performance management, through leadership issues from change leadership to the painful questions surrounding service reduction or shut down. Hence, the book is structured in three parts—Part One: Startup and Structure; Part Two: Methods; and Part Three: Leadership. Most chapters include one or more case examples, from which the authors derive lessons to help readers in their own nonprofit business venture. You may start at the beginning and read through the end, or start with the chapter that promises to answer your most pressing questions.

Here is what you can expect to gain from each chapter.

PART ONE: STARTUP AND STRUCTURE
Chapter One: Aligning Mission and a Social Venture

Mission is the heart of a nonprofit. Unless a nonprofit's social venture is truly aligned with its mission, the venture is just another business, albeit one owned and operated by a nonprofit entity. True social ventures aim to do more with their fee-based services than generate profit. They aim to generate a social return on their investment. And that's what author Keith Artin teaches in this chapter. Artin is chief operating officer of TROSA, an innovative, multiyear residential program that helps substance abusers become productive, recovering individuals by providing comprehensive treatment, work-based vocational training, education, and continuing care.

Founded in 1994, TROSA generates revenue through several businesses, including lawn care, moving, catering, furniture, custom framing, and holiday sales. TROSA's client-workers are involved in all levels of the business, learning valuable and transferable work skills even as they improve their recovery skills and help TROSA continue its operations. This chapter helps you see how the alignment of mission, the organization's unmatched understanding of its clients' needs, and carefully selected business opportunities can create win-win-win results.

Chapter Two: Doing Good Versus Doing Well: Balancing Impact and Profit

A social enterprise needs both mission and margin to be successful. Of course, those two drivers are often in conflict. Authors Kevin Lynch and Julius Walls, Jr., argue that this tension is valuable: it pushes you, your staff, and your organization to work to your very best while grappling with numerous paradoxes. The authors offer a template for developing guiding principles that help you continually rebalance this tension, and show you how these principles have been applied in real life to the great benefit of clients and consumers. Lynch is president of Rebuild Resources, a $2 million nonprofit that serves chronic addicts in St. Paul, Minnesota. Walls is chief of staff for Greater Centennial AME Zion Church in Mount Vernon, New York, CEO of Greyston Bakery (a social enterprise), and a professor at New York University (NYU).

Chapter Three: Business Planning for Enduring Social Impact

How does one write a business plan that shows *both* financial and social impact? How does a social enterprise show its funders that there will be an enduring positive outcome as well as an enduring organization? Author Andrew Wolk consults with nonprofits, businesses, and government agencies to help them find innovative solutions to social problems. In this chapter, he presents a four-step planning process to help your organization accelerate its social impact. The process addresses concerns such as financial sustainability, organizational capacity to implement social impact strategies, and risk mitigation. This chapter will be especially useful for organizations considering whether and how to embark on a social impact business.

Chapter Four: Aligning Staff and Board Around a Venture: Sometimes It's Best to Ask for Forgiveness Rather Than Permission

Wendy Baumann and Julann Jatczak founded Coffee With A Conscience in 1996. It began as a coffee kiosk at the Milwaukee Public Library, and now has two locations, caters events, and sells whole beans. Its full-time manager and six staff deliver impacts of global awareness, economic sustainability, and environmentalism while serving up fair trade organic coffee, purchased from women-owned microbusinesses. Coffee With A Conscience is housed within Wisconsin Women's Business Initiative Corporation (WWBIC), a statewide microcredit organization, and an important part of the story is how the authors generated the energy for an upstart start-up within a larger organization. Baumann and Jatczak credit their success to several aspects: seeking unexpected opportunities, ensuring that the core business is in order, asking for forgiveness rather than permission, finding board champions, and having fun with the business. Nonprofits interested in starting a microbusiness within a larger agency will find excellent advice in this chapter.

Chapter Five: The Life Cycle of Social Enterprise Financing

A nonprofit venture can't go anywhere without access to capital. Moreover, it needs different kinds of capital from different sources at different points in its life. Typically, ventures move through four stages: start-up, establishment, expansion, and maturity. Authors Jeannine Jacokes and Jennifer Pryce explain these stages, the challenges at each, and how the right kind of funding can help the venture succeed but the wrong kind can threaten survival. Just as important, they explain where to find the right kind of capital to succeed at any given phase. They argue persuasively that success or failure in social enterprise depends on your ability to manage these ever-changing life cycles. Jacokes is CEO of Partners for the Common Good, which works with Community Development financial institutions to finance a variety of projects. Jennifer Pryce is senior investment officer at Calvert Foundation, where she oversees its social enterprise portfolio and other social investments.

PART TWO: METHODS

Chapter Six: Product or Service Development

Any start-up—for-profit or nonprofit—is risky. The same goes for the development of new products or service lines *within* a nonprofit. The reality is that many will fail; hence the need for good planning processes that mitigate risk and help you sort and pick the most feasible business ideas. Author Mark Loranger profiles his own experience as president and CEO of Chrysalis, a Los Angeles workforce development agency that helps homeless and economically disadvantaged people become self-sufficient through employment services and opportunities. The five-step process he describes here ties the organization's mission to possible earned income strategies and then helps the organization pick the best candidates for development.

Chapter Seven: Image, Advertising, and Communications

"If you build it, they will come," may have sounded great in *Field of Dreams*, but nonprofits often learn the hard way that the advice was offered by a writer, not a business builder. In this chapter, Martin Schwartz, president, Vehicles for Change, shows how his organization created a strong brand image by offering great products and customer service. He followed that up with an advertising and media campaign to bring in more customers. A great and needed product, excellent promotion, and top-notch service is still the best formula for business expansion. Schwartz has initiated half a dozen social ventures, including Freedom Wheels, which provides reliable, affordable used cars to customers and worthy families, generating more than $2 million in revenue.

Chapter Eight: Generating Sales Through Great Customer Service

Generating sales revenue while generating good work is the holy grail of social enterprise. In this chapter, you learn how great customer service leads to both outcomes. Author Martin Schwartz (who also wrote Chapter Seven) shows how his organization built great customer service via an in-depth examination of the competition, price, the target market, analysis of cost of goods sold, and a deep understanding of the market. For his organization, this means delivering a good quality car at the right price with a great warranty in a way that always leaves the customer happy—even when the car doesn't work out quite right. The great lesson of this chapter is that when you treat customers well and address inevitable problems with good cheer and honesty, you build the kinds of relationships that generate an ever-growing customer base.

Chapter Nine: Advocacy and Social Enterprise

This chapter makes the case that social enterprise is about social change. Lasting social change often requires a comprehensive shift in the systems that create the problems that nonprofits arise to treat. Because a network of laws, regulation, and enforcement create maintain systems, advocacy is the way to change them. Author Charles King is founder and president of Housing Works, Inc., which provides housing, health care, mental health services, chemical dependency services, legal advocacy, and job training and placement for homeless men, women, and children living with HIV/AIDS. The organization operates on a $45 million budget, one-third of which is earned income. King argues persuasively that advocacy must be a part of social enterprise efforts.

Chapter Ten: Innovation and Technology Strategies

MissionFish, now more than a decade old, launched itself as the solution to the challenge of in-kind donations. The organization developed an online environment where donors could offer in-kind services and goods to nonprofits and where the nonprofits could auction the donation and convert it to a cash one. But any technology-based enterprise faces the reality of rapidly changing platforms, methods, and improvements. In this chapter, MissionFish leaders Sean Milliken, Clam Lorenz, Oktay Dogramaci, and Nannan Chen share five strategies that have helped them stay on top of the best benefits of ever-changing technology: (1) don't go it alone; (2) make your service relevant and convenient; (3) focus on "what," not "how"; (4) ask your customers what they want; and (5) trust the data and make the change. Though every enterprise differs, the strategies make sense whether yours is a low-tech, high-touch one or, like MissionFish, enabled by the newest online and database technologies.

Chapter Eleven: Building a Performance Measurement System: Using Data to Accelerate Social Impact

Social impact organizations need to know whether they are really making a difference. This chapter shows how a performance measurement system can help an organization get a clear picture of its progress toward goals and mission, understand how to analyze its data for organizational strengths and challenges, use data to fuel continuous improvement, demonstrate performance improvements, and show funders why they should continue to invest in the organization. Andrew Wolk (who also wrote Chapter Three) is founder of Root Cause, an organization focused on advancing innovation in the nonprofit sector. The five-step process presented in this chapter, in combination with the case study, will help your organization understand how to accelerate social impact.

Chapter Twelve: Value Versus Waste: Leaning the Enterprise

Successful social enterprises need to learn to function leanly—to get the right things done with a minimum of waste. This chapter shows that lean operations contribute to social good. Various tools can help the organization become more efficient—so long as those tools are customized by the organization for its specific environment. This chapter introduces three techniques to help the organization become more lean in ways that fit the organization's unique profile: *value-stream mapping*, which looks at the processes of the organization; *Kaizen*, a Japanese method that emphasizes a continuous stream of incremental improvements; and *5S*, which is a systematic method for removing clutter and thus exposing areas where waste may occur. Authors Kevin Lynch and Julius Walls, Jr. (also authors of Chapter Two) have extensive experience with these methods.

PART THREE: LEADERSHIP

Chapter Thirteen: Good Board Governance Is a Good Business Practice

When a traditional nonprofit starts a social enterprise, the board has to grapple with how to create a culture that maintains the organization's strong, mission-centered core, that minimizes risk, and that still encourages the entrepreneurism that marks a successful enterprise. Author Sonia Pouyat has more than twenty-six years' experience as an executive director, fifteen of them with kidsLINK. Her cautionary tale of the failure of IMPACS, a social enterprise, focuses on the board's role and five key mistakes it made. Her story of board success at the Canadian charity Notre Dame of St. Agatha helps illuminate the factors that contribute to board effectiveness. Readers of this chapter who lead social enterprises will want to be sure their board members study both stories carefully.

Chapter Fourteen: Leading Change

Goodwill Industries of San Francisco, San Mateo, and Marin Counties had a problem: people were dumping their old computers at their pickup sites. Goodwill had to dispose of the computers, a costly endeavor. But the organization found a way to convert the cost center into a profit center—certainly a dream for any self-respecting social entrepreneur. Author Deborah Alvarez-Rodriguez tells the story of how she facilitated this change and the lessons she learned about budgeting time to think and plan, changing the organizational culture, prioritizing internal communications, and about the leader's role in staying out of the way of creative staff. The lessons learned will benefit the executive wishing to lead her organization toward a new enterprise. Of course, the story of the conversion of a cost center to a profit center is an inspiration for any social entrepreneur.

Chapter Fifteen: Leadership Succession

Unless handled carefully, leadership succession puts an organization at risk. This is especially true in social enterprises, which often rely heavily on the leader's energy and a small cadre of talented staff. The loss of such a leader can rob the enterprise of knowledge and competitive advantage.

In this chapter, Jim Schorr profiles cases of leader succession at Juma Ventures, a prominent social enterprise organization in San Francisco. Schorr, professor of management at Vanderbilt University Owen School of Management, succeeded the founder at Juma and then paved the way for his own successor. He shares lessons learned about managing the time line of leadership succession, mining the opportunities in transition, maintaining continuity during transition, the role of the departing executive, and how to communicate during a transition.

Chapter Sixteen: Scaling Back or Shutting Down the Venture
Many start-up businesses fail in their first years; it is expected. But what does this mean for a nonprofit that enters a social enterprise? Nonprofits are notoriously risk averse, and the idea of accepting program reduction or shutdown flies in the face of nonprofit culture. This chapter covers the high-profile closure of a respected United Kingdom charity, One Plus: One Parent Families. Authors Gerry Higgins and James Finnies of CEiS, a social enterprise business support agency, explain how the shutdown occurred and how impacts on service recipients, staff, and others were minimized. Their case study reveals lessons about mistakes made at the governance level, by staff, and by One Plus's commissioners and funders. Though the lessons are painful, the story of successful transfer and maintenance of mission-oriented services is one that all organizations looking at reductions need to consider.

Readers who have been part of the nonprofit world for some time—as well as their colleagues in the private sector—may be excused if they have some doubts about the use of words such as "enterprise," "venture," and "entrepreneur" in the same sentence as "nonprofit." In this book, they'll find ample evidence that the nonprofit sector, and private, for that matter, are filled with highly creative and energetic entrepreneurs, willing to place time, treasure, and talent in the service of social good and nonprofit profit. Enjoy the stories.

PREFACE

Different periods in human history have given rise to new innovations that then became incorporated into the fabric of society. Business is one such institution that began to emerge several thousand years ago starting with barter and trading, and has evolved to its current position of driving the global economy and providing us with an ever-expanding array of goods and services that have elevated our standard of living. Government is another innovation that has progressed through various iterations to the form we're familiar with here in the United States that provides for many social needs, from national parks to Social Security and many more. Nonprofits as corporations set up to advance social good emerged more recently in the grand scheme of things. Together with government and philanthropy, the nonprofit sector has played a huge role in addressing social needs and challenges, including stewarding the common good and assisting populations on the margin of society. Yet, despite the growth of all these institutions, social challenges have by and large become larger or more entrenched over the past fifty years. To name just a couple of indicators, the United States ranks low among developed nations on scores of educational excellence, we have the highest incarceration rate in the world, and social and economic mobility has remained stubbornly out of reach for a growing underclass in America.

What has become increasingly clear by reflecting on the past couple of decades of growth in the nonprofit sector is that the traditional nonprofit approach to social and environmental challenges is not adequate for resolving those challenges. The scale and scope of the challenges require something different. If we want to go beyond responding to these challenges to actually tackling and reducing their root causes, we must employ a different approach. For example, a homeless shelter and kitchen responds to hunger in a community, but is not designed to reduce the number of people needing food assistance.

Fortunately, courageous and creative people have innovated new approaches to social challenges, approaches that combine a nonprofit mission with the power of business for greater impact and sustainability. These new approaches are represented in established social enterprises that have broken new ground that others may follow. In many cases, these leaders, working in all mission areas and sectors from human services to education, from community development to the arts and everything in between, have honed their innovative approaches for two or three decades now. This book brings you the best learning and advice from these innovators. In the following chapters you'll benefit from their mentoring on all aspects of operating a social enterprise.

The lessons learned, the tips and advice provided, can help existing or new social enterprises be more successful. The hard-earned knowledge shared by our contributing authors, selected from social enterprises across the country, will help speed the uptake of best practices, so that more social enterprises can successfully tackle and fully address more of our social challenges. The social enterprise approach goes beyond helping mission-based organizations to be more financially sustainable. The mission-based purpose of these enterprises, whether it is social or environmental or a combination, complemented with powerful business techniques, represents a new way of organizing and building communities that is much needed to help generate a society that works better for more people. Social enterprise is an innovation that is destined to grow and evolve into a powerful sector, and this book makes an important contribution to the establishment and maturation of this relatively new discipline. I hope you enjoy and benefit from the wisdom offered in the following chapters.

The wisdom contained in the following chapters was generously contributed by Social Enterprise Alliance members, and I'd like to thank all of these leaders for sharing their expertise. Thanks also to Vince Hyman, who played an invaluable role in coaching the contributors and shaping the final manuscript.

Kris Prendergast
President and CEO
Social Enterprise Alliance
Washington, D.C.

Succeeding at Social Enterprise

PART ONE

Start-Up
and Structure

Aligning Mission and a Social Venture

*By **Keith B. Artin**, Chief Operating Officer, TROSA, Inc.*

For some, the idea of starting a social venture may seem like an exciting new frontier, something that energizes an organization and brings with it the promise of greater social impact or financial freedom. For other people, it is something they feel pressure to pursue—they see others realizing success with social ventures and don't want to be left behind. And then there are those who simply view it as part of doing business. But regardless of the perspective, the alignment of a social venture to an organization's mission must be considered. In the case of nonprofit organizations, there may be legal and tax reasons for this, but it goes beyond that. Getting swept up in a business opportunity that is inconsistent with your mission can take you away from your main purpose. A new venture can absorb a lot of resources, financial and otherwise, and the organization needs to consider what it hopes to gain and at what cost.

Before we continue, perhaps it is important to clearly define the terms *mission* and *social venture*. Merriam-Webster defines mission as, among other things, "a preestablished and often self-imposed objective or purpose." For the purposes of this chapter, we will assume that the objective or purpose is to have some type of social impact on individuals, communities, or society. A social venture is a business enterprise that also has, as one of its goals, some type of social impact on individuals, communities, or society.

In effect, a social venture is the combination of mission and venture, in varying degrees. The importance and emphasis applied to the different goals of a social venture affect how integrated it should be with mission. Though some ventures may focus primarily on profit, while placing some emphasis on mission, we will be looking at lessons learned and conclusions drawn from ventures where, without ignoring basic business viability, the emphasis is skewed more toward mission. On the surface, it may seem that all organizations would strive for this type of social venture, but striking this balance isn't always realistic. In some cases, mission or profit may need to be compromised. Deciding what compromises need to be made (and when) is often the challenge.

According to a survey conducted by Community Wealth Ventures in 2003, nearly 90 percent of nonprofits operating social ventures reported their ventures related strongly with their mission.[1] The insights that follow will be most relevant to those "high mission" ventures. The goal of this chapter is to help you understand what it means to align the concepts of mission and venture in a way that achieves social good and makes money. But first, let's look at the journey of one organization—Triangle Residential Options for Substance Abusers (TROSA)—that has consistently achieved such alignment in more than a decade of operations.

CASE STUDY: FROM $18,000 TO $10 MILLION IN FIFTEEN YEARS

My perspective on social ventures is shaped by my experiences over the past seven years with Triangle Residential Options for Substance Abusers. TROSA is an innovative, multiyear residential program that helps substance abusers to become productive, recovering individuals by providing comprehensive treatment, work-based vocational training, education, and continuing care. Founded in 1994 by Kevin McDonald and located in Durham, North Carolina, TROSA has become the largest residential therapeutic community in the state. The program gives individuals an opportunity to rebuild their lives in a structured and supportive environment where they can overcome their addiction, learn new behaviors, and become productive members of society. A 501c3 corporation with all business operations run through a nonprofit corporate structure, TROSA's revenue in the fiscal year ending June 30, 2008 (including in-kind donations and other philanthropic support) was just over $9.8 million, and the organization has close to fifty staff members.

TROSA employs an entrepreneurial business model that generates revenue through the operation of several businesses in the community. These businesses also serve a critical role in TROSA's program, because they are staffed almost entirely by clients in the residential program, providing them an important opportunity to learn job and leadership skills. Other key outcomes include rebuilding self-confidence and discovering the therapeutic value of teamwork and peer-to-peer counseling. TROSA clients are involved in all aspects of running the businesses, which include a moving company, lawn care service, catering, custom framing, a used furniture store, and holiday sales. In addition to working in TROSA's businesses, clients also staff many of TROSA's internal departments and work in such areas as office administration, transportation, construction, facility maintenance, and solicitation of in-kind donations, among others. Revenue from TROSA's businesses makes up approximately 60 percent of the organization's revenues, with an additional 30 percent generated through in-kind product donations. The remaining 10 percent comes from traditional philanthropic sources (individual donors, corporate donors, government grants, and foundation grants).

At TROSA, we always have to keep in mind both the mission of our organization and the limitations that our self-imposed rules place on business operations. For example, the peer-based focus of our program means that solitary work is not of interest to us—we look for businesses whose work can primarily be done in teams (or in pairs at a minimum). As one of our goals is to have our clients responsible for the majority of the work performed, any business that would require a significant investment in outside staffing isn't a very good fit. And because TROSA is a two-year program, we have found that businesses that primarily require skilled staffing aren't appropriate. Although we're able to train some of our clients in very specialized areas (for example, helping them obtain a commercial driver's license so they can drive a moving truck), we are limited by the length of time clients are with us.

In tough financial times, it can be tempting to make mission-related compromises in order to pursue a lucrative opportunity. TROSA faced this dilemma in early 2008. Downturns in the housing market had resulted in moving organizational revenues well below budget, and we were working on a number of ways to reduce costs and also find new business opportunities. We were approached by a corporation for which we had done quite a lot of work in past years (more than $1.8 million in business over the previous three fiscal years), and which had employed a number of our graduates in recent years. But the weak economy meant they had less work for us—down more than 50 percent from the previous year. Although their demand for our traditional labor was down, they expressed a need for help in a very specialized area of their business. It would mean much higher hourly rates for us (close to double what they were currently paying us), regular work, and our clients would learn a highly marketable skill. However, the work would be fairly individualized, and we wouldn't be hired until our clients passed rigorous training and subsequent testing. Our previous experience with this type of work on a smaller scale had been discouraging, as a few of our clients had become isolated and ultimately left prior to completing the program. These concerns outweighed the potentially lucrative upside, and we passed on the opportunity.

This situation and others that I have encountered in the past seven years have led me to some conclusions as to how TROSA has progressed from its meager beginnings in 1994. TROSA started with only $18,000 in the bank, was located in an old dilapidated elementary school, and had fewer than ten clients in the program. TROSA now serves more than four hundred clients daily between its long-term residential and supportive housing programs and has more than twenty residential and commercial properties throughout Durham. We have always maintained a focus on the program's mission, as displayed in the previously outlined case, but there are more aspects that have allowed us to hold true to our mission.

Finding a Good Fit

One area where TROSA has been extremely successful is in finding a good core business and building on the foundation that it creates. Moving services are the flagship business of TROSA, and it was chosen after careful thought and consideration. It must be noted that the knowledge and experience that TROSA's founder, Kevin McDonald, brought to the table was very significant. He was the main driving force behind TROSA's starting its moving operations within a year after opening its doors.

From a business perspective, there was a fairly low financial barrier to entry. To perform contract labor for national carriers with local offices took nothing more than manpower. No equipment was required, no operating license was required, and no specialized skill was required. Kevin started with the goal of becoming a licensed moving company, with the understanding that it would take some time to develop basic skills and deal with the legal barriers of obtaining a license. The work ethic that TROSA instilled in its clients was enough to get us off to a strong start. As some of our clients developed leadership and moving skills, we were ready to start our own moving company on a very small scale. We secured an operating license with the help of an attorney, purchased a single moving truck, and continued to supplement our growing business by doing work for outside carriers. Over time, we built up our fleet, built up our program, and built our reputation. It has taken us a long way. The ratio of moving to contract labor has improved significantly over the years—in 2000, it was roughly 1:1, in 2006 it was 3:1, and in 2008 it was 5:1. This speaks to the growth of TROSA Moving, which is now the largest independent moving company in the Raleigh-Durham metropolitan area.

From a mission perspective, moving is an ideal business. All jobs are done by teams, so team building and leadership skills get practiced daily in real-world situations. Clients have the opportunity to represent TROSA in the community and see the respect they get for a job well done. This helps build self-esteem and helps them see that they can and should be treated not as recovering addicts but as honest, hard-working people. Also, operating a full-service residential and commercial moving company takes a lot more than "lumpers" who can lift heavy things. Individuals have the chance to be trained in truck driving, sales, office administration, customer service, dispatching, logistics, scheduling, packing, and warehousing. And we make sure to stay current on moving and office technology so when clients graduate our program they are ready for the workplace.

Using One Business to Build Another

If an organization can establish an initial social venture that aligns well with its mission, organic growth can take place looking for business opportunities that complement the existing venture. With TROSA Moving, we went beyond the obvious fits such as residential and commercial storage. For instance, we regularly received donations of used furniture from moves. Individuals either were replacing old furniture during their move, or found that their new home couldn't accommodate all of their old furniture, and so were donating their unwanted furniture to TROSA. We needed to furnish our residential housing, but as the moving business grew, the supply of donated furniture far exceeded our internal needs. But we weren't sure we had enough furniture or expertise to open our own used furniture store.

So we started small, partnering with a local foundation that focused on developing earned income and other nontraditional funding sources for local nonprofits. They had been thinking about opening up a consignment store whose consignors would be local charities. But they weren't sure how to stock the store from day one, and also had staffing concerns. We worked out an arrangement whereby TROSA would help with the staffing of the store on a commission basis, thereby shouldering some of the financial risk without having any obligation for other overhead costs of the operation. TROSA also provided a significant amount of the original used furniture stock needed for the grand opening. Through our staffing arrangement, we were able to learn the basics of the business operation without making a financial investment. After about two years, the foundation turned the business over to TROSA, and we have operated the store with steadily increasing sales and revenues ever since.

Once we took over the used furniture store, we folded in another TROSA business that had stagnated in recent years. TROSA had done custom picture framing since its earliest days, mostly for in-house needs but also on a small scale for outside customers. The used furniture store provided the opportunity for a commercially viable storefront operation that didn't previously exist. In April 2007, the combined used furniture and custom framing business moved to a location in a newly resurgent downtown Durham and has experienced steady growth ever since. An expanding employment base in downtown Durham, combined with an increasing base of regular customers, promises continued growth.

What Makes You Successful

In order to continue to extend its operations, and add successful new ventures, TROSA needed to identify what its customers value most. It became clear based on feedback, not only from customers but also employers of TROSA graduates, that customer service was one area where we really excelled. The work ethic displayed on the job made customers feel like they were really getting their money's worth. We believed an enterprise that could play to those strengths would have a good chance of success. Our next step was to identify another enterprise that would highlight those qualities, and we realized we had one already under way that was ripe for expansion.

Although we have been doing some form of lawn care work for nearly ten years, it wasn't until the previous four or five years that we started seriously pursuing residential and commercial customers. Like moving, lawn care is labor intensive and is a business where customer service can be a big differentiating factor. The two ventures complement each other in establishing our local reputation of providing high-quality service at competitive prices. We have taken great care to grow the business at a manageable pace in order to keep on top of appropriate training and customer relations. People have come to learn that when they hire TROSA, they can count on both the quality of the work performed and the customer service they receive. As a result, business has more than doubled in the past two years, and lawn care has become the largest business TROSA operates next to moving.

Unexpected Advocacy

Don't underestimate the potential for your social venture to shape the public's view of your organization while simultaneously serving your mission. For better or worse, many people in the local metropolitan area think of TROSA primarily as a moving company. This isn't a huge surprise. We do more than five thousand jobs each year, and the majority of these jobs are local. People see our trucks all over town with the TROSA logo proudly displayed. It's not that we try to hide who we are in any way. We take care to instill in our clients a sense of pride in themselves and the TROSA program, and those assigned to the moving department recognize that they are the public face of TROSA. They openly discuss the program with any customers who have questions. And from a programmatic standpoint, rebuilding self-confidence is one of our goals over the course of the two-year TROSA program. We believe it helps with ongoing success and sobriety when a person graduates the program. But this confidence grows stronger as a result of the overwhelmingly positive reaction that our moving crews get almost everywhere they go. From 2006 to 2008, readers of the *Durham Herald-Sun* voted TROSA the "Best Movers in the Triangle" (this includes Raleigh, Durham, and Chapel Hill). And this respect for TROSA's moving company leads to a respect for the larger TROSA program, and changes public perception of what recovery from addiction can really mean.

I wouldn't claim that the warm acceptance of TROSA is purely a result of the moving company and its reputation. TROSA does a lot of volunteer work in the local community, and people know that we make possible many community events simply by our involvement. When the local neighborhoods experienced natural disasters such as hurricanes or ice storms, we have been out to lend a helping hand to those in need. And we take pride in our residential properties the same way we take pride in ourselves. We know their appearance and maintenance reflect on the TROSA program and are careful not to let those things slide. The result is arguably unique in the world of substance abuse treatment. Forget about "not-in-my-backyard" issues that many in our field face; we have people asking us to buy houses in their neighborhoods. And we've experienced the same sort of response to our business operations, where people look past the fact that they are hiring recovering substance abusers and ex-offenders and actively seek ways to work with TROSA.

The Double-Edged Sword

Social ventures can present some unique challenges, not the least of which are preconceptions people might have. From the onset, someone might have low expectations about the quality of the work or product because they might view it as a "training business" or otherwise less than professional. This leads to expectations of lower rates. Your performance and products can go a long way toward overcoming this type of mentality. Just remember that no matter how hard you try, some customers may still feel like they are "doing you a favor" by hiring you.

Another obstacle that you might face may not seem like an obstacle at first. There are some people who so strongly believe in your cause that they will hire you almost regardless of cost or quality. Taking advantage of these customers is not a way to realize long-term viability and success. Though your social cause may provide a competitive advantage, for many people this will be true only when all other things are equal. By offering high quality, professionalism, and fair pricing, you can earn business without people even needing to take your cause into account.

And if you are providing job-training opportunities for your clients, you do them no favors by running anything less than a top-notch business. Think about what your organization or social venture might look like on a résumé and if it's anything less than positive you might want to rethink how you conduct business. TROSA has had such success with its moving company and other operations that many local businesses are eager to hire TROSA graduates, in some cases even making exceptions to existing hiring policies. Coming from TROSA gives our graduates an upper hand in a lot of cases, despite the fact that employers know that, by definition, a TROSA graduate is a recovering substance abuser.

If you are an organization that relies on philanthropic support in addition to the revenue generated by your social ventures, you may also find that you are "punished" for your success. There are donors who like the idea of social enterprise but think using your for-hire services or purchasing your products is a suitable replacement for giving. If additional financial support is needed, whether it is over the short term or ongoing, making a compelling case can be surprisingly difficult if you have a successful social venture. Therefore, though there is no argument that building a customer base is important, be sure to make it clear to your donor base how social enterprise fits into your complete picture.

One other way that being a social enterpriser can create unwanted obstacles is in the case of outside support. You may encounter potential benefactors who want to support your cause, and think the best way they can help is to give your organization a business or business idea. In some cases this can be a great opportunity, and the insights of an experienced entrepreneur or business leader can be quite valuable, but the flip side is that often these supporters don't understand your organization as well as you do. This means they may not have thought about alignment with your mission and the details that may create serious problems for your organization. These suggestions and offers of help need to be vetted as carefully as something generated internally.

CRITERIA FOR ALIGNING MISSION WITH BUSINESS IDEAS

Drawing from TROSA's experience, we can see a number of factors regarding a social venture that might be taken into account. Although not all of these are quantifiable, and in many cases they are tested intuitively rather than formally, you should consider at least some of these criteria when considering whether a venture makes sense.

Fit with Mission

Though obvious, this can't be repeated enough: you need to remember why you do what you do. In moving services, TROSA has found a venture that is perfectly suited to the structure of the program and the values of teamwork, responsibility, and work ethic that we try so hard to instill in our clients. And it provides a wide range of vocational opportunities for people of varying physical and mental capabilities. The venture works on many levels, building individual confidence and greater respect for our program and the people we serve.

Potential Profitability

Profitability is not always essential, but a losing venture is very difficult to justify unless no other alternatives exist to accomplish your mission. TROSA has made some mistakes along the way, and we have chosen to shelve or simply not pursue opportunities that don't have sufficient margins. There are exceptions; for example, we are currently exploring the idea of opening a grocery in an economically disadvantaged neighborhood. Profits will likely be slim or none, but we see other benefits that are making us strongly consider moving forward. But again, a case like this is the exception, and more often than not there are less costly (or more profitable) ways to accomplish the same things.

Fit with Competitive Advantages

Look at what you already do well. Is there a way to modify it and create a successful business venture? Is there a new opportunity that is a natural fit with or an expansion on an existing venture? Starting up a used furniture store took advantage of two things we did well: accumulating donated items and providing outstanding customer service. The business has grown over the years, and for many Durham residents it is the place where they can most easily interact with TROSA and its clients.

Financial Limitations

Business ventures can be risky. Though some believe you need to spend money to make money, or some variation thereof, be careful to not take unnecessary chances. Test the waters with a low level of commitment if possible, as we did with our used furniture store, or grow the business slowly and steadily, as we did with our moving business. Or, if you are able, line up donors or investors to underwrite the start-up costs of a new venture. It might be an exciting way to get new people involved who might not otherwise support your organization as strongly in terms of traditional philanthropic support.

The People You Serve

You need to consider the impact of your venture on the people who should benefit from your mission. Does the business opportunity make them vulnerable in some way? Is that vulnerability sufficiently offset by the possible benefits to them? What effects will failure of the venture have on the people you serve? Consider the case where TROSA passed up a lucrative contract opportunity because we were concerned that the work environment might compromise our clients' stay in our program. Once that was taken into account, the decision was easy to make.

Reputation

How will this venture reflect on your organization? Will it cause people to think better of it? Will it lead to greater acceptance and understanding of the people you serve? Or will it reinforce negative stereotypes and foster animosity? At TROSA, we are very aware that public opinion of our program is often shaped not by the services we provide to our clients but by the businesses we operate. For that reason, we will not pursue opportunities where we doubt our ability to deliver anything but the highest level of customer service. As a result, many people have a positive perception of our program without really knowing much about the services we provide—but they can see clearly what TROSA can help people become.

This is by no means an exhaustive list. New opportunities may bring to light possible benefits that you had not previously considered. Ask yourself what you stand to lose if things don't work out (or even if they do work out) and what you are hoping to gain.

CONCLUSION

A social venture can be a powerful tool in magnifying the impact of an organization. It can, among other things, raise public awareness of a social cause, be a source of critical financial support, or help you accomplish some aspect of the social service you aim to provide. In some fortunate cases, it can do all of these things and more. But a social venture is not to be entered into lightly. As you develop any new entrepreneurial endeavor, keep in mind the effects that such a venture may have on your mission. Though the primary goal will weigh on your assessment of the venture, don't develop tunnel vision. Consider not just the obvious, but also the potential ripple effects. Organizations that have a mission to achieve a social impact have a responsibility to consider factors that a traditional entrepreneur could otherwise ignore.

Bear in mind that alignment with your mission may change over time, and be prepared to respond. This could be by changing the way you approach a venture, or it may be as simple as rethinking what you want to get out of the venture. Look for synergy not only with your mission, but with other social enterprises in which you are engaged. Take advantage of not only the expected but also the unexpected benefits that your venture generates. Understand that it may be necessary to educate your customers and other supporters if you hope to maximize the potential of your venture. Finally, even if your primary motivation is profitability, never lose sight of your mission and the impact you seek.

Note

1. "Survey of Organizations Running Enterprises." *Powering Social Change: Lessons on Community Wealth Generation for Nonprofit Sustainability.* (Washington, DC: Community Wealth Ventures, 2003): 57.

ABOUT THE AUTHOR

Keith B. Artin joined the TROSA team in 2001 and has served in the role of chief operating officer since 2003. At TROSA, Keith draws on his past professional experience in managing TROSA's day-to-day operations. Keith began with TROSA following two years of work with entrepreneurial for-profit ventures. He also spent over five years as an associate in the Public Finance Department of Robinson-Humphrey/Salomon Smith Barney, where he structured more than thirty-five publicly traded municipal bond transactions totaling over $1.7 billion. Keith currently serves on the board of directors of Habitat for Humanity of Durham (NC) and the Social Enterprise Alliance, a membership organization serving the social enterprise movement in North America. Keith received his B.S. in commerce from the University of Virginia and his M.B.A. from the Fuqua School of Business at Duke University. He lives in Durham, North Carolina, with his wife, Kate, and daughter, Phoebe.

TROSA is an innovative, multiyear residential program that enables substance abusers to become productive, recovering individuals by providing comprehensive treatment, work-based vocational training, education, and continuing care. Founded in 1994 by Kevin McDonald and located in Durham, North Carolina, it has become the largest residential therapeutic community in the state. The program gives individuals an opportunity to rebuild their lives in a structured and supportive environment where they can overcome their addiction, learn new behaviors, and become productive members of society.

TROSA employs an entrepreneurial business model that generates revenue through the operation of several businesses in the community. These businesses also serve a critical role in TROSA's program, because they are staffed almost entirely by clients in the residential program, providing them an important opportunity to learn job and leadership skills. Other key outcomes include rebuilding self-confidence and discovering the therapeutic value of teamwork and peer-to-peer counseling. TROSA clients are involved in all aspects of running the businesses, which include a moving company, lawn care service, catering, custom framing, a used furniture store, and holiday sales. In addition to working in TROSA's businesses, clients also staff many of TROSA's internal departments and work in such areas as office administration, transportation, construction, facility maintenance, and solicitation of in-kind donations, among others.

Doing Good Versus Doing Well

Balancing Impact and Profit

*By **Kevin Lynch**, President, Rebuild Resources, and **Julius Walls, Jr.**, Chief of Staff at Greater Centennial A.M.E. Zion Church, former Chief Executive Officer, Greyston Bakery*

I s yours a business idea that creates the common good? Or a social idea that gets carried out through a business model? Late at night, at social enterprise gatherings, the bars and lounges are filled with people debating this core paradox. As Shari Berenbach of Calvert Foundation says, "Mission versus margin is not an abstract trade-off." (For the sake of this discussion, we use "margin" as shorthand for "earned operating income" simply because "mission versus margin" rolls off the tongue better than "mission versus earned operating income.")

While the trade-off defines the decisions that need to be made, you must look at the question broadly. You don't have to settle for an either-or

Reprinted with permission of the publisher. From *Mission Inc*, copyright © 2009 by Kevin Lynch and Julius Walls, Jr., Berrett-Koehler Publishers, Inc., San Francisco, CA. All rights reserved. www.bkconnection.com

option. In fact, the moment you do, you cease being a social enterprise. Without your mission, your commitment to the common good, your desire to cure an ill, you are not *social*. But it is equally true that without margin, you cannot define your organization as an *enterprise*.

You need both mission and margin to be a successful social enterprise. Naturally, these two concepts will create some tension. This tension—and there *must* be tension—will push on you, your decisions, your staff, your culture, and your customer relations. It will permeate every facet of your business. You had better give it as much thought as any other part of your business, be it your financing, marketing, or administration, or else leading a social enterprise will bring out the closet schizophrenic in you and your employees.

If you find yourself thinking it is one way or another, then you are in an unhealthy place. Using the body as an analogy, is one part of your body more important than another? Would you rather do without your hands or without your feet? Would you rather have no eyes or no ears? Would you rather have a brain or a heart? What choice would you make? How would you participate in the conversation about those choices?

The body thrives when all bodily functions work in unison, each part supporting the other. So it is with the world. So it is with a social enterprise and with mission and margin. On balance, mission and margin are absolute equals. And yet on any given day, the proportions might appear to be 70–30 one way or the other. Just as it is with the body. In a track race the feet are more important to the body than the hands, but at a backyard cookout the hands carry the day. Sometimes the mission will feed the margin, and other times the margin will feed the mission. Depending on the situation, you may need to protect the mission by defending the margin or defend the margin by protecting the mission.

Mission versus margin (and margin versus mission) is, intellectually, a macro paradox. But in the day-to-day operations of a social enterprise, it is played out in an endless series of micro paradoxes.

GUIDING PRINCIPLES

In order to maintain some level of sanity for yourself, your board, and your employees, you must tackle these paradoxes head-on. One way to do so is by establishing a written set of guiding principles that gets all stakeholders on the same page in defining success.

Establishing these principles before you begin to operate the business is key. Doing so in the heat of battle will lead to wasted energy going in directions that will only accidentally achieve your desired outcome. You would not go to a meeting at a bank and, in front of the banker, calculate for the first time how much money you need to start your business. Nor would you sit in front of your customer calculating the cost of raw materials to determine your sales price. You recognize the obvious need to be prepared in those instances. Similarly, you need to be prepared for the larger decisions that will confront you. All stakeholders need to know where the values of the business lie. They need to know where you, as the business leader, stand. They need to know what will drive you and your decisions.

Guiding principles are more descriptive than a mission statement. They describe what can be expected of you in various situations. They should be prepared in cooperation with your board and employees and be readily available to them. State them as overarching principles that do not handcuff management but do provide structure and guidance. Your strategic planning and goal setting should flow from your mission and guiding principles, which should be changed only with a great deal of deliberation.

Your guiding principles should be brief, simple, and few in number. Six should be about right. Although we have prepared a longer yet incomplete list to illustrate some of the potential areas your guiding principles might cover [see Table 2.1], your mileage may vary. The key principles that are important to you will depend entirely on the industry you're in and the particular "brand" of common good you are seeking to create.

Table 2.1
Sample Elements of Guiding Principles

Area:	Ask Yourself:
Employees	What is your role with our employees? Are they a means to an end or are they an intricate part of who you are? How does that manifest itself in your business and its structure?
Community	What is your relationship to your community? Is it simply a place of business? Could you move a hundred miles away without any loss of impact or connection? Or would your community miss you because you were having a positive impact?
Environment	What will you do and not do to earn a profit? What are your profit goals? Who is rewarded when a profit is made?
Wages	How will wages be calculated? What is your commitment to moving in the direction of a living wage? What type of benefits are you committed to providing?
Governance	To whom is the organization accountable? To whom are you, the leader, accountable?
Decision Making	From whom are you going to seek input, counsel, and advice? Will things be decided by consensus or chain of command? Where will the buck stop?
Business Ethics	What will be the basic business terms by which you will conduct commerce?
Diversity	Whom will you welcome into your organization and how hard will you work to get them there?
Personal Development	To what degree will the enterprise be a vehicle for personal growth? To what degree will you seek to encourage spirit at work? What about fun?
Advocacy and Public Policy	Which social issues is the organization passionate about? Will you seek to affect those issues with your work alone? Will you be a public voice? Will you seek to influence public policy?
Impact	How will you measure your impact, and what will you call success? What are you willing to spend on measurement? How open will you be to the course corrections that measurement suggests?

Here is an example of guiding principles for Greyston Bakery, a social enterprise organization run by author and CEO Julius Walls, Jr.

The Principles We Practice

- We don't hire people to bake brownies; we bake brownies to hire people.
- The bakery will strive to be a model for inner-city business development committed to Southwest Yonkers.
- The bakery should consistently achieve an operating profit.
- The bakery will maintain an open-hiring policy.
- The bakery will actively integrate itself into the Greyston Mandala.
- A central purpose of the Greyston Bakery is to generate profits that can help sustain the work of the Greyston Mandala.
- The bakery will rigorously measure, document, and monitor its progress toward all non-financial goals.
- The bakery will empower its employees by compensating them fairly for their efforts and move towards a living wage.
- The bakery will strive for stable employee turnover rates for post-apprenticeship employees.
- The bakery will automate its production whenever such changes are fiscally appropriate.
- The bakery will support the individual growth of its employees through its PathMaking Program.

Source: Greyston Bakery's Web site, www.greystonbakery.com. Used with permission

Greyston maximizes the benefit of its guiding principles by promoting them. The principles leave no confusion about what the CEO and his team aim to accomplish.

Communicate your principles widely, including on your Web site, for all to see. You will attract the stakeholders you want to work with and will repel those you don't. Life is short!

Once you've done the hard work of creating your guiding principles, your life will become a lot simpler. The world with which you and your enterprise interact will know where you stand.

PRACTICALITIES BEYOND PRINCIPLES

We firmly believe that a well-thought-out model, a clear set of operating principles, a combination of deep passion and commitment, and sufficient attraction of capital will, taken altogether, allow you to have both mission and margin. But again, that is a macro concept. Out there in the trenches, where you spend most of your life as the leader of a social enterprise, you face constant individual decisions where you *do* have to give more or less weight to one or the other of these imperatives.

Joan Pikas, founder of The Enterprising Kitchen, recognizes the conundrum as it relates to pricing issues in the highly competitive soap market in which she operates. She says:

> I am thrilled that we are making soap, and I think that makes us special. But at the same time, what I care about is that we are giving people an opportunity to get some work experience and get on their feet. If I thought there was a big customer out there who would buy $50,000 worth of product, which would give us a lot of work to do, but I needed to lower the per item price, which meant that we were just barely covering our costs . . . I would say "okay we are going for this because it means we are going to have x number of women here working on this project."

Now, mind you, that's not a trade-off Pikas can make every day. She may need to augment that big $50,000 customer with lots of smaller, high-margin customers. Or she may need to improve the efficiency of her operations to lower her break-even point. She may need to amass more purchasing clout to lower her raw material costs. Or she may need to accept a larger portion of her budget via public support. But it's hardly an either-or, and that's the important point.

Most daily decisions aren't made in perfect mission-margin balance. They will tip in one direction.

MISSION LEVERAGE

Jeffrey Hollender, founder of Seventh Generation, says his company has a variety of missions:

> On the one level [our mission] is to provide safer and healthier household products to consumers. Wrapped into that is—probably equally important—our goal to both educate people about environmental, social, and health issues as well as inspire them to believe that through their actions they can make a difference. On another level—and no less important—it is to create a working experience for the people at the company that is better and more fulfilling than they have had anywhere else and that allows them an opportunity to grow and develop as human beings. In a third area, we very much wanted to be a model for what was possible in business terms of integrating our mission with our financial objectives.

It is not a coincidence that Hollender has managed to build one of the most successful social enterprises (if you consider $100 million in sales and nearly 50 percent margins successful) around not just one but at least three missions—because not only can you make money while pursuing a mission, pursuing that mission can *help* you make money.

Let's start with your employees. You'll quickly notice that they'll operate with a higher level of passion if they resonate with your cause. You will have the opportunity to attract better talent because your company provides more than just a paycheck. Don't use this knowledge to underpay your employees: pay them what they deserve. Their commitment to the mission will provide you an opportunity to connect with them in ways of which other businesses can only dream. People really *do* care about their planet and their fellow humans and are just waiting for an opportunity to express this. Your mission-driven business will give them that chance.

Now on to your customers. Does it matter to them that yours is a mission-driven company? The short answer is yes. Consider Rebuild Resources, the social enterprise run by coauthor Kevin Lynch that provides transitional employment to recovering, reentering persons. Its primary business is screen printing and embroidering corporate apparel and promotional items. A substantial portion of Rebuild's customer base comes to it over the Internet. In testing various campaigns, Rebuild has definitely concluded that messages incorporating its social mission attract more inquiries than those that don't. But once the lead comes in, Rebuild then must be every bit as good on quality, service and price as its non–social enterprise competitors. If it's not, it loses the deal, every time. Mission is a door-opener and a tie-breaker—but not a crutch that can support poor execution.

Mission also provides positive leverage to your operations. Being good in one area tends to make you good in others. For example, before you know it you may end up greening your facilities, which tends to reduce costs, liabilities, and regulatory problems. Or you may end up getting your staff involved in community projects, leading to new customers, better suppliers, better real estate and facility options, or political support when you most need it.

Mission leads to financial leverage. In general, banks tend to be nicer to organizations that are doing good because it makes *them* look good. In the worst-case scenario (one we sincerely hope you never face), shutting down or foreclosing on a "do-good" enterprise is the last thing a bank would ever want to do. In the best case, remember that banks lend on a combination of character, capacity, and collateral and will often give more than a passing nod to the superior character of social enterprisers.

In fact, in just about every area of your enterprise, you can create a positive trade-off between mission and margin. Use this trade-off to create competitive advantage.

Of course, mission-versus-margin creates a whole set of challenges, too, but those are the stuff of another chapter. The next time someone asks whether your mission is more important than your margin, tell her that your mission and margin are equally important. Tell him that you started your business because you had a yearning to change the way the world operates, that the institution having the most effective impact on the world today is business, and that you are going to use that power for good. Tell her that you wouldn't have started your business if you did not have this yearning for change. Tell him that you couldn't be successful without margin and wouldn't want to be without mission. Tell her that your business can't sustain itself without profits, and that the world can't sustain itself without your business.

Tell him that you run a social enterprise—where mission and margin are *not* an either-or.

ABOUT THE AUTHORS

Kevin Lynch is president of Rebuild Resources, Inc., a $2.2 million nonprofit social-purpose business in St. Paul, Minnesota, that helps chronic addicts and alcoholics find a path to sobriety through a program of spiritual recovery and work. Rebuild's business operations include a custom apparel and promotional-items business and a contract manufacturer. These businesses provide the recovery environment for Rebuild's student-employees and serve as the economic engines that fuel the enterprise.

Lynch is currently a board member of the Social Enterprise Alliance and has served on several national and local boards, including those of Social Venture Network, Headwaters Foundation for Justice, Twin Cities Community Gospel Choir, and (as the cofounder) Responsible Minnesota Business. Lynch has started several successful businesses, including a direct-mail business (while in college) and Lynch Jarvis Jones, a social enterprise ad agency whose mission was to create positive social change through the power of advertising and marketing.

Julius Walls, Jr., is chief of staff for Greater Centennial A.M.E. Zion Church, a five-thousand-member church in Mount Vernon, New York, as of July 2009. Walls supports the pastor, Rev. Dr. W. Darin Moore, in overseeing their more than fifteen ministers and over one hundred ministries. As CEO of the Greyston Bakery, Walls grew the Bakery to a $7 million social enterprise. Walls is a professor at the business graduate schools at NYU and Bainbridge Graduate Institute, the coauthor of *MISSION, INC., The Practitioners Guide to Social Enterprise*, 2008, and participates in Harvard University's Executive Session on Transforming Cities Through Civic Entrepreneurs. Born in Brooklyn, New York, Walls attended college seminary before receiving his B.S. from Concordia College. Walls served as vice president of operations for a chocolate manufacturing company and founded his own chocolate company, Sweet Roots, Inc. Core ingredients in Walls' life are his spiritual practice, family, and service. Walls serves on several local and national nonprofit and government boards.

Business Planning for Enduring Social Impact

*By **Andrew Wolk**, Founder, Root Cause*

The past decade has seen the emergence of scores of social-entrepreneurial organizations dedicated to developing innovative new solutions to social problems. Among the most prominent of these organizations are Teach for America, for which Wendy Kopp was named one of "America's Best Leaders" by *U.S. News & World Report*; Muhammad Yunus's Grameen Bank, which was awarded the Nobel Peace Prize; and Benetech, for which founder Jim Fruchterman received a "genius" award from the MacArthur Foundation. To turn their social innovations into successful organizational models, these organizations draw on private-sector strategic thinking. Business planning is an essential tool for facilitating such thinking.

In the private sector, a *business plan* is a road map for carrying out an organizational strategy that is tied to an innovative business model. The plan describes the steps a company will take to generate profit. It also establishes exacting methods to measure impact, provides guidelines for making data-driven decisions, and helps secure reliable streams of financing and resources. Of course, a key underlying intention is to provide a "sales pitch" to attract investors who will invest in the organization—based on ongoing, proven results.

Business planning for organizations whose primary mission is social impact—including nonprofits, government agencies, and for-profit enterprises—demands the same strategic rigor and financial savvy. Typically, the business plan for an organization focused on social impact outlines a three-to-five-year course of action that guides the organization toward its mission. The plan also explains to social impact investors how their money will be put to use, in addition to articulating the "social returns" they can expect. (The term "social impact investor" refers to anyone who provides resources to fund a business plan for enduring social impact.)

Business plans for organizations dedicated to social impact, then, are important tools that play multiple roles:

- **Serve as a road map**: delineating a course of action for the organization's leadership, governance structure, and social investors to follow in carrying out the organization's mission, making day-to-day decisions, and ultimately creating enduring social impact.

- **Support the acquisition of resources**: serving as the most important fund-raising tool for soliciting new and returning investments from corporations, foundations, government, and individuals, the business plan can also aid in seeking sources of earned income and in-kind goods and services.

- **Provide a method of measuring and monitoring performance**: establishing a common point of reference for stakeholders outside the organization (such as board members), enabling them to ensure that their money is being used well.

- **Help establish partnerships**: becoming an essential recruitment tool for identifying partnerships and soliciting political support from a variety of stakeholders.

- **Enrich the field**: providing practical insights by articulating the organization's approach to the problem in a form that can be shared with practitioners, social investors, researchers, and policy makers.

The business planning approach described in this chapter draws on Root Cause's unique methodology developed through its consulting work with organizations throughout the United States, as well as with a number of international organizations. Root Cause, a nonprofit organization, supports and brings together social innovators and social impact investors.

ITNAMERICA—USING BUSINESS PLANNING TO HELP REPLICATE A FLAGSHIP PROGRAM

To illustrate the promise of business planning, consider the experience of Independent Transportation Network® *America* (ITN*America*). This nonprofit organization offers a safe, sustainable, consumer-oriented transportation service for older drivers. In 2005, Executive Director Katherine Freund received funding from The Atlantic Philanthropies, the Great Bay Foundation for Social Entrepreneurs, and the Sam L. Cohen Foundation to develop a business plan. The objective was to enable her ten-year-old program based in Portland, Maine, to increase its impact in addressing the lack of transportation options for seniors across the United States. The organization articulated its innovative model and explored opportunities to expand its flagship program in Portland to other cities.

The final business plan outlined a set of strategies and action plans to help the organization increase its social impact by expanding to new sites. It also included a performance measurement system to provide the organization with data that enable the organization to identify opportunities to improve its model and estimate current and future impact. The plan also outlined a financial sustainability strategy, which showed the way to cover the costs of implementing the plan by raising $5.4 million over five years.

Because of the compelling story that the business plan told investors about ITN*America*'s approach to achieving social impact, the organization secured $3.5 million within just three months of completing its business plan. Today ITN*America* serves seniors in Portland, Maine; Charleston, South Carolina; Lexington, Kentucky; Los Angeles and San Diego, California; Middletown and East Windsor, Connecticut; Orlando and Sarasota, Florida; and the Quad Cities of Iowa and Illinois.

THE PROCESS OF BUSINESS PLANNING

At Root Cause, we know firsthand the value of business planning as a tool for guiding organizational actions to achieve social impact. At the same time, we understand the demands that business planning makes on an organization's people, time, and resources. Before proceeding with a business planning process, an organization's leaders should gauge their readiness. Answering such questions as these will help: What do we want to accomplish through business planning? Are we prepared to make difficult decisions based on what the process discovers? Can our leadership team, planning group, and the board make the necessary commitments and resource allocations for planning over the next four to nine months? Do we have what we need to ensure a rigorous process?

After making the decision to move ahead, an organization can build an effective business plan through a four-step process: (1) planning to plan, (2) articulating a social impact model, (3) developing an implementation strategy, and (4) finalizing and putting the business plan into action. Figure 3.1 shows this process.

Step 1: Planning to Plan—to Get the Business Planning Process Up and Running

Don't skimp on this important step. Thoughtful preparations will strengthen the business planning process from front to back. Step 1 includes the following substeps.

Select the Right "Working Group" for Planning   Typically, the working group represents a mix of perspectives, including the organization's leader, the board chair, and members of the management team (where one exists). This group decides how to develop the plan over the next four to nine months, gives feedback on plan drafts, and decides when sections of the plan are ready to share with other stakeholders to get "buy-in." The working group also establishes a process for updating key stakeholders, creates a work plan that specifies approval dates, plans a "road show," and conducts a gap analysis. An organization can expect to spend the equivalent of one senior-level staff person working full-time for 120 days.

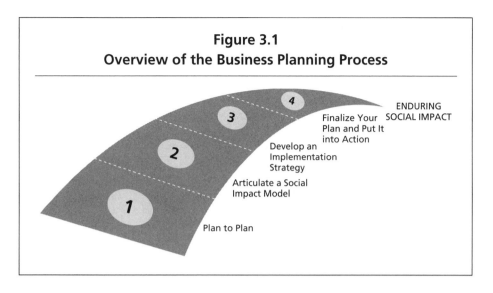

Figure 3.1
Overview of the Business Planning Process

4 — ENDURING SOCIAL IMPACT
Finalize Your Plan and Put It into Action

3 — Develop an Implementation Strategy

2 — Articulate a Social Impact Model

1 — Plan to Plan

Implement a Support and Approval Process   This process will become critical in raising resources for the final business plan. Begin by listing all stakeholders. Include the board of directors, who can help create buy-in for the plan. Consider others who can influence the plan's success, such as local politicians, partner organizations, current and past clients, past funders, and other leading organizations in the field. Let stakeholders know the planning process is under way, and update them periodically. If the business plan is financially supported by a foundation, keep that foundation informed of progress.

Develop a "Work Plan"   A good work plan serves as a to-do list and time line for the working group. The work plan sets meeting dates and establishes deadlines for progress check-ins, drafts, feedback, and approval. For example, if board approval will be needed for the business plan, look ahead to select which board meeting to use for that process.

Plan a road show. In the private sector, a "road show" refers to the process of securing financing before a company issues a public stock offering. The nonprofit context is similar. The organization's leaders use the road show to announce the completed plan and set up meetings with potential social impact investors to seek an investment to implement "phase one" of the plan. Early in the planning process, begin to develop a list of current and potential social impact investors, inform them about the planning process, and send brief updates. Once the plan is complete, the organization's leader will prepare to pitch the business plan to those investors.

Conduct a Gap Analysis to Avoid Duplicating Work At the outset, identify what information has already been gathered to support sections of the business plan, and list areas requiring additional information. Relevant information might include recent financials, performance indicators, a recent strategic plan or an older business plan, and background information about the field and research on peer organizations.

SIDEBAR

Outline of a Business Plan for Enduring Social Impact

I. Executive Summary

II. Need and Opportunity

   A. Overview of Social Problem

   B. Current Trends

   C. Root Causes

   D. Environmental Landscape

   E. Barriers

   F. Opportunity

III. Social Impact Model

   A. Overview of Organizations

   B. Social Impact Model Diagram (including social problem definition, mission, indicators, and vision of success)

   C. Description of Operating Model

   D. Description of Social Impact Strategies

IV. Implementation Strategy

   A. Business Plan Time Line

   B. Phase One Strategy Goals

SIDEBAR

    c. Organizational Capacity Building

        1. Team and Governance

        2. Financial Sustainability

            a. Financial Projections

            b. Capitalization Strategy

        3. Marketing

            a. Brand

            b. Target Market

            c. Partnerships

        4. Technology

        5. Public Policy

        6. Performance and Social Impact Measurement

            a. Indicators and Targets

            b. Feedback Loop

        7. Risk Mitigation

   v. Phase One Action Plan

  vi. Appendix

Step 2: Articulating a Social Impact Model—to Guide the Organization's Work

Though this may seem surprising, the biggest question for an organization to answer as it moves ahead with business planning is: What "core work" will we do to address the social problem we want to solve? Thus, a key objective is to develop a Social Impact Model that will connect the organization's innovative approach (core work to address the target social problem) with the organization's mission, strategies, operational capacity, intended impact, and vision of success. The Social Impact Model (Figure 3.2) provides a framework to guide the organization's work for the

Figure 3.2
The Social Impact Model at Work

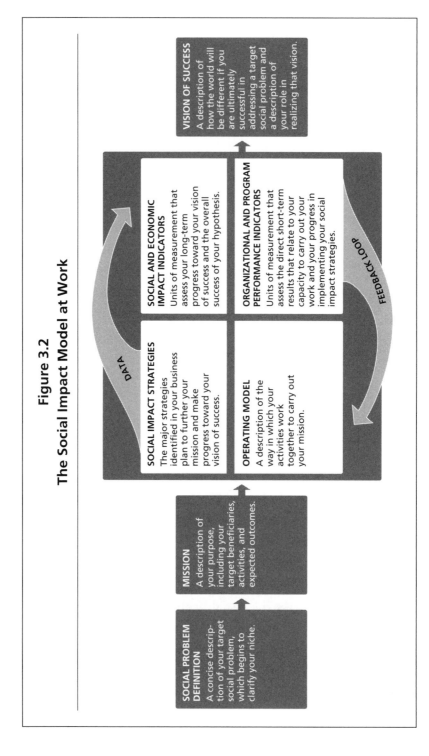

life of the business plan (three to five years). The model culminates in a set of social impact strategies that will lead the organization to realize its vision of success. The key components of the model follow—in the order they are best developed by the working group.

Define the Social Problem   A "need and opportunity analysis" will help define the target social problem and the organization's niche in addressing it. Include a description of the social problem, current trends, a research-based theory about the root causes of the problem, a description of approaches used by other organizations working on the same problem, and potential barriers to solving the problem. The analysis should also frame an "opportunity" to test the group's hypothesis for how to accelerate progress to address the problem.

As an example, consider the Social Impact Model that Root Cause developed in working with another organization focused on aging issues. Two of the conclusions drawn from the organization's need and opportunity analysis include:

- Currently, little collaboration and coordination exists among service providers for the country's senior citizens.
- Many seniors in this country do not know what services are available to them.

The social problem definition that evolved was: "The current national infrastructure required to meet present and future needs of people entering their aging years is not adequate and will have a dramatic impact on their lives."

Envision Success   To start developing a social impact model, articulate a long-term goal that is ambitious enough to be motivating, yet grounded in what is realistic. For example, the organization focused on seniors that was introduced in the previous paragraph has this vision: "We envision a day when—through collaboration and coordination of government, non-profit, and the business sector—all seniors, regardless of economic status, will have access to a seamless integration of the high-quality, affordable services they need in order to live healthy and productive lives." One organization alone could never hope to meet all the needs of senior citizens, but our example organization could hope to organize a network that makes this possible.

Identify Impact Indicators   Next, identify three to five social and economic impact indicators that will help determine whether the hypothesis is helping to solve the target social problem. For instance, the indicators chosen by the organization focused on seniors include the number of seniors matched to services and the number of service providers who meet senior's needs by making improvements to their services or by serving a new geographic area.

Develop a Mission Statement   A well-conceived mission statement describes the *target beneficiary*, the *activities* conducted by the organization to address the target social problem, and the *expected outcomes*. For our organization focused on seniors, the mission became: "to determine the needs of seniors [target beneficiaries] and link them to necessary resources [activities] so that they can lead healthy and productive lives in their aging years [expected outcomes]."

Shape the Operating Model   The operating model defines how the organization's activities will work together to carry out the mission. To shape that model, it often becomes necessary to identify opportunities to improve current activities. Consider these questions: What are the organization's mission-based activities? Who is the target market? How does the organization measure performance and long-term impact? What staff positions are needed? What are the costs of the organization's activities? With the answers to questions like these, the working group can illustrate how the organization's programs work toward the mission, where groups come together, how to integrate evaluation into the work, the cost of activities, and so on.

Develop the Social Impact Strategies   Social impact strategies are the major actions that an organization needs to engage in to carry out its mission. Based on the results of the "need and opportunity analysis," identify the core actions necessary for achieving the mission. A common conclusion at this stage is that an organization is doing too much. Decisions may follow to cut one program or strengthen another. For example, prior to the planning process, the organization that focused on seniors was primarily an advocacy organization. Only recently had it started to connect seniors to services, and the planning analysis uncovered the need to better link services to the country's seniors. The operating model analysis also revealed that the organization's direct-service programs held promise for greater social impact. Thus, the organization identified the opportunity to partner with government to meet seniors' needs, rather than advocating to government. It then developed social impact strategies with that in mind.

With social impact strategies in hand, the working group can develop three to five organizational and program performance indicators to measure the organization's capacity to implement its plan—and to help ensure the organization accomplishes what it intends to in the short term. The example organization focused on seniors selected these performance indicators to measure (among others): the number of members, the number of volunteers serving its programs, and the number of seniors assessed.

Two components of the Social Impact Model, the operating model and the social impact strategies, are always works in progress. In fact, as Step 3 will describe, a feedback loop will establish systems to help ensure that the team returns regularly to make improvements to the operating model and social impact strategies, based on data generated by the measurement system. In contrast, the mission and vision of success will remain unchanged over the course of the business plan.

Step 3: Developing an Implementation Strategy—and Outlining Needed Actions

The rest of the business planning process focuses on the implementation strategy: setting a time line and building capacity to implement the social impact strategies.

Set the Time Line The time line generally has two or three phases spanning three to five years (Figure 3.3). The implementation strategy focuses primarily on Phase 1, which is a pilot to test the social impact strategies over twelve to twenty-four months. The working group begins

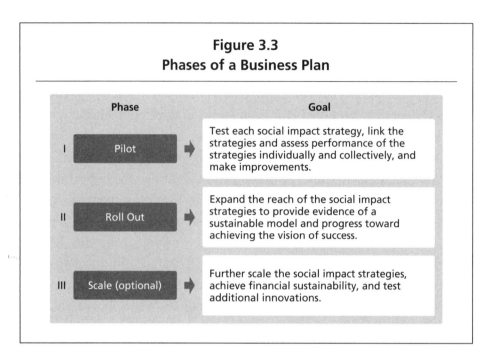

Figure 3.3
Phases of a Business Plan

Phase		Goal
I	Pilot	Test each social impact strategy, link the strategies and assess performance of the strategies individually and collectively, and make improvements.
II	Roll Out	Expand the reach of the social impact strategies to provide evidence of a sustainable model and progress toward achieving the vision of success.
III	Scale (optional)	Further scale the social impact strategies, achieve financial sustainability, and test additional innovations.

by restating each social impact strategy as a goal and listing the activities needed to help accomplish that goal.

For example, OASIS is a national nonprofit organization providing lifelong learning and service opportunities for older adults. One social impact strategy that resulted from the OASIS business planning process focused on *"increasing the services and tools that the national headquarters, known as the OASIS Institute, provides to local OASIS centers."* In Phase 1, OASIS attached the following goal to that social impact strategy: *"To streamline and strengthen the training and other services that the institute provides to centers."* Then OASIS listed five concrete actions to meet this goal, including the following:

- Define a menu of all available services, looking at both the cost to the institute and the value to the centers or directors.

- Develop and implement a training and professional development model with input from the director.

Determine Organizational Capacity to Implement Social Impact Strategies To determine how to build the capacity to implement the social impact strategies, the working group will need to work on seven focus areas. This is an iterative process. As the group makes decisions about each area, they write a summary of that area for inclusion in the final business plan. (The sidebar "Outline of a Business Plan for Enduring Social Impact" provides an overview of what to include in the business plan.)

1. Team and Governance

The organization must plan for the necessary human resources to implement the social impact strategies. Start by listing the roles, responsibilities, and skill sets of the current key team members, board members, and volunteers. Compare that with a list of the human resources needed to implement the social impact strategies—typically calling for new roles for current staff and new hires. Next, create a new organizational chart. Go through the same process for the board roles and any volunteers who will participate in implementing the business plan. In writing the "Team and Governance" section in the plan, include the roles of current and new staff, plus the time line for new hires.

2. Financial Sustainability

The objective here is to include the total capitalization required to implement the plan, a full set of financial statements based on the plan's time line, and a description of how to achieve financial sustainability. Critical questions to address include: How much money will our organization need over the life of the business plan? How will we capitalize our business plan? What mix of reliable resources will we need in order to achieve financial sustainability?

Staffing is typically the greatest expense in implementing the plan. With an understanding of that expense, the working group can estimate the costs to implement all other aspects of the plan. Phase 1 is the primary focus of these projections (because so much can change by the time the organization reaches Phase 2 or 3). Also, look carefully at the business plan aspects that require a significant capital investment, such as technology, new staff hires, or consultants.

Next, estimate the required capitalization. Review current and projected revenue to determine funding needs for each implementation phase. Begin with earned revenues, if any, and subtract estimated expenses for implementation. After subtracting committed and likely philanthropic revenue, the group will arrive at what capitalization is needed to implement each phase of the business plan.

Now proceed to develop a plan for capitalizing Phase 1 and achieving financial sustainability. The capitalization plan will differ greatly depending on the type of social problem, but all tend to include two fundamental components:

- *Predictable revenue sources*—long-term, repeat, and performance-based funding sources (including foundation, individual, government, corporate, and fee-based) that the organization thinks it can rely on with reasonable certainty
- *Nonfinancial resources*—skilled or unskilled volunteers and in-kind donations that enable organizations to increase the sustainability of their initiatives

Capitalizing the business plan requires seeking philanthropic and other revenue sources that will move the organization toward financial sustainability—essentially seeking investors who will invest and reinvest in the organization. Moreover, earned income streams from government fee-for-service and membership fees, in addition to individual donors and corporate partners, are often core elements of an organization's financial sustainability model.

The following two pie charts (Figure 3.4) illustrate a sample strategy for shifting an organization's revenue toward more predictable funding sources over the course of four years. Notice the shift away from unpredictable revenue toward earned income, individual donations, and corporate sponsorships—all of which tend to be more reliable.

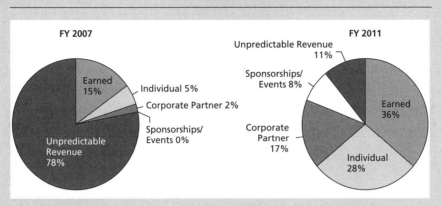

Figure 3.4
Sample Strategy for Shifting Revenue to Predictable Funding Sources

FY 2007

Earned 15%

Individual 5%

Corporate Partner 2%

Sponsorships/ Events 0%

Unpredictable Revenue 78%

FY 2011

Unpredictable Revenue 11%

Sponsorships/ Events 8%

Corporate Partner 17%

Earned 36%

Individual 28%

3. Marketing

Strong marketing and communication activities are essential to attract new social impact investors, partners, and participants for the organization's continuing and new programs. To increase the plan's impact, effective communication systems and strategies must support brand building, target marketing, and partnership development. The leadership team will need to create an "action plan" to ensure that communication standards and systems are in place to tell the organization's compelling story.

4. Technology

A robust technological infrastructure is a critical factor for expanding an organization's reach, sustainability, and competitive advantage. The right technologies—such as tools to help measure organizational performance, contact and other kinds of informational databases, and proprietary technology—can enhance the ability to serve the target population and connect with stakeholders. For example, ITN*America* built ITNRides, a customized technology system that uses a geographic information system (GIS) and a database to manage all aspects of the

ITN operating model. ITNRides became one of the cornerstones of the organization's national expansion plan.

5. Public Policy

Public policy "investments" can help an organization achieve large-scale social impact. In its first years of operation, ITN*America* discovered that a Maine state law that regulated car dealerships also prevented the organization from receiving car donations for its Portland-based service. Working with the legislature's transportation committee, ITN*America* helped to bring about new legislation that makes an exception for organizations that use automobile donations to provide transportation to seniors.

Begin by researching public policy initiatives that could strengthen the operating model, and build relationships to help change policies in a beneficial way. Alternatively, simply building an understanding of the policies surrounding the social problem will increase the ability to implement the business plan successfully.

6. Performance and Social Impact Measurement

Performance measurement helps to maintain quality and develop a track record to secure investments. The performance indicators identified for the Social Impact Model now become part of the organization's self-evaluation system to assess performance and improve the operating model and social impact strategies. For each indicator, the team will need to establish a baseline from existing data, and set "targets" to measure against that baseline. Then the team can establish a feedback loop to help make corrections based on data. Progress reports (such as dashboards and report cards) will let the team analyze the data, identify improvement opportunities, and communicate progress and social impact.

7. Risk Mitigation

The working group identifies potential risks that may limit the plan's prospects for success and describes how to minimize those risks. This section often includes a contingency plan addressing a common risk question: *What will happen if the organization brings in less revenue than the predicted success?*

By the end of Step 3, the organization will have already reviewed, discussed, and written each section of the business plan as it was developed throughout the planning process.

Step 4: Finalizing the Business Plan—and Putting It into Action

The working group should compile all business plan elements into a full document that tells the compelling story of the organization's planned social impact. The underlying objective is to interest current and future stakeholders to get involved, including social impact investors. When the completed draft meets the working group's expectations, they should write a two-to-four-page executive summary. This summary will help interested parties learn about the organization's future plans.

In keeping with the approval schedules developed at the outset of the planning process, the working group can distribute the full plan to the appropriate reviewers with a deadline reminder. Also prepare to launch the "road show" by scheduling meetings with potential social impact investors. In that way, the process of raising money for the plan can begin the moment the business plan receives final approval. The immediate financial goal is to raise the necessary resources to complete Phase 1. With those resources secured, management and the entire team can focus their time on executing the plan.

Action While Planning

SIDEBAR

Inevitably, the social innovators that act confidently and build momentum during the planning process have the most success in securing investments. Begin by choosing one or two projects that you feel confident in undertaking during the planning process.

SIDEBAR

This is "action while planning." It can be as simple as testing ways to market to your target beneficiary or learning how to design a new service for which you have discovered a need. The operating model (Step 2) is one of the first parts of the business planning process that uncovers such opportunities.

Successful Action While Planning

Partners for Youth with Disabilities (PYD) connects youth with disabilities to adult mentors who provide guidance in meeting their personal, educational, and career goals. PYD decided to develop a business plan to launch a technical-assistance arm of the direct service program. During the planning process, PYD identified target markets for selling its mentoring approach to other organizations serving youth with disabilities.

PYD moved ahead to make test sales calls to peer organizations (particularly those who inquired previously). These calls let the organization practice something new, while testing price points, and while understanding how much time was involved in this sales process and learning how to set sales targets. As a result, PYD uncovered good "sales leads" for follow-up as the business plan was complete.

Engaging in "action while planning" helps an organization avoid a major pitfall: getting caught up in worrying about raising the money before implementing the plan. It shows potential social investors that the plan is not just an idea, but truly a course of action that is already under way.

CONCLUSION: BUSINESS PLANNING ACCELERATES SOCIAL IMPACT

Business planning may feel daunting at the outset. Yet, when done well, planning transforms organizations so that they can achieve a level of social impact that previously seemed unimaginable. In fact, an organization can strengthen the probability that the plan will be effective—while reducing risk at the same time—by undertaking "action while planning" throughout the process (see sidebar).

The business planning process provides the organization with opportunities to talk with social impact investors, board members, and other stakeholders in new ways—while providing the organization with a clear path forward. Moreover, the recent boom in the field of social innovation and entrepreneurship demonstrates the need to approach social problem solving with the strategic thinking that business planning enables. Our own experience at Root Cause has shown us that there is no better way to lead a successful organization and to pursue enduring social impact.

ABOUT THE AUTHOR

Widely recognized as a leading social innovator and a pioneering teacher of social entrepreneurship, **Andrew Wolk** founded Root Cause in 2004 and continues to lead its strategic direction. He consults to organizations across the nonprofit, for-profit, and government sectors that are seeking to advance effective solutions to pressing social problems. In addition, he has authored a number of publications on social innovation. They include a report for the Aspen Institute on policy recommendations for advancing social innovation, a chapter on social entrepreneurship and government in the Small Business Administration's 2007 annual report to the president of the United States, and Root Cause's first how-to guide, *Business Planning for Enduring Social Impact*. In 1999, Andrew designed and taught one of the first courses on social entrepreneurship in the country. For the past five years, Andrew has taught social innovation and entrepreneurship at MIT. He is also a Gleitsman Visiting Practitioner in Social Innovation at the Center for Public Leadership at Harvard University's Kennedy School of Government.

Root Cause is a nonprofit organization dedicated to advancing innovative, proven solutions to our most pressing social and economic problems. We support social innovators and educate social impact investors through advisory and consulting services, knowledge sharing, and community building.

Aligning Staff and Board Around a Venture

Sometimes It's Best to Ask for Forgiveness Rather Than Permission

*By **Wendy K. Baumann**, President and Chief Visionary Officer, WWBIC, and **Julann Jatczak**, Vice President and Chief Operating Officer, WWBIC*

If it were easy, everyone would be doing it!

—Grandma Baumann

These cherished words have guided us through the growth of our nonprofit organization, and even more importantly, through our fifteen-year journey with our own social business venture, Coffee With A Conscience™.

As with most ventures into the unknown, launching our enterprise was complete with highs, lows, and everything in between. We learned early on that sometimes success only comes from "going for it." This means that the traditional nonprofit channel of "asking for permission" is often a bureaucratic road block that allows perfect opportunities to slip away.

We are a pair of seasoned nonprofit managers who have never thought like our social sector colleagues. We look at social enterprise not as a "special project" or "flavor of the day"; rather, it is inbred to the core of our small agency. Earned revenue is not a luxury; it is the tool of our long-term success.

Are we rogues? No. Are we roguish? Definitely, yes. Our approach with the board of directors and our staff is driven by our unyielding vision, leadership, and raw guts. There are times when a decision had to be made, and a committee structure would have surely killed it. We aren't always right, but we've earned the respect of our board and staff as our organization's guide toward self-sufficiency.

Although we write this from a not-for-profit lens (rather than the private sector or government perspective), the dual struggles of "financial reward" and "mission balance" still apply. We're here to tell you, You CAN do it! The journey will not be easy and painless, but with a clear vision and grasp of *risk versus reward,* it can become a reality. So gear up your intestinal fortitude and let's take a ride.

RUNNING WITH AN IDEA

Vision is the art of seeing things invisible

—Jonathan Swift

The Wisconsin Women's Business Initiative Corporation (WWBIC) is a statewide microcredit organization founded in 1987. As the parent organization of Coffee With A Conscience (CWAC), WWBIC has an annual operating budget of $2.5 million and a staff of thirty. We provide business education, individualized counseling, and access to capital for more than three thousand microentrepreneurs each year. Our passion is to assist women, minorities, and low-income individuals in achieving their dream of small business ownership.

Our approach to earned income has always been simple: we don't want to put all of our eggs in one basket; we want many eggs in many baskets. As such, we've woven together a patchwork of income streams to augment our grants and donations. We manage several fee-for-service contracts, primarily with government entities. We earn revenue on our core business through workshop fees and interest on our microloans. We provide consulting services to other nonprofits and nongovernmental organizations domestically and abroad. And . . . we own a coffee shop.

In 1996, we were struck by a vision—literally. Wendy was attending a conference in Denver and went for a run to start off her day. She passed many small businesses on her journey—from candy boutiques to bakeries to pretzel carts to sandwich shops. All of these businesses were just like our WWBIC clients back home. Wouldn't it be great to have a place to showcase their wares and earn a buck for WWBIC at the same time.

Back home in Milwaukee, the coffee scene was in its fledgling stages. Starbucks hadn't made it to town yet, and there were only a handful of coffee roasters and cafés.

Then the idea struck: because what we do for a living is help other people start businesses, why not start our own? By the time the plane landed in Wisconsin, Coffee With A Conscience was born.

We started humbly with a small coffee kiosk at the main Milwaukee Public Library. Today, we have two locations that are managed by a full-time manager and staffed with six part-time baristas. The focus of Coffee With A Conscience is to provide our customers with a great cup of coffee while also remaining true to our three consciences: global awareness, economic sustainability, and environmental concern. We serve only fair trade organic coffee, we only purchase from women-owned businesses and microbusinesses, we recycle, and we use environmentally sound products.

In addition to our two café locations, we also offer catering services and whole bean sales (we're proud that the Wisconsin governor's residence has selected Coffee With A Conscience as its exclusive coffee provider). Furthering our mission, we have integrated our coffee operation into WWBIC's small business curriculum. We created an experiential learning experience for participants in our education programs using the day-to-day operations of Coffee With A Conscience. Through the development of five "learning labs," students have a hands-on opportunity to learn skills in customer service, merchandising, human resources, inventory control, and basic bookkeeping.

Admittedly, the journey has been bumpy at times. In the early years, revenue was low and profits slim to nonexistent. However, we're excited to report that the contribution of revenue from Coffee With A Conscience now represents 10 percent of WWBIC's annual operating budget.

We consider ourselves researchers from the school of hard knocks, with a great deal learned via trial and error. We plan, and plan again. We study. We haven't always been liked by our stakeholders. But at the end of the day, we do what we feel is right and what will help us achieve that illusive balance of money and mission.

In the following, we share the lessons we've learned. Our hope is to highlight some of the things we did right and the things we should have done differently with our board and staff.

LESSONS LEARNED

_____

The ability to convert ideas to things is the secret of outward success.

_____

—Henry Ward Beecher

Look for Unexpected Opportunities

Opportunities and ideas come at the oddest moments—in the shower, during vivid dreams, or when running through the streets of Denver. The challenge is to know when the idea is truly an opportunity or when it's just another wacky scheme.

Not all nonprofit leaders profess to be entrepreneurs. This may be true, but we challenge all leaders to think entrepreneurially. What can I do to improve my agency's programs and bottom line at the same time? What market opportunities are out there that fit with our core competencies? What should we be doing to help others share the vision?

Our standing joke is that Wendy (as CEO) thinks of twenty new ideas every day, and Julann (as COO) thinks of twenty ways to shoot them down. Over the years we've developed a system to ferret out the gems from the rocks. Our complementary skills and backgrounds have taken our earned income from less than 1 percent of our annual revenue to more than 30 percent. Coffee With A Conscience is one of the ideas that passed both the Wendy and Julann smell tests.

After an opportunity has been identified, the next step is to engage a support team—your board, staff, advisors. Know the tools that can help you—a business plan, for example. This was a tangible tool that helped us launch the coffee business, especially with stakeholders who "need to see it in writing." By no means was it perfect, but it gave us a template to sell the idea. A simple two-column chart listing the venture's "Upside" and "Downside" may even suffice. You want things that everyone can touch, hold, and keep as a roadmap.

Another useful tool is the financial statements of the parent organization. A poorly performing organization can demonstrate that "desperate times call for desperate measures," so exploring a business is a necessity for survival. Conversely, a strong balance sheet can demonstrate that there is a cushion to allow the organization to take more risks to augment growth even further.

The bottom line: although ideas should be vetted, they shouldn't be so overanalyzed that you talk yourself out of everything. Balance risk versus reward, but stretch your risk tolerance to allow yourself freedom to explore cool ideas. Embrace failure—it's what we learn from.

Make Sure Your House Is in Order

There are no secrets to success. It is the result of preparation, hard work, and learning from failure.

—Colin Powell

You may be all fired up to venture into social enterprise, but is your "house"—your core operation—in order? A quick S.W.O.T. (Strengths, Weaknesses, Opportunities, and Threats) Analysis provided a starting point for us to determine that we were ready to adopt earned revenue opportunities in a more strategic way. In hindsight, one of our best decisions was to ensure that our organization *as a whole* (which at WWBIC we fondly call "the mother ship") was in order before plunging into owning a social enterprise.

Here are the key issues we challenged ourselves to address...not just with cursory answers, but with real, root-cause thoughtfulness. This foundation allowed us to proactively answer stakeholder concerns before they arose. There's power in the ability to respond with, "We already thought about that."

Do We Have a Business Model in Place?   We were at an advantage in that the core mission of WWBIC is small business development. We had a business plan written for our operation (yes, nonprofits should have a business plan!) and conducted much of our day-to-day operations with a business sensibility. Nearly half of our staff came from the private sector and brought extraordinary assets—marketing expertise, accounting, and business consulting.

The other half of the staff, however, had a singular social service philosophy. While they were excellent service providers and supported the cause, our sense was that they didn't truly grasp the concept of "without money, there is no mission."

Before we proceeded, we knew that we had to develop not only a common business language among all staff but we also had to foster an entrepreneurial culture. We educated the staff on our budgets and financial statements. We began using business terminology regularly. For example, Wendy's position is not the typical nonprofit title of "Executive Director," instead it's "President/CEO." It's a small but powerful distinction.

We also benchmarked our staff's understanding by using a survey. This provided solid indicators on what we had to address first.

Using humor is a great way to engage all levels of employees and stakeholders. The *Entrepreneurial Culture Pop Quiz,* Exhibit 4.1, is a light-hearted tool that we used (and share with others today) to get our folks thinking about social enterprise in general and its relevance to our organization. Though it is definitely not scientific, you may be surprised at some "aha" moments that surface from it. Give it a try!

Do We Have the Time, Talent, and Treasure to Make This Happen?
A full understanding of the stress that a new venture can put on the parent organization is key. We had to make sure that we had the time to dedicate to successfully growing this business and that we had the appropriate business talent on our team.

Frankly, we didn't have much of either in the beginning. We decided that Wendy would allocate 25 percent of her position to overseeing the café. Sometimes, it meant working sixty-hour weeks instead of the typical fifty. Julann picked up the slack with the mother ship's operations.

Our internal survey also showed that we had the financial and marketing expertise with existing staff and board, but we lacked the retail and coffee business talent. To address this, we specifically recruited an experienced on-site manager. We were fortunate that those with expertise on our board were also gracious in giving of their "spare" time (in specific legal and accounting support).

Perhaps the most challenging piece of the equation is treasure. How does a venture get financed? Can the mother ship afford the risk?

Our first step was to set realistic expectations for Coffee With A Conscience. We probably should have reduced our financial projections by 25 percent and extended our profitability window by several years. We overestimated the Milwaukee Library clientele's interest in spending three dollars for a cup of gourmet coffee. Our advice: really, really understand your potential payer market.

But we purposefully started small with one location; we could grow bigger later. (Too many businesses start too big and are forced to downsize when expectations aren't met.) Our capital outlay was minimal, so we

---

Exhibit 4.1.
Entrepreneurial Culture Pop Quiz

---

1. **What percent of your agency's revenue is from earned income?**

☐ 100% ☐ 75–100% ☐ 50–75% ☐ 25–50% ☐ 1–25%
☐ None ☐ I'm not sure

2. **What percent of your *board* is from the private sector?**

☐ 100% ☐ 75–100% ☐ 50–75% ☐ 25–50% ☐ 1–25%
☐ None ☐ I'm not sure

3. **What percent of your *staff* has solid private-sector experience?**

☐ 100% ☐ 75–100% ☐ 50–75% ☐ 25–50% ☐ 1–25%
☐ None ☐ I'm not sure

4. **When you walk into your offices, you feel like . . .**

☐ You are at a nonprofit organization
☐ You are at IBM's headquarters
☐ You are at a professional and friendly business
☐ You are in the Twilight Zone

5. **Your agency uses a business operations model (that is, it runs like a business).**

☐ True ☐ False ☐ In some things

6. **Your staff, board, and committee meetings are scheduled for the entire year.**

☐ True ☐ False ☐ I'm not sure

7. **Your staff and board could readily recite your agency's mission.**

☐ True ☐ False ☐ I'm not sure

Exhibit 4.1.
(*continued*)

8. When talking about your agency's services with your staff or board, they are likely to say, "Oh, we offer our agency's services for free."

☐ True   ☐ False   ☐ I'm not sure

9. Your *board* thinks it's wrong to make money.

☐ True   ☐ False   ☐ I'm not sure

10. Your *staff* thinks it's wrong to make money.

☐ True   ☐ False   ☐ I'm not sure

11. The word "profit" is a dirty word.

☐ True   ☐ False   ☐ Depends on the day

12. You feel like you are a lone wolf and nobody else "gets it."

☐ True   ☐ False   ☐ Really depends on the day

Source: WWBIC, 2008.

bootstrapped the finance package together. We did outreach to local foundations and philanthropists, but met with mixed success.

Although the funder arena today is savvier about social enterprise, it is still evolving. We're not quite there yet as a field, so know your donors' appetite for social enterprise before you mentally rely upon them too much.

Why Do We Want to Do This Social Enterprise in the First Place?   It's important to make sure the board and staff understand the "why" before the "what" or the "how." Are we pursuing a social enterprise to diversify our funding base? To stabilize our agency? To take advantage of an unmet market need? To expand our scope? To survive?

In our work with Coffee With A Conscience, our goal was to earn revenue to support the mother ship and provide a hands-on training vehicle for our small business clients. Of course, being the entrepreneurs that we are, in the beginning we tried to do too much. We quickly learned that coffee shops don't earn as much money as you'd like; so we revised our projections. Maybe Coffee With A Conscience wouldn't make WWBIC self-sufficient, but it can cover its program costs and contribute to our earned revenue.

Do We Have the Stomach for This? Face it, mistakes will happen. Business start-ups are risky already, let alone with a double bottom line imperative. You have to be able to weather the storms and critics. You also have to be prepared. And you have to get used to the idea of asking for forgiveness rather than permission.

Ask Forgiveness, Not Permission

It's easier to ask forgiveness than it is to get permission.

—Grace Hopper

Nonprofit leadership typically gravitates to one of two models: board-led or staff-led. In the best scenario, both board and management staff colead the organization to successful outcomes. Of course, even if the staff has a strong voice in leading the organization, the board never relinquishes its responsibilities in governance, strategic planning, and checks and balances. But most successful organizations recognize the skills and insights of those closest to the ground . . . the staff.

At WWBIC, we have a strong board-staff relationship and lean more toward a staff-led model. We have worked hard to earn the trust and confidence of our board; because of this, they afford us the latitude to make operational and low-risk decisions. Under this model, sometimes it's okay to ask for forgiveness rather than permission. It may be a bit tongue-in-cheek, but this way of thinking has met with success at Coffee With A Conscience.

The concept for Coffee With A Conscience was perhaps born on a whim during a morning run, but the time had to be right for the board to be in a position to accept this as within the realm of possibility. WWBIC was on solid ground. It was time to color outside the lines. But admittedly, not one board member or other staff member was thinking we should start a coffee business.

Sometimes, as a leader, it is important to take others on the run with you. For example, when we rolled out Coffee With A Conscience, we literally had to help our board touch and feel this opportunity. The business plan would help, but we needed something even more tangible, more visual to sell the idea.

We told everyone that we were holding our regular WWBIC board meeting off-site—at a quaint coffee shop in the Milwaukee Public Library. When they began arriving we heard comments about the warm café environment and the blend of business and books. (Remember this was in the day before large book retailers had on-site cafés.) One board member even suggested that WWBIC could use this location as a training venue. At that pivotal moment Wendy said to the board: "I'm glad you like this place . . . we own it!" After picking some folks up off the floor, we discussed the stream of events that had brought WWBIC to owning a business.

Though the executive committee knew of our plans ahead of time, we knew that there would be several board members who would loudly object to our purchase. Our board was nearly twenty-five strong and the naysayers could have swept this opportunity right out from under us. It was one board member—a respected attorney in town who was this project's biggest champion—who shared the rationale and potential with his fellow board members.

To us, there was no downside. The deal was low risk and high gain—a minimal $2,000 investment for the previous owner's coffee kiosk and supplies with a ninety-day exit clause. Our landlord, the library, gave us the space for free in exchange for assisting their used-book program volunteers.

Our risk was minimal in terms of money and investment, reputation, and brand. We were definitely starting off small, but with high hopes to grow bigger down the road.

After we convinced the board of our plans (and exit strategy, just in case), it was time to talk with the staff. This was almost more challenging than the board. Although we were continually building an internal culture of entrepreneurial thinking, not everyone thought this was a great idea. It was change. And everyone loves change until it affects them.

But here, too, we led by example and with our own enthusiasm. We never gave in to staff members who thought we were more crazy than usual. And, yes, we lost some team members along the way who couldn't embrace the new direction. Having a few internal staff become our front-line champions proved a valuable resource.

Have a Champion (or Two)

Champions keep playing until they get it right.

—Billie Jean King

It's important to get used to the fact that one person cannot make a venture successful alone. No matter how smart you are or how hard you work, there will be time when you need help. We've all experienced the power of the respected "voice" in the room . . . the one who can cause an idea to sink or swim within two sentences. You need one—or two—of these advocates on your side.

When launching Coffee With A Conscience, we identified several staunch champions—those to guide the board of directors and those to support our staff rollout.

On our board, our two champions were both members of our executive committee. One was our board chair and the other was the attorney mentioned before who guided us through the planning and acquisition process. They both were well respected and others followed their lead. They remain our champions today.

With our staff, Wendy's role is that of the driver and visionary. Julann's role is that of behind-the-scenes advocate and support. Wendy had the passionate voice and unwillingness to say "NO." At the time, Julann had just joined WWBIC from a sales position in the private sector. We made a complementary launch team. A few staff members, who strongly believed in the potential of the venture, were our front-line champions. In the early days, they even volunteered to pour coffee at weekend events. That's a true champion.

Even after years in business, our champions still play a vital role. Their support held the operation together when we churned through eight managers in fifteen years, faced pricing and delivery issues from the micro-businesses supplying our cafés, and experienced employee theft and fraud. It was our champions who not only supported us, but helped our other WWBIC constituents see the continued value of the venture.

Here's another example where champions were integral to an expansion decision we faced with Coffee With A Conscience.

Our original location in the library was struggling, while our second location in an office park was holding its own. The library location was off the charts on the mission fit, but we were still losing money. Finally, we closed that location. Coincidentally, at the same time, we received a call from the Milwaukee Art Museum wondering if we'd consider opening Coffee With A Conscience in their main entrance foyer.

Still stinging from the closure of our first "baby," we met with the museum staff. We couldn't believe our luck—typical art patrons have more disposable income (to spend on cappuccinos and biscotti) than typical library patrons. But, how to convince our board and staff that this was a good idea, especially after we just closed a location two months earlier?!

Here's where our champions came into play. First, Wendy took Julann mysteriously to the art museum one day out of the blue and asked, "Don't you think this would be a great place for Coffee With A Conscience?" That visual moment turned Julann into a believer. Then we engaged our original two board champions who were pivotal during the original launch. They were renewed supporters right away. Without their commitment, the road could have been bumpier . . . or even a dead end. (As a note: we were MUCH smarter negotiating the financial and lease arrangements the third time around!)

Having both internal and external champions serves us well . . . we still have them today. While a board member is ideal, your champion could also be a partner, investor, or advisor. Internally, champions at all levels of the organization can facilitate buy-in. It's just as important that your CFO welcomes social enterprise as it is that your receptionist feels like part of the movement (the power of the receptionist's phone is often underrated).

In addition to the champions, having a dedicated project leader to guide through the nitty-gritty is important. Though this could be the CEO, the job may more appropriately rest with your COO or a program director. This person will be a vital link to your social enterprise manager and his or her team.

SIDEBAR

Characteristics of a Social Enterprise Champion

- Understands business
- Recognizes that without money, there is no mission
- Risk taker
- Optimistic believer
- Embraces change
- Stays the course, even when things get bumpy (because they will!)
- Truly wants organizational stability and growth (walks the talk)
- Recognizes that running a social enterprise *is different* from running a nonprofit
- Good salesperson; willing to "spread the gospel" with fellow stakeholders

Sell the Sizzle

A leader is a dealer in hope.

—Napoleon Bonaparte

Entrepreneurs are by nature optimistic, but not everyone shares that enthusiastic passion. Your job is to sell the sizzle. Of course, everyone wants you to be realistic, but the naysayers will come out of the woodwork, especially when the words "social enterprise" pop up. A leader's role is to transform the "why nots" by selling the "whys."

Here is where Marketing 101 principles come in handy. We've created a checklist of talking points and considerations for launching your social enterprise.

☐ Clearly and concisely communicate the current operational capacity and financial status of the mother ship

☐ Describe the current financial pressures of organization (for example, reduced government or philanthropic dollars)

☐ Illustrate the unmet market trends and opportunities that are staring you in the face:

    ☐ Use visuals, not just a list of numbers and facts

    ☐ Use the concept of market pull versus market push to strengthen your views

    ☐ Sell, sell, sell the sizzle

☐ Educate board, staff, and stakeholders on the double (or triple) bottom line concept

☐ Overcome the negative thoughts some stakeholders will have that anything new and out of the box is "mission drift" (it truly is "mission lift"!)

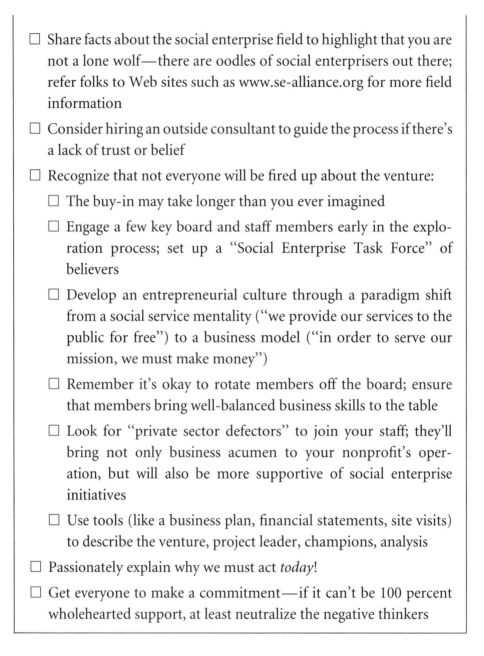

- ☐ Share facts about the social enterprise field to highlight that you are not a lone wolf—there are oodles of social enterprisers out there; refer folks to Web sites such as www.se-alliance.org for more field information

- ☐ Consider hiring an outside consultant to guide the process if there's a lack of trust or belief

- ☐ Recognize that not everyone will be fired up about the venture:
  - ☐ The buy-in may take longer than you ever imagined
  - ☐ Engage a few key board and staff members early in the exploration process; set up a "Social Enterprise Task Force" of believers
  - ☐ Develop an entrepreneurial culture through a paradigm shift from a social service mentality ("we provide our services to the public for free") to a business model ("in order to serve our mission, we must make money")
  - ☐ Remember it's okay to rotate members off the board; ensure that members bring well-balanced business skills to the table
  - ☐ Look for "private sector defectors" to join your staff; they'll bring not only business acumen to your nonprofit's operation, but will also be more supportive of social enterprise initiatives
  - ☐ Use tools (like a business plan, financial statements, site visits) to describe the venture, project leader, champions, analysis

- ☐ Passionately explain why we must act *today*!

- ☐ Get everyone to make a commitment—if it can't be 100 percent wholehearted support, at least neutralize the negative thinkers

You may specifically find that some board members will require a little more TLC to "see the light" of social enterprise. If this sounds like your situation, here are several lessons that we learned during our Coffee With A Conscience journey that were helpful in transforming some of our board members from "nonbelievers" into "believers."

First, share what is working. Provide constant, consistent, and concrete exposure to similar examples of successful business models from around the world. Expose your board to a variety of social enterprises, risky and less-risky types of ventures, and generated revenue models via e-mails, media articles, discussions, and case studies. Take field trips. Invite guest speakers to board meetings.

Second, present a realistic vision of both the risks and the rewards. Board members may need to see it on paper and discuss it to understand it. Be patient. Not everyone will "get it" as quickly as you.

Third, harness the talent and passion of your champions. Ask them to have candid and passionate discussions with their fellow board members. They are champions for a reason.

Finally, change the board. Although you need to respect board terms and limits, there is nothing wrong with slowly bringing on more risk-tolerant members. We fervently believe it is essential to have those self-made millionaires and bootstrapping entrepreneurs representing our organization. It works. Nurture the board you want.

HAVE FUN

Talk doesn't cook rice.

—Chinese Proverb

If it appears that the only way to align the board and staff around social enterprise is to be freewheeling buccaneers, we apologize. We recognize that nerves of steel aren't inbred in all managers (especially those in old-line nonprofits). The foray into social enterprise could shake your leadership confidence.

But we challenge you to bring out your adventurous side. Don't let fear paralyze you. Don't overthink. Be realistic, but be brave. People will understand that you come from a place of goodness, not exploitation.

Not only has Coffee With A Conscience been a successful venture for us, but it has also been our badge of honor—for trying something avante garde, for taking knocks along the way, for standing tall to still talk about it. Coffee With A Conscience is more than just a great cup of coffee. It is a way of thinking.

ABOUT THE AUTHORS

Wendy K. Baumann has served as president and chief visionary officer of the Wisconsin Women's Business Initiative Corporation (WWBIC), a respected statewide economic development corporation, since 1994. She is a dynamic force on the local, national, and international scenes specifically relating to microcredit, social entrepreneurship, business incubation, and women in business. Through her leadership and vision, WWBIC has grown from a $200,000 budget and staff of two, to a $2.5 million operational budget today that includes several social enterprise initiatives. Wendy served and continues to serve on numerous national and regional boards including Consumer Federation of America-America Saves, The Association of Enterprise Opportunity, The Chicago Federal Home Loan Advisory Board, Johnson Bank New Markets Tax Credit Advisory Board, and the Governor's Council on Financial Literacy. Wendy resides in a log cabin in Wisconsin with her border collie, Amy, and fat red cat, Sandee. Wendy has four lovely children and enjoys jogging, reading, cooking, and travel in her spare time.

Julann Jatczak, vice president/COO of the Wisconsin Women's Business Initiative Corporation (WWBIC), heads the organization's business development programs and oversees agency operations for all four of its offices. She is recognized for her workshops on small business management and has worked with more than fifteen thousand entrepreneurs since joining WWBIC in 1996. Julann is author of two microenterprise publications for the NxLeveL Education Foundation on money management and business planning. She is active on numerous boards and committees, including serving as secretary of the Social Enterprise Alliance. Prior to joining WWBIC, Julann held positions in advertising, marketing, and sales in Wisconsin and New York. In 2008, Julann was selected by the U.S. Small Business Administration as the nation's "Women's Business Champion." When she's not discoursing about social enterprise, Julann cherishes the time spent traveling with her family, reading too many novels, and hanging out on her back porch in Wisconsin.

The Wisconsin Women's Business Initiative Corporation (WWBIC) is a leading-edge economic development corporation celebrating nearly twenty-five years of entrepreneurship, opportunity, and success. WWBIC offers quality business education, one-on-one business assistance, direct loans and access to other capital, financial awareness, and asset-building programming. Through innovative initiatives, WWBIC focuses its efforts on those individuals most likely to face barriers from traditional financial or educational resources. With several earned revenue strategies and a social business venture, Coffee With A Conscience, WWBIC is a leader in social entrepreneurship as well as microcredit (www.wwbic.com).

The Life Cycle of Social Enterprise Financing

*By **Jeannine Jacokes**, Chief Executive Officer,*
Partners for the Common Good,
*and **Jennifer Pryce**, Senior Investment Officer,*
Nonprofit Finance Fund and Calvert Foundation

You have a great earned-income idea. You've done the market and feasibility analysis. You have a solid business plan for a venture that will not only make money—but will make the world a better place. The *only* thing standing between you and success is the money to make it a go! Whether you are a social or traditional entrepreneur, this is the age-old dilemma for anyone who has ever tried to start a business.

"Too many dreams die in the parking lot of a bank," is an oft-quoted saying. You may ask, "Why do people with money lack vision? Why do they doubt the entrepreneurial spirit? Why aren't they persuaded by cold, hard market analysis that proves an idea is a home run? What *is* the problem?"

The problem may be *capital mismatch*. Knowing what type of capital is needed at what time in the life cycle of your venture is critical to success. Infused into the organization at the wrong time, some types of capital may hurt your business more than help it.

Within the traditional for-profit sector, businesses are generally recognized as traveling through a life cycle. As time passes, a successful business will move through the various stages. At each juncture, the needs, challenges, and financing options of ventures change. Just as the parenting strategies that work for a toddler do not work for a teenager, the financing strategies of a start-up are unlikely to succeed with a mature venture and vice versa.

Finding the right mix at the right time is a perennial problem for organizations—both for-profit and nonprofit. This problem, however, is not insurmountable if your business plan recognizes what you need . . . and when you need it. Understanding the stages of enterprise development and knowing where your organization falls on the continuum will provide guidance on the most appropriate form of capital to seek.

Over time, an enterprise will move through four distinct stages of development:

Start-Up or Seed Stage: The start-up or seed stage is the birth or infancy of your enterprise. You have a good idea for a product or service—but it needs to be developed. You will need to match your skills, experience, and entrepreneurial enthusiasm to the business opportunity and make sure that you have the right people to make the venture successful. As a new player in the market, your challenge will be to gain market acceptance by identifying and soliciting your first customers. With no proven track record, it will be difficult to obtain start-up capital from anyone unless he or she knows you very well and is willing to take a risk.

Survival or Establishment Stage: Your business is up and running and you have your first customers. At this stage (sometimes referred to as the "proof of concept" stage), you may find yourself engaged in significant product or process refinement as you receive feedback from customers about what they like or don't like about your product or service delivery. A key challenge for your enterprise is that initial seed capital from internally generated sources and grants may be running low while you are not yet generating a profit. As your enterprise gains momentum and moves toward profitability, its demands for capital will likely outstrip resources available from the nonprofit parent. Some philanthropic sources may still be available but are limited. Your challenge will be to expand your customer base and market penetration while preserving precious capital.

Growth or Expansion Stage: Your enterprise has established a foothold in the market and begun to realize some efficiencies in its operations. Revenues and customers are growing and you have hit or surpassed the break-even point where revenues exceed expenses. You may also experience greater competition as others recognize the value of the products or services you provide and want to get in on the act. At this point, you may need more employees to keep up with growing demand and, as the scale of your activity expands, you may need to invest in better internal management systems to keep operations moving efficiently. At this point, initial seed capital is exhausted, cash reserves and net worth are thin—but capital is needed to fuel the growing business. Once breakeven is achieved, the business may be able to begin to access sources of debt and establish a credit history. Cash flow may still be thin and collateral limited. Socially motivated lenders may still be able to provide flexible or subordinate debt for your cash-hungry growing social enterprise.

Mature Stage: Your enterprise has evolved into a successful business. You have a solid foothold in the market, strong brand identity, customer loyalty, and solid production and distribution systems. The enterprise has achieved stabilized operations through at least one growth phase and achieved a regular pattern of profitability. Now that the business has finally hit a stable plateau, the challenge will be to remain competitive as new players enter the market with innovative products or more aggressive pricing strategies. Your challenge will be to stay ahead by continually improving the efficiency of your operations and making sure your products stay ahead of the pack. Your social enterprise may be in a position to take advantage of new opportunities through further expansion requiring a new round of capital. The mature business may also have substantial permanent working capital needs. Debt capital will likely be the preferred instrument at this stage because it is flexible and easier to raise from banks and others.

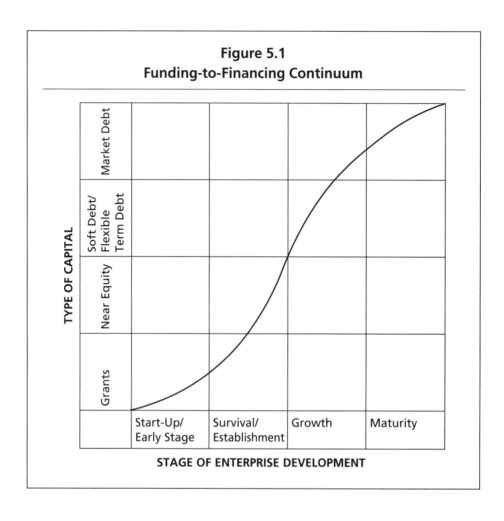

Figure 5.1
Funding-to-Financing Continuum

TYPE OF CAPITAL — Market Debt / Soft Debt/ Flexible Term Debt / Near Equity / Grants

Start-Up/ Early Stage · Survival/ Establishment · Growth · Maturity

STAGE OF ENTERPRISE DEVELOPMENT

Figure 5.1 illustrates the relationship between the stage of enterprise development and the type of financing that is most appropriate.

Start-Up or Seed Stage
What Are Your Challenges?

- Turning your idea into a marketable product or service
- Bootstrapping your start-up capital
- Making sure you have the right people and skill sets
- Securing your first customers and gaining market acceptance

Your business is an idea and must be built from the ground up. This is the birth of a new business; like any new baby, it needs everything. Capital is needed to conduct market research on product or service demand and to write a business plan. Having the right people with the right skills and experience is also paramount for success. It may take a few years of ground work to move a business from the concept stage to the launch pad. Once you have determined a concept is viable, capital is needed to buy equipment, build production and delivery systems, bridge receivables, and pay operating expenses. And . . . you need to let the world know you are open for business, and then work on gaining market acceptance.

Above all, a start-up business needs to keep focused. A social entrepreneur cannot have a new idea every minute. You must be disciplined enough to focus on a single opportunity and market niche and not spread your money or time too thinly.

With all of these demands, your main challenge will be to minimize the "burn rate" on your precious cash. Visiting a local bank for a business loan seems the obvious solution. Or is it? Debt payments can eat up thin cash flow at a time when every dollar is precious. To put it more pragmatically, if your business has no track record, has not yet built loyal customers, and has no history of cash flow, how are you going to make your monthly loan payment? Even a concessionary-priced Program-Related Investment (PRI) from a local visionary foundation can't help you before you generate sales and cash flow.

What Kind of Capital and Where to Find It?   What you really need is "equity" capital—the most difficult money to find. Only sources that can afford to lose it all can or should provide capital at this stage. As the business has yet to be tested, there is a great chance it might fail. An oft-quoted sobering statistic reports that 97 percent of all new for-profit businesses close within the first year.

Within the traditional business sector, friends, family, and the entrepreneur are the most common sources of equity. For social entrepreneurs, "friends and family" might roughly translate into grants from foundations, government, or committed individual contributors. Some social entrepreneurs believe that salvation lies in finding that one venture capital fund or investor who has vision and "gets it." This strategy is akin to finding a four-leaf clover and usually results in wasted time and energy. Rarely can a social enterprise meet the return requirements of even "visionary" venture capital investors.

Like a traditional business, a social entrepreneur's most likely route is "bootstrapping" (meaning reaching into its own pockets or convincing people who are already loyal, proven supporters to give one more time). Just like the for-profit entrepreneur, a social enterprise should expect to put some equity "skin in the game" if they are asking others to support them.

The vast majority of social enterprises do not function as "stand-alone" businesses. In the observation of the authors, most social enterprises and ventures are started by or housed within a larger "parent" organization. The social enterprise is often a venture that complements the mission and activities of the sponsoring parent nonprofit. Support from accumulated unrestricted net assets of a sponsoring "parent" nonprofit will likely be a necessary component to your equity pool.

An interesting dilemma about nonprofit capital markets is that "true equity" in the for-profit sense of the word does not exist. The Internal Revenue Service prohibits anyone from "owning" a nonprofit created for charitable purposes. By contrast, a for-profit entrepreneur can exchange an ownership interest in his business and its future revenues for cash by selling stock or a partnership interest. In doing so, the entrepreneur must be prepared to share the financial returns or windfall once the business is profitable and, in some cases, he may also need to share control over the future direction of the venture. Yet, within the nonprofit sector, our "investors" must "give it all away" without anything but a promise that the nonprofit will deliver the social "returns" promised. For good or bad, our tax code and the legal parameters of nonprofit status make it difficult for social entrepreneurs to infuse the same for-profit motive within the capital structure of a nonprofit-controlled social enterprise. (An interesting note is that the Good Capital Fund [www.goodcap.net] is experimenting with creating new high-engagement investment instruments to provide social enterprises during early phases of the business life cycle.)

The distinction between the nonprofit and for-profit sectors often allows a for-profit business to grow and respond to market demand more quickly than a nonprofit business can. You may wish to consider designing your social enterprise business plan with conservative projections related to the amount of time it may take to raise sufficient start-up capital. Without adequate capital, a social enterprise may find that it is chronically understaffed in an effort to maintain a low expense profile. A planning rule of thumb: No matter how much capital you think you need, double it! Extra capital will be needed through the fundraising period. You should also be creative about exploring opportunities to utilize in-kind services or donations.

Figure 5.2 illustrates the array of capital sources that are available to a nonprofit or for-profit social enterprise as it grows and evolves through the various stages of the business life cycle.

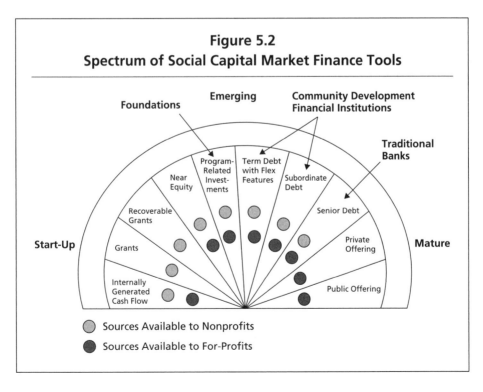

Figure 5.2
Spectrum of Social Capital Market Finance Tools

Survival or Establishment Stage
What Are Your Challenges?

- Solidifying market position by expanding customer base
- Refining your product or service in response to customer feedback
- Conserving precious capital
- Building the internal infrastructure to support growth

Your business is starting to generate revenue. The good news is that, as you gain momentum, your business is no longer a baby. The bad news is that it is now a budding toddler with a host of new issues and challenges that you did not have before. To generate more income, you need to solidify market position by expanding your customer base. At the same time, your existing customers may tell you that product refinements or service delivery changes are needed. The old adage in business is, "Your best customer is a returning customer"; keeping existing customers happy is key. Changes, however, may mean you need to rethink how you build the product, how your staff deliver services, and how your production and delivering systems function—you may even need to rethink the whole business plan. Building internal systems to manage growth also becomes a new priority to scale up your production capacity.

Despite your early success, you have probably not yet achieved "breakeven." Within the world of nonprofit program delivery, "breakeven" can be a difficult concept. We are accustomed to subsidy. As a sector, we are generally unfamiliar with the for-profit world's discipline of tracking costs. Most nonprofits do not understand how much it actually costs to deliver a product or service to a single customer. Nonprofits' collective motives are to make the world a better place and do what is needed to help our clients or constituents—regardless of whether a client can pay to cover the cost of the service. By contrast, to run a successful social enterprise, we need to make the world a better place within a self-sustaining business model.

What Kind of Capital and Where to Find It?   More equity will be needed to sustain the organization through this period. Your initial seed capital from internally generated sources and grants may be running low. As your enterprise gains momentum and inches toward profitability, its demands for capital may outstrip resources available from your nonprofit parent. Some philanthropic sources may still be available, but were probably limited from the start. Your goal will be to preserve cash and survive until breakeven is reached. Again, your best bets for capital are a sponsoring entity and your "friends and family." Prepare yourself to make another "ask."

In communities with the benefit of enlightened philanthropic supporters, Program Related Investments (PRIs) may be available. A PRI is a loan provided at below market rates, with a patient payment schedule, and in a subordinate position to other creditors or obligators (such as suppliers). The PRI movement within the national foundation community is growing—but still small. The number of foundations making PRIs has been historically limited because of the significant investment of staff time and infrastructure necessary to run a PRI program. PRI Makers is a national network of foundations and philanthropic organizations interested in expanding the use of this instrument. PRI investments must be made to support charitable activities and involve a potential return of capital within an established time frame. Yet, access to PRI capital may require a guarantee from a sponsoring parent organization or a third-party supporter or a pledge of collateral (for example, real estate owned by a nonprofit, pledges of grants, or contract income). A guarantee may ask for a commitment of up to 100 percent of the principal amount of a PRI, but it can be less. For more information on PRIs, visit www.primakers.net. PRIs are clearly a highly favorable form of debt financing for social enterprises. The problem is that they are not widely available, and they may be unavailable in your community.

Growth or Expansion Stage
What Are Your Challenges?

- Dealing with more competition
- Continuously finding ways to improve efficiency to reduce costs
- Needing more people and systems to sustain growth

- Staying focused

- Feeding the growing working capital needs of the enterprise

You may have achieved or are hopefully close to breakeven. Your social enterprise is an established presence in its market. Your business survived the toddler years and is a growing child. Experience and trial and error are paying off—and haven't killed the business along the way!

Your customer base is growing and so are revenues. You may also be seeing new opportunities for products and services that will enhance your current offerings. As your social enterprise grows, one of your greatest challenges will be to stay focused as a wide range of new operational challenges compete for your time and money. You will need to be highly selective in evaluating the costs and benefits of any new offerings. They can distract you from strengthening core profitability.

At this growth stage, you will likely need to revisit your business plan and growing staffing needs. The more you grow, the more formality and structure (for example, accounting, information technology, personnel systems) you will need to manage growth. You will need to be constantly evaluating and reevaluating operations and delivery systems and improving efficiency. As the enterprise teeters past breakeven, net worth and cash flow are thin, but increasing. Growth and expansion will be necessary to reach real sustainability.

Profits are growing, but don't get too comfortable! Look over your shoulder! Others may be eyeing your profitable niche, and competition may be increasing. You will continually need to make sure your product is better, cheaper, or a better value than what your competitors offer. As competition increases, the window to capitalize on new opportunity or differentiate, your offerings will narrow. You may find additional pressure to gain or maintain market leadership quickly.

What Kind of Capital and Where to Find It?   Capital is needed to fuel the growth of the business. Your early-stage capital is likely to be depleted while cash reserves, net worth, and cash flow are thin. The good news is that new sources of capital are opening up for you.

Social enterprises are established to meet the following goals: (1) to fill a market need; (2) to advance mission; and (3) to attain financial sustainability through the generation of profits. When your enterprise expands to the point where operating expenses can be paid through sustainable recurring revenue (that is, when you reach breakeven), you may be able to support debt payments of principal and interest.

Debt has three key advantages over equity for social enterprises. First, it is available in relatively greater quantities than equity. Second, raising debt is quicker. Third, it often is more flexible than equity provided by philanthropic organizations that often limit the use of funds for specific expenditures or activities.

Within the nonprofit sector, debt is often mistakenly viewed as a sign of poor management. Within the for-profit sector, it is regarded as a key business tool to support capacity building and growth. Debt allows a business to grow quickly, respond to market demand in a timely manner, and build assets that will strengthen the viability of the business over the long run. Social entrepreneurs from the nonprofit sector may need to reevaluate their assumptions about the role of debt lest they forgo using a tool that has been found to be invaluable to the for-profit sector in operating successful businesses.

Debt is available through a variety of sources. Traditional sources include banks, trade credit, credit cards, factoring companies, and others. Social enterprises may also be able to access financing from Community Development Financial Institutions (CDFIs). CDFIs are social enterprises that deliver capital to markets that are underserved by traditional lenders, including low-income individuals or neighborhoods, green businesses that create jobs, and social enterprises that make the world a better place. CDFIs are generally more flexible, patient, and willing to tailor products to borrowers' needs than traditional providers are.

Banks often do not understand nonprofits as well as they understand for-profit businesses. Our financial statements are often more complex and take more time to understand. We often have many different types of revenue—restricted and unrestricted funds—and income statements that make it impossible to distinguish reliable revenue from one-time money. Finally, differences in how the FASB requires nonprofits to report some financial items can confuse and make due diligence difficult.

What Do Lenders Look For?   As the manager of a social enterprise, your goals are straightforward. You need sufficient cash to grow your business. You need payments that are manageable while you build cash flow and profits. You want capital that will enable you to operate your enterprise in a manner that will meet both your financial and social goals.

When you talk to a lender, he or she will look at you first—and foremost—as a business. The lender is providing a loan, not a grant, and does not forgive a loan no matter how worthy the cause. A lender's goals are also straightforward. Your lender wants to preserve capital and get full repayment of principal and interest, as well as to cover the costs of doing business. If your lender is a traditional lender, he or she will be primarily concerned with the preservation of his or her capital and the return on the loan. If your lender is a socially motivated lender (such as CDFI or a foundation), he or she will want a financial return but will also be interested in the borrower's ability to create social impact.

Your lender will need to fully understand your business. By understanding the business, lenders will know whether a loan can be approved, how much money they can provide, and the terms or conditions under which they can offer the loan. You need to have your business plan and financial statements ready when you meet. The first question the lender must assess is whether debt is appropriate at your current stage of development. Lenders use an underwriting methodology often called the "five Cs of credit." The five Cs are: Character, Capacity, Context, Cash Flow, and Collateral.

In assessing *character*, a lender is trying to figure out whether a potential borrower will honor its financial obligation. Potential lenders will look at your track record in honoring past obligations. They may do due diligence to determine what customers say about the quality of services received. They may inquire about your credibility within the community or industry, and among your peers. They will want to know about the reputation of the team running the enterprise.

A lender assesses *capacity* to determine whether the social enterprise team and organization have the ability to successfully run the business over the long term—and hence have the ability to repay the loan. The most critical question is whether the leadership and the people in decision-making roles have the track record and right expertise to run the enterprise in the context of its industry, products and services, target customers, and geographic market. In the case of a social enterprise within a larger organization, your lender may also want to know how much time key managers or staff dedicate to the venture (versus other responsibilities of the larger organization). Your lender wants to be assured that key people are not too distracted by other responsibilities to pay attention to the business.

Your lender will examine your financial condition and infrastructure. He or she needs to know whether you have the financial capacity to repay interest and principal *after* paying day-to-day operating expenses. Your lender will likely ask for audited financial statements. Annual audits cost money, but they are a critical tool for assessing creditworthiness. You should budget an audit as a regular expense. Your lender will want to see that you produce at least monthly financial statements and use the reports to make sure you are meeting your targets. He or she may want to talk to the people who handle the finances of the enterprise to ensure they understand accounting rules and have systems needed to run a money making entity.

As lenders to nonprofits, the authors of this chapter believe that a set of questions around cultural capacity is appropriate for social enterprise borrowers. Given that most social enterprises operate within a larger mission-focused institution, we examine the degree to which the mission and activities of the enterprise and the sponsoring nonprofit are complementary. Our observation is that the closer the mission-activity linkages, the less likely it is that there will be cultural conflicts between the parent and enterprise over "mission drift" or that the venture will be abandoned when the going gets tough. We also assess whether you have demonstrated an entrepreneurial ability in the past. Operating a successful social enterprise requires a shift in thinking—a bottom-line orientation that many non-profits lack. Finally, we would assess the degree to which a social enterprise is "market oriented" versus "mission oriented." As a double-bottom-line business, a social entrepreneur needs to balance both. You need to know ahead of time where and how you will sacrifice one objective for the other if faced with a conflict. There is no wrong or right answer! But you need to know the right balance for your venture, manage to it, and demonstrate to the lender how you will be able to repay the loan despite these conflicts.

You will need to demonstrate to your lender that you understand the market *context* in which you are operating. Your lender wants to know that your leadership is in touch with the realities of your target market. Is there demand for your product or service? Can you distinguish your product from competitors in the market? Do you have the capacity to adjust and adapt to changes in the market? You should share any market analysis you have conducted and be prepared to explain how you keep on top of your ever-changing market.

The bottom-line *cash flow* question your lender wants to know is: Are you consistently generating sufficient revenue *after* paying day-to-day operating expenses to pay the monthly interest and principal on your loan? Your lender will need to examine your sources of revenue and how reliable they are over time, evaluating the extent to which you are covering costs, how close you are to breakeven, and whether you are making progress toward sustainability. Your lender will ask you to make financial projections about your social enterprise's expected performance. He or she will need to make a judgment call as to whether your cash flow projections and assumptions are realistic given historic performance and the market for services. Finally, in the case of a social enterprise operating within the larger organization, your lender will want to examine the financial condition and projections of the parent. These questions will focus on whether the sponsoring parent has the cash flow or sufficient net asset liquidity to step in and make payments if the venture cannot repay the loan.

Collateral is often the most difficult issue for both the social enterprise and its nonprofit parent. Collateral is essentially the commitment of an asset by the borrower. If a borrower cannot repay the loan, it gives the lender the right to take ownership of the asset. Typical forms of collateral include buildings, land, equipment, contract receivables, and accounts receivable. In the case of a nonprofit-owned enterprise, this may also include revenue from grant receivables. For mature nonprofits that have built a strong net asset position, a few lenders allow borrowers to make a general pledge against the assets of the institution. Your lender will want to see collateral that has a value at least equivalent to the value of the loan. If not, your lender may ask that you find a third-party stakeholder to provide a guarantee or pledge their assets.

Mature Stage
What Are Your Challenges?

- Keeping up with a dynamic, competitive market
- Improving efficiency
- Taking advantage of new opportunities while keeping an eye on core profitability
- Managing the growing working capital needs of the business

Your enterprise has stabilized. You have successfully managed at least one growth phase—maybe even several cycles. Sales growth is no longer explosive, but steady and manageable. You have built brand identity. Your customers are happy and loyal. You have worked the bugs out of your production and distribution systems. You have evolved into a thriving company. Things are just humming along . . . or are they?

As a mature business, it could be easy to sit back. But the market is dynamic and competitive. To stay profitable, you may feel a need to constantly keep an eye on the competition, shifts in customer needs, new developments in your industry sector, and the economy. Your efforts may be focused on improving productivity and becoming a leaner, meaner machine to stay ahead. You may also see opportunities for expansion into new markets. You may be faced with making decisions, such as whether to expand market share within your niche or move into new products and markets. All options offer potential rewards, as well as potholes that could send your business into a downward cycle of decline. You must choose carefully.

What Kind of Capital and Where to Find It? As you have scaled the mountain past breakeven to steady profitability, your social enterprise has matured into adulthood. Along the way, however, the working capital needs of your business have grown. You now have substantial permanent working capital needs.

Working capital is an investment of *cash* into operating assets (for example, accounts receivable or inventory) that is needed to generate revenues. Deficits in working capital can cause a cash crunch. If a successful business cannot pay suppliers and creditors when needed, they can go out of business despite strong demand and capacity. A cash crunch can be caused by a variety of factors (such as timing of receipts, collection problems, timing of disbursements, changes in revenue sources or payment structure, unexpected events affecting income and expenses). If your working capital dips too low, you risk running out of cash.

Most businesses have three types of working capital—short-term, seasonal, and permanent. Short-term working capital bridges short-term cash needs and receivables (that is, you need to pay staff today to generate sales and revenue you will collect later). Seasonable working capital is temporary financing tied to business cycle (for example, holiday gifts, ice cream stands) or specific contracts. This type of capital is often not used during off-season. Long-term working capital is needed to finance steady growth over time. As a business grows, its working capital and need for ongoing cash grows with it. The need for working capital is a function of the pattern of sales and revenue growth.

Ongoing working capital is needed to fuel the growth of the business. At this point in your life cycle, debt is probably the only outside source that will be able to satisfy your voracious need for ongoing cash. At this point in your development, you will probably want to have relationships with a bank and maybe more than one large financial institution to ensure that you have ready access to working capital. Assuming you have maintained steady and growing profitability and demonstrated your ability to manage debt, you will be in the driver's seat. Banks will be competing for you as a customer!

CONCLUSION

Your success or failure as a social enterprise business will ultimately depend on your ability to manage your ever-changing life cycles. Finance can often seem like the greatest obstacle to your success. Many practitioners find finance questions among the most difficult to sort through to find the best option. But understanding where your business fits on the life cycle will help you anticipate new challenges and find the right capital that meets your needs today and into the future.

ABOUT THE AUTHORS

Jeannine Jacokes is chief executive officer of Partners for the Common Good (PCG). As a national wholesale participation lender, PCG works with regulated and nonregulated Community Development Financial Institutions (CDFIs) across the United States to finance working capital, affordable housing, community facility, and commercial revitalization projects that create benefits for low-income people and communities. PCG helps CDFIs manage liquidity and other capitalization challenges that would otherwise inhibit their ability to maximize social impact and service to borrowers. Jeannine also serves chief executive and senior policy advisor to the Community Development Bankers Association, the national trade association of the community development banking industry. She serves on the board of directors of Opportunity Finance Network and the CDFI Coalition.

Jeannine previously served as a senior member of the management team at the U.S. Department of the Treasury's CDFI Fund and played a leadership role in designing and implementing the Fund's programs and operations. Formerly senior policy staff for the U.S. Senate Committee on Banking, Housing, and Urban Affairs, she played a key role in drafting many of the laws that currently govern Federal housing and community development programs and which impact the availability of credit in underserved markets. Jeannine also served at the U.S. Department of Housing and Urban Development.

She formerly served as the president of the board of directors of the Women in Housing and Finance Foundation, a District of Columbia community foundation that promotes financial literacy among low-income individuals. She is also a former board member of the Social Enterprise Alliance, a national trade association promoting earned income strategies for high income social ventures. She holds a master's degree in city and regional planning from the University of North Carolina at Chapel Hill and a B.A. from Aquinas College in Grand Rapids, Michigan.

Jennifer Pryce, senior investment officer, oversees the management and growth of Calvert Foundation's domestic investments, which includes the social enterprise portfolio as well as investments in community development finance institutions, fair-trade organizations, and affordable housing development. Prior to the Calvert Foundation, Ms. Pryce worked with Nonprofit Finance Fund, a national CDFI, as the director of the Washington DC-Maryland-Virginia office. Before NFF, Ms. Pryce also held positions at Wall Street firms, working at Neuberger & Berman as an equity research analyst and Morgan Stanley's London office in the investment banking division. Ms. Pryce was a Peace Corps volunteer in Gabon, Africa, and worked at the Public Theater in New York City. Ms. Pryce received a B.S. in mechanical engineering from Union College and an MBA from Columbia University. She serves as the finance chair on the board of Appletree Institute, a Washington, D.C., public charter school, and OneWorld, an international media organization. Ms. Pryce also serves as a member of the selection committee for the *Washington Post* Award for Excellence in Nonprofit Management.

PART TWO

Methods

Product or Service Development

By Mark J. Loranger, *President and Chief Executive Officer, Chrysalis*

The process of developing a product or service for a social enterprise is similar to that used for any entrepreneurial venture, with one big difference: the product or service must have a strong connection to the organization's social mission. A social enterprise without a strong connection to the organization's core mission will face significant challenges.

The reality of starting a business, whether a traditional commercial business or a social enterprise, is that it is inherently risky. The U.S. Small Business Administration (SBA) notes that about half of all businesses close within four years of start-up. Further, the SBA's research shows that businesses that are larger (in terms of revenue and employee base) and better financed are more likely to succeed. For this reason, thorough planning, preparation, and assessment are crucial. This is particularly important for a nonprofit, as it has unique fiduciary and ethical obligations to its clients and stakeholders.

Business plan development in the for-profit sector has been exhaustively documented. A quick search on Amazon.com will find thousands of titles on this topic alone. Although virtually all of the same principles apply when developing a plan for a social enterprise, the one key difference is that the social enterprise plan will have a social benefit component whose costs must be accounted for in the plan. This chapter will highlight the differences between traditional business planning and planning for a social enterprise and suggest a process framework for the venture's development.

My perspective on this topic has been formed as both a for-profit and not-for-profit entrepreneur (although given their financial returns, some of my "for-profit" concepts might have been better organized as nonprofits!). My experience is that the discipline, focus, and credibility that form the basis of for-profit entrepreneurial ventures will serve social entrepreneurs well.

WHAT'S DIFFERENT ABOUT PLANNING A SOCIAL ENTERPRISE?

The steps might be the same, but the decisions made along the way when planning a social enterprise can be quite different from those for planning a for-profit venture. Let's take a look at some of the most significant differences:

Business Purpose

A traditional business has as its primary purpose profit maximization. A social enterprise has a different reason for existence. This may seem obvious, yet it drives much of the planning process. The search for funders, marketing approaches, customers, and employees—all can be different when profit is not the most important objective of the business.

Funding Sources

A social enterprise will most likely be funded by foundation or government grants, or by philanthropic contributions from generous supporters. Although alternative business structures (such as LL3's and B Corporations) are beginning to gain traction, I believe that most social enterprises will be under the umbrella of traditional not-for-profit organizations for the foreseeable future. This means that the written business plan, financial projections, and investor sales pitch must be tuned to the particular needs of nonprofit funders, rather than the needs of investors accustomed to achieving a financial return.

Customer Acquisition and Marketing

This is an area where social enterprises may have advantages over traditional businesses. Depending upon the product or service provided, the social enterprise may be able to leverage its social mission and network of supporters to produce a compelling sales proposition that combines a great product with an important social objective.

Operations Plan

A traditional business will hire the best available talent and maximize efficiencies when developing its operating plan. Because the social enterprise has objectives other than profit maximization, it might choose another path. Rather than use machines to produce a product, for example, the social enterprise might prefer to employ more workers. And rather than hire the most experienced workers, the social enterprise might choose to employ low-skilled workers, or workers with significant barriers to employment, in order to execute its social mission.

CASE STUDY: GROWING A GREEN BUSINESS

In order to bring this topic to life, I'll refer to my experience as president and CEO with Chrysalis, a nonprofit in Los Angeles.

Chrysalis's mission is to help homeless and economically disadvantaged individuals become self-sufficient through employment opportunities. Since 1984, Chrysalis has assisted over thirty thousand people on the path toward regaining their dignity and becoming self-sufficient at its centers in downtown Los Angeles (near Skid Row), Santa Monica, and Pacoima in the San Fernando Valley.

Chrysalis offers a host of employment services, through a unique synergy of supportive social services and paid transitional employment, to strengthen clients' (those who receive services from the organization) employability and help them secure and retain work. The program instills good work habits in the clients—the soft skills that are crucial to success in any work environment. The staff provides encouragement and boosts self-esteem, which clients often desperately need due to their troubled backgrounds. In addition, in order to fully meet the needs of all its clients,

Chrysalis partners with over fifty organizations that provide mental and physical health care, substance abuse rehabilitation, shelter and transitional housing, and education services in Los Angeles County.

As part of its program, Chrysalis operates a transitional jobs program for those clients with the most significant barriers to employment. Transitional jobs deliver marketable experience and job skills and provide a closely supervised, supportive working environment that allows clients to prove themselves as reliable, capable workers. Chrysalis Enterprises is comprised of *Chrysalis Works*, a professional street maintenance company that provides work experience in street maintenance—trash and recycling pick-up, landscaping, graffiti removal, hauling, sweeping—that clients can market to future employers; and *Chrysalis Staffing*, a temporary staffing agency that allows clients to reenter the job market through short-term, full-time, and part-time work assignments. Combined, the two businesses generate $4 million in annual revenue and employ about two hundred clients per week. The businesses are financially self-sustaining. Profit generated from the businesses is used to help support Chrysalis's programs and administrative overhead.

A Good History . . . But Demand for Jobs Grows

Although Chrysalis Enterprises was able to offer transitional employment opportunities to over six hundred clients in 2007, the demand for such positions significantly exceeded the supply of such jobs. In early 2008, management began an intensive examination of the core competencies of Chrysalis Enterprises, the needs of its clients, and opportunities for expansion.

From this work the management team began to review various business opportunities, and quickly began focusing on environmental initiatives. In Southern California, industries that focus on developing solutions to environmental problems are thriving and generating new jobs. In addition, management believes that the "triple bottom line" of a business with a social mission, earned income, and a solution to environmental issues would be well received by Chrysalis' stakeholders. Most of Chrysalis Works contracts have an environmental focus, in the sense that they involve cleaning, the removal of trash and graffiti, and power washing, all done in an environmentally responsible manner. In addition, in partnership with the City of Los Angeles, Chrysalis had been operating a recycling program focused on the collection of recyclables from small offices, apartment buildings, and public rights-of-way. A logical extension of this program would be to consider other recycling, reuse, or landfill diversion efforts.

Through conversations with customers, board members, government officials, and other social entrepreneurs, a business model for *Chrysalis Green* began to take shape. As of the summer of 2009, Chrysalis Green is in the feasibility analysis phase. The intent is to launch a pilot program focusing on the disassembly and recycling of large, bulky items, such as mattresses, in the first half of 2010. As currently envisioned, the business will create 150 transitional jobs per year, generate $1 million in annual revenue, and be self-sustaining.

LESSON LEARNED: FOLLOW A STRUCTURED PROCESS

The creation of a new social enterprise within Chrysalis did not come about overnight. The management team followed a *process*, and carefully considered the *mission* when weighing alternative enterprises. The needs of *customers* and the basic question of "Who will pay for this product or service?" were carefully considered. *Scale and scope* are factors, along with the buy-in of *stakeholders*. Finally, after all of this groundwork has been completed, a solid *business plan* was developed.

Although entrepreneurship can be a solitary endeavor, in the context of social enterprise, it will undoubtedly become a team effort. In most cases, an organization chooses to develop an earned-income strategy as a way to diversify its funding base. This means that a cross section of the organization's staff should be involved in the venture's development: program staff, finance, development, and external stakeholders should all play a role.

At Chrysalis we found it important to convene a working group representing different parts of the organization to develop our strategy for a new venture. If, like many nonprofits, your organization experiences regular staff turnover, the convening of a working group that not only represents a wide variety of interests within the organization, but also represents a variety of tenures and institutional knowledge about the organization can be helpful. Rather than "reinvent the wheel," the group is able to build on research and task force work from the past.

One approach to focusing the venture development process is to structure the process as follows:

1. Determine whether the organization's mission connects to an earned income strategy.

2. Consider what the organization's stakeholders (clients, board members, supporters) need.

3. Find where the mission intersects with the needs of the stakeholders.

4. Identify potential ventures that have characteristics consistent with this intersection.

5. Select and plan the venture.

Lesson 1: Determine Whether the Organization's Mission Connects to an Earned-Income Strategy

As a starting point, dust off the organization's mission statement. Is it still relevant to the needs of today's clients, funders, and governmental entities? If not, now would be an excellent time to update it, as the mission should drive the development process for the social enterprise.

For a workforce development organization like Chrysalis, the link between our mission and our social enterprises is clear: jobs. Other organizations may not have such a clear linkage. How does the mission of a health care agency link to a social enterprise? Perhaps an element of the services that the agency provides can be extended to a broader audience on a fee-for-service basis. How about a provider of hot, prepared meals? Maybe their large industrial kitchen can be leased to caterers or other training programs that can take advantage of the significant infrastructure investment that has already been made.

If the linkage between mission and the venture is missing or weak, there may be negative consequences. Consider a housing agency that is building a new facility. The agency has ground-floor retail space available and is interested in developing a social enterprise in the space. In addition to all the issues that any retail business must address in the start-up phase, this agency must also determine how the new venture will fit into its existing program. The basic question is, "Why do we want to do this?" Given the risks and failure rates of start-ups, the leaders of an organization must be able to concisely, confidently, and honestly answer this question.

Lesson 2: Consider Stakeholder Needs

Once agreement is established by the stakeholders on the linkage between the mission and social enterprise, the process can move on to consideration of what the organization's core constituencies might need. Client needs should be at the forefront of this discussion. Although clients may not play an active role in the venture, the point of the venture must be to benefit the clients in some way.

If the intent is for clients to be employed in the venture, then the demographics, skills, and backgrounds of the clients are key factors to consider. Is the venture intended to be a job program or a training program? Are the jobs transitional or permanent? Do clients need a consistent routine in which to develop soft skills?

Alternatively, if clients are not employed in the venture, will the social enterprise become a distraction to the organization? One topic for early discussion is whether staff resources dedicated to the development, operation, and oversight of the new venture would be better spent on client-focused services. In addition, the existing staff might not have the necessary business or entrepreneurial skills to launch the venture.

Board members and other external stakeholders also have needs that must be considered. Boards have varying degrees of risk tolerance, particularly if an organization is considering its first social enterprise. Because fund-raising will be required to get the venture off the ground, the board must buy into the concept and become actively engaged in supporting it.

The needs of other external constituencies should also be considered. If the organization has strong ties to governmental agencies, how might the social enterprise benefit from these connections? Can the venture provide services for these agencies in exchange for increased funding?

Will the creation of a particular type of earned-income venture position the organization for increased funding from government or foundation programs? Alternatively, will pursuing an earned-income strategy jeopardize existing funding relationships?

Lesson 3: Find Intersections Between Mission and Stakeholders

The intersections of the mission and needs of clients and other stakeholders by now are beginning to take shape. These intersections now become the criteria by which new ventures may be evaluated.

In the case of Chrysalis Green, the team determined that the following characteristics were important in any future business venture:

- **Routine**: Clients should be placed in jobs that involve a regular, daily routine that help support stability and build confidence. In addition, clients working in the venture should have the opportunity to work three to five days per week.

- **Simple, Consistent, and Predictable**: The venture should be relatively easy to manage and have a steady and consistent flow of work (and not be unduly focused on seasonal variations) in order to be a consistent source of jobs for Chrysalis clients.

- **Large Volume**: There needs to be a sufficient number of jobs (at least twenty full-time equivalents) and enough revenue (at least $1 million) to justify the management focus on the venture.

- **Single Location**: The ability to have workers in a single facility is attractive for a number of reasons. Supervision is simplified, and the logistics of managing a large field force of workers is reduced. Most importantly, a single facility provides Chrysalis with the opportunity to deliver its program elements in a more effective manner to a receptive audience.

- **Supervision**: Most of our clients need intense supervision and case management. Therefore, the current Works model, which requires Chrysalis supervision of workers, will be followed.

- **Fits Southern California Economy**: Any new venture should be contemporary with the changing Southern California economy.

- **Minimize Worker Displacement**: Ideally, the new venture will produce net new jobs, rather than displace existing workers by winning a contract from an incumbent vendor.
- **Acceptable Margins**: The venture must produce gross margins that are consistent with Chrysalis's philosophy of its businesses being sustainable on an operating basis.

The criteria developed through this process serve as a powerful tool when evaluating potential ventures.

Lesson 4: Identify Potential Ventures

Using the criteria to focus the search for a venture, the process can finally move to the selection of appropriate businesses. The creativity of the group will likely generate plenty of ideas, but the discipline instilled in the process through the earlier phases will help to focus the effort on those ventures that have the best fit with the unique needs and opportunities facing the organization.

Lesson 5: Select and Plan the Venture

You've developed a list of products or services that meet the criteria. Now the difficult part: choosing a specific business and planning for its success.

As mentioned earlier, there are many resources available to the entrepreneur that discuss business plan development. Rather than trying to add to this existing large body of work, the following section will highlight questions that are particularly important for the social entrepreneur to consider.

Will Our Product or Service Be the Best at Addressing the Specific Issue, Niche, or Problem?　A business venture is, by definition, created to address a need. How will your business succeed at doing this, particularly in light of the competition? Don't expect that your business will attract customers primarily because of its social mission. The mission might end up being a contributing factor, but the business still needs to stand on its own two feet.

Will Anyone Buy Our Product or Service at a Price That Allows Us to Reach Our Financial Goals?　Once again the mission issue comes up. In most cases, customers are unlikely to pay a premium for the product or service simply because of the connection to the social mission. Because your product or service will be comparison shopped, be prepared to defend your price point. In some cases, breaking even is not a necessary objective of the social enterprise. Some organizations are willing to absorb losses from the venture as a cost of the social mission. If that is the case, determine early in the process the tolerance for such losses (or investment) and the source for funding them.

Are We So in Love with a Particular Concept That We Are Missing the Forest for the Trees?   Yes, you built a process, and you have diligently followed it. But along the way you fell in love with a particular business idea. Although you may find it difficult to disassociate yourself from this idea, it is crucial to objectively evaluate each concept on its merits. This is an excellent opportunity to ask for help from external stakeholders. Outsiders are more likely to take a dispassionate view of the selection process, particularly if they have a business or entrepreneurial background.

Who's Going to Run the Venture?   When venture capitalists make investment decisions, one of the most important criteria is the venture capitalist's confidence in the management team. It's common to hear investors say "I'd rather invest in a 'B' company run by an 'A' leader than an 'A' company with a 'B' leader." Venture capitalists can teach us an important lesson when it comes to leadership. If this is the organization's first social enterprise, it is critical to recruit a competent general manager with extensive commercial business experience. This general manager must also be given flexibility to select his or her own team. A growing number of MBA graduates have an interest in nonprofit or social enterprise management, so the availability of candidates with the right mix of social consciousness and business skills is increasing.

Will It Scale?   There's lots of discussion in social enterprise circles these days about "scalability." For the purposes of this discussion, I'm referring to the scale of the venture relative to the parent organization and the local market opportunity. Establishing a business is hard work under ordinary circumstances. Doing so within a social enterprise framework is even more difficult. If the business isn't going to be of significant size and contribute substantial revenue to the organization, produce many jobs for the organization's clients, or otherwise make significant progress toward meeting the organization's mission ... why do it? Nonprofits historically have a challenging time finding the resources to meet their traditional mission; adding the challenge of a new social enterprise should only be attempted if the payoff is expected to be substantial.

LET MISSION DRIVE ENTERPRISE

Choosing the right product or service for a social enterprise is an exciting challenge for nonprofits searching for an earned-income venture. The excitement comes from the opportunity to advance the organization's mission by implementing a venture that may diversify the funding base and at the same time put clients to work, monetize the organization's unique expertise, or otherwise take advantage of the organization's assets. The challenge comes from the additional burden of planning a venture within the framework of a nonprofit or socially responsible business. Because the mission is the key driver of the organization, so too must it be the driver of the business.

As we look to the future, expect new funding options for social enterprises that are hybrids of traditional venture capital and foundation giving. In addition, loan programs will become a viable option for nonprofits looking to create such ventures. However, just as in the private sector, these investors will be asking the following:

- What's the big idea, and why is it better than the other funding opportunities under consideration?
- Who's on the team?
- How will I earn a return, whether the return is defined in monetary terms or based on social or environmental outcomes?

These questions can be addressed by a thorough business planning process, which, if done properly, will position the new venture for success.

ABOUT THE AUTHOR

Mark J. Loranger is the president and chief executive officer of Chrysalis, a workforce development agency whose mission is to help homeless and economically disadvantaged individuals become self-sufficient through employment opportunities. Prior to becoming CEO of Chrysalis in March of 2009, Mark held the position of vice president for Chrysalis Enterprises, the social enterprise division of Chrysalis. In that position he was a key member of the senior management team and was responsible for social enterprises that produced $4 million in revenue, were financially self-sustaining, and employed over two hundred.

Early in his career, Mark held various sales and technical positions for IBM in both Washington, D.C., and New York. After leaving IBM Mark became an entrepreneur. Among his entrepreneurial ventures he counts the founding, operation, and sale of a leading logistics and marketing firm in Southern California. Prior to joining Chrysalis, Mark served as a consultant to such not-for-profit organizations as the Alzheimer's Association, the Avon Products Foundation, and the Leukemia and Lymphoma Society in the development and execution of large-scale fundraising walks. He holds a B.S. in electrical and computer engineering from the University of California–Davis and a master's in international business from George Washington University.

Image, Advertising, and Communications

*By **Martin Schwartz**, President, Vehicles for Change*

Andre Agassi stated in his Canon commercials many years ago that "image is everything." That statement says it all about your advertising and communications. We can build the best organization in the world, but if the public views it differently, for whatever reason, success will be difficult to attain.

Your business plan drives the image of the organization. That image says who you are, what you do, and how you do it. The look of your physical organization, the office (inside and outside), the staff, your Web site, and communication pieces tell your story long before your public will ever meet you in person.

Ultimately, you ask yourself and the management in your organization: "What do we want people think about us?" Everything you touch as an organization must consistently answer this question.

Advertising and communications—your message—drive customers to your door and, ultimately, drive your revenue. Advertising is the means by which you will communicate your message to your potential customers, convincing them to take a desired action. That action is to make a purchase or visit a Web site, thus generating revenue for your organization. Advertising includes a variety of purchased items in various media such as radio, television, print, Internet, and direct marketing.

It also should include creative means of directly reaching your customer base (these will be discussed later in the chapter).

AN IMAGE MUST BE GROUNDED IN REALITY

Vehicles for Change (VFC) opened in 1999 with a $30,000 grant and began awarding cars to worthy families in one rural county in Maryland. Starting with a staff of two, a small office, a parts partner, and a dream of assisting low-wage families attain their "American" dream by providing them with reliable transportation. Since then, VFC has grown to awarding over three thousand cars and changing the lives of more than nine thousand individuals. Today, VFC has twelve full-time team members awarding cars in most of Maryland, Virginia, and Washington, D.C., awards thirty to fifty cars per month, and runs a wholesale and used car business, Freedom Wheels, that generates as much as 30 percent of our total revenue. In 2007, VFC awarded five hundred cars to worthy families, generated over $2 million in revenue and was highlighted in Public Television's Business Connection and Motor Week, *AAA Magazine*, the *Wall Street Journal*, the *Baltimore Sun*, the *Washington Post*, and appeared in a documentary created by the Anne E. Casey Foundation called *Pursuit of the Dream*.

Vehicles for Change attained this massive growth and success by:

- Providing a quality product
- Creating the image of an organization that puts the customer first
- Doing whatever it takes to increase the number and quality of cars to families in need by communicating to the public that there is no better place to retire your old car than allowing Vehicles for Change to award it to a worthy family.

Freedom Wheels is a revenue-generating arm of Vehicles for Change. In 2003 VFC was looking to increase revenue to fund an expansion in the number of cars awarded to worthy families. Freedom Wheels was the result.

Knowing that the used car business was one with a very negative reputation, we set out to design a used car business that would directly address that trend. The great thing about starting a business from scratch is the ability to design it from the bottom up.

Freedom Wheels, building on the reputation established by Vehicles for Change, set out to create the image of a trustworthy organization providing reliable, low-cost, used cars. This was achieved by:

1. Pricing quality cars at below market prices

2. Donating 100 percent of net proceeds back to VFC

3. Providing a three-day return policy, no questions asked

4. Providing a six-month/six-thousand-mile warranty (typically not something done by used car dealers)

5. Providing customers the opportunity to review competitors' deals while at our location via Internet

6. No hassle pricing

7. Standing behind the product and offering exemplary customer service

8. Understanding our primary customers (parents of high school kids and low-wage families)

9. Sales staff with a simple and soft approach

Each of these choices combined to create our desired image. Our customers now sell the image for us. About 30 percent of our customers are either repeat or referred by prior customers.

Satisfied customers build our image and bring in new customers. Word-of-mouth is the best form of advertising. Freedom Wheels regularly surveys its customers to make sure the image we think we are portraying is in fact how they see us. Listen to your customers. They are the only ones who can tell you if you are as good as you want to be!

LESSONS LEARNED: LEARN ADVERTISING BY TRIAL AND ERROR

Your advertising messages are driven by the image you want to portray as an organization and must take into account a number of key factors. These are

- Who your potential customer is

- What you want him or her to do

- When and how you can reach customers in the most economical fashion
- How many times will they need to hear your message before they will act
- How much they need to spend in order to make your venture profitable

Every car that Vehicles for Change provides to a low-wage family is obtained through donation. In addition, VFC generates 30 percent of its operating funds through donation of cars that cannot be awarded to a family. Consequently, we spend a considerable amount of resources, both financial and human, in generating car donations. At VFC car donations are our life blood. Purchasing successful advertising to generate donations is one of the most difficult activities I have undertaken.

There is no better learning experience than doing. I was fortunate to be able to start several social ventures over the years, not all of them successful, but all of them have been great learning experiences. Thomas Edison once said, when asked about how he felt about the many times he had failed, "I have not failed. I have just found 10,000 ways that won't work."

Your social venture will provide you with many learning experiences of how your marketing and advertising won't work. Each one provides you the opportunity to make the next better. Constantly tweak your advertising and communications by collecting data from your customers as to what works and what works *really* well.

There is a plethora of information available to assist in directing your advertising purchases. For a social enterprise dealing with vehicles, radio is an excellent medium, and so most of our successes have come through radio advertisements. There are ratings available of the area's top radio stations, providing statistics on which stations have the most listeners, and the demographics of the listeners. The information even reveals a breakdown of which station has the most listeners at specific times of day. There is also data stating how many "impressions" are necessary before a listener will be moved to action. This in essence means a listener must hear your commercial X times before he or she will be moved to make a purchase, visit a Web site, or donate a car.

It is important to know your customers. VFC had a professional organization complete a study of our donor base in 2005. We discovered that our donors had household incomes of $75,000 and higher, were married couples with two or more children, and lived in mainly four different counties in our region. This study helps us direct our advertising efforts to the individuals meeting these demographics. Fortunately, it is possible to identify the radio stations reaching this particular market.

Creating the Optimum Advertising Campaign:

- Match the most suitable station with the demographics of your potential customers
- Identify which times you need to place your message to achieve the desired number of impressions
- Design a message that will inspire your customers to act

Even then, there is no guarantee that your ad campaign will generate sales, or in the case of VFC, car donations. Obviously, this is easier with an unlimited budget. Unfortunately, very few have that luxury. Research and tracking can help you determine which campaigns to continue and which to cut.

Our approach to purchasing advertising on a new radio station is to purchase a three-month package, usually buying spots during three out of four weeks and targeting those spots on morning and evening drive time (6 A.M. to 9 A.M. and 4 P.M. to 8 P.M.). We track the donations from that station to determine whether the number of cars donated is meeting expectations—for example, one car donated for every $200 to $250 spent. If the station meets expectations, we continue with the program; if not we invest those funds in another station or media.

The approach we have devised, purchasing three months during drive time only, is one that we feel is successful. It allows a station enough time to build an awareness of VFC and to build donations to the desired level. We monitor each new station very closely. At the end of the period, we make a decision based on hard data. VFC tracks the source of each donation by asking the donors where they found out about us. This is how we evaluate the effectiveness of each advertising campaign, partnership, or marketing event.

Over the past five years we have used this approach with eight radio stations. Each of these had our required listener demographic. We took the same approach with each station and, for the most part, used the same message in each. Of the eight, only two proved to generate the desired car donation results. These two have been very successful, and we continue to advertise with them. It is important to note that we continue to evaluate their effectiveness each month and continually tweak the run times and message to generate the greatest possible yield.

There are no guarantees in advertising. At one point VFC engaged a professional firm to design a new message specifically targeting the "VFC donor." The new message was different from the one we were currently using in a successful campaign. The program selected and designed by the professional organizations was a disaster. It resulted in only five car donations over the three-month period and cost VFC $12,000. The end result had little to do with the organization's lack of expertise, but more to do with the lack of guarantee one can expect from an advertising campaign, particularly when funding is limited.

Develop a strategy and budget that will work for you and your customers. Identify the medium or various media that will give your strategy the best opportunity for success. Monitor your results and be willing to reinvest your advertising dollars when necessary.

Use News Media to Your Advantage

The media, newspaper, Internet, and television, are a great way of communicating your message without spending scarce funds. An item in any of these has several benefits.

1. Provides your organization a third-party endorsement
2. Typically tells your story to a wide audience
3. Often includes testimonials from customers
4. Provides your organization with a piece that you can use for your own promotions

VFC is always examining our daily operation looking for stories the press may find interesting for their readers or viewers. Our service region covers the states of Maryland and Virginia and Washington, D.C. This is a fertile area for newspapers (major and local), television stations, and Internet options. Stories we have exposed to these groups include:

1. New expansions into counties (local papers and television stations)
2. Major expansions
3. New board members
4. Recipients who, as a result of receiving a car, achieved new heights
5. Awards received
6. Changes in the tax law
7. Monumental numbers that demonstrate success, such as three thousand car awards

It is important to utilize your board members, friends, customers, and anyone else with connections to writers, producers, and so on. An "inside connection" is always helpful. If you or one of your team members can build an ongoing relationship with these individuals, it will reap great rewards.

Media should be a part of your overall communications plan. Vehicles for Change has a goal of achieving two articles per month in one of these options. It is one of the focuses of our marketing coordinator and public relations team. One article placed in a major newspaper generated sixty-eight car donations over a two-month period. Publicity like this is invaluable and has a very long shelf life.

Employ Constant Creativity

Often start-up organizations and social ventures do not have an abundance of operating capital. Look at all the options and find ways to generate exposure while minimizing expenditures. This is an ongoing effort at VFC; it is part of our overall corporate culture. Our team members, board members, customers, and friends are encouraged to contact us with ways they think we can generate car donations. Many of them do just that.

Examples include:

- A car recipient once requested a hundred promotional flyers that she would distribute at an event she was attending. Simple but effective.

- At one of our regular marketing committee meetings we were discussing creating a new marketing packet to be designed and mailed to potential partners. One of the committee members suggested we take advantage of technology and use a flash drive to achieve this. The flash drive is a simple item to mail, can include a news piece recently published by one of the local news celebrities, and is very inexpensive to create.

- Another board member who has a contact at a major accounting firm volunteered to get his contact to send an e-mail to every employee at the firm. No-cost, huge impact!

All of these are low-cost and effective ways of gaining exposure to the individual who has the means of donating a car. They also give your constituents a sense of contribution to the organization. They will keep coming back!

One of our most innovative ideas grew from a chance meeting and letting the creative juices flow. Attending a golf tournament, I met the director of development of a local hospital. When first meeting an individual in this kind of position, I attempt to discover as much about his or her organization as possible, particularly his or her challenges. Then I look for ways in which VFC can assist in solving these challenges, ultimately building a win-win partnership.

This particular hospital had a problem retaining lower-wage employees due to a lack of transportation. This is a common problem in hospitals and an obvious challenge that VFC could help overcome. VFC has an ongoing need to find donated cars and ways to reach individuals in our target demographics who may have cars to donate. In this instance, the hospital has doctors, nurses, and other staff who meet those demographics. We struck a partnership whereby the hospital informs the staff of the opportunity of donating cars to VFC. Working with the human resources department at the hospital, VFC identifies individuals who would be able to maintain their current positions or obtain a promotion as a result of owning a car.

This was a great partnership for VFC and, through the connections of our board and other constituents, we are creating similar partnerships with other nonprofit organizations, including private high schools, associations, and others.

Create a culture of open thinking within your organization. Encourage your staff to think creatively and reward them for new and creative ideas. Some managers have a tendency to squelch ideas if they do not initiate with themselves or other management. The more you can engage your team members in thinking about how they can contribute to the success of the organization, the greater your chance of success and the more engaged they will become.

Use People Power

Your best sales people and marketers are those individuals who have purchased your product. Your ultimate goal is to get the general public so buzzed about your product that everyone is talking about it. Your customers create a buzz that generally pushes you over the top; this is known as the "tipping point." In a book by the same name, Malcolm Gladwell defines the tipping point as "the moment of critical mass." What a great way to look at the situation: imagine your customers, all buzzing about your organization and your product, creating a critical mass of marketers.

The phenomenon of teen fads is a perfect example. How often have we seen clothing manufacturers attempt to create their own tipping point? They attempt to use the hip teens, those seen by others as the individuals to follow, to promote their products. Back in my day it was Chuck Taylor high-top tennis shoes. Today it is Nike and Under Armour. They reach the tipping point by getting the top athletes to wear their shoes or line of clothing. Then they get the younger athletes to wear it. Under Armour started as an athletic clothing line, mainly for use by football players under their uniforms. Their clothes have now become a fashion statement.

Freedom Wheels adopted this same approach to selling cars. The Freedom Wheels cars are priced at a level where they are attainable for high school students and their parents. Our goal is to get the "hip" kids at the school to purchase cars from Freedom Wheels. Because making a car purchase is much different from purchasing clothing, this is a much more difficult task, but the steps are similar.

1. A "cool" logo was designed by a local university graduate school design class at the University of Baltimore.

2. Several of these logos were reviewed and voted on by a group of high school students who were considered the cool kids in their schools.

3. The logo was then put on shirts and decals.

4. Each individual who purchases a car from Freedom Wheels receives a tee shirt and is encouraged to wear the shirt to school.

5. Partnerships are established with the "sports boosters" groups in the nearby high schools. These partnerships pay the booster programs $50 for each car sold to students at that school. The goal is to get the sports boosters to promote the benefits of purchasing a car from Freedom Wheels. They focus particularly on the student athletes, as they are often some of the more popular individuals in the school.

6. In addition, a student marketing team is created. This consists of one student from each of the ten local high schools. These students receive community service credit for their work on the committee, and students who complete their assignments during the year also receive a $500 scholarship to the college of their choice.

The goal is to get the students and parents to spread the word that the best place to purchase a car is Freedom Wheels. Currently 35 percent of all car sales are made to high school students.

IMAGE BUILDING NEVER STOPS

As Agassi said, "image is everything." What he did not say is that creating that image is not easy, is all-encompassing, and is never over. Your image not only identifies who you are but will also have the final say as to your level of success. It takes daily diligence and years of hard work to build the image you desire. Unfortunately, it takes just a short period of time, when you let your guard down, to tarnish that image.

Image, advertising, and communications are the meat of your organization. The best products in the world do not sell themselves just because they are the best. They need a plan to bring them to market. The combination of an outstanding product and a great marketing plan will give your organization the greatest chance of success.

ABOUT THE AUTHOR

Martin Schwartz, president of Vehicles for Change, initiated more than five social ventures over the past twenty-eight years, starting with an adult education program in a private high school in 1981 and concluding with Freedom Wheels in 2005. In between, he directed the attendance record–setting NCAA Men's Lacrosse Championships in 2003, 2004, and 2007, received the Baltimore Area Visitors and Conventions Bureau "Salesperson of the Year" award and University of Baltimore's "Social Entrepreneur of the Year" award. Vehicles for Change is currently under a strategic plan to expand the number of cars awarded to worthy families from five hundred per year to two thousand per year by 2013.

Generating Sales Through Great Customer Service

*By **Martin Schwartz**, President, Vehicles for Change*

Sales are the ultimate goal of the earned-income venture. That is what generates your bottom-line success. As you will see, the way to gain sales is through exemplary customer service. That's because customer service is what keeps your customers coming back.

The advantage we have, as organizations dedicated to social good, is that customer service is what we are all about. Our organizations are evaluated on how well we provide our particular service. As the social venture arm of a nonprofit, you can take that service experience and duplicate it in your earned-income venture—by focusing on providing the best service possible.

Marketing and advertising may drive customers to your door. But customer service will keep them inside the door. *Customer service* is everything you do to make your customers feel they can trust your organization and your product. Customer service "is a series of activities designed to enhance the level of customer satisfaction—that is, the feeling that a product or service has met the customer expectation."[1]

If you think about it, you already know what makes *bad* customer service; everyone has had poor customer service experiences. And today, the outstanding customer service experience is less and less the norm.

But the prevalence of bad customer service is good news for your nonprofit social venture, because nonprofits already know how to provide excellent customer service. The one thing that will close a sale is customer service and, more important, it will bring your customers and their friends back for more. And that means that exemplary customer service can be your competitive advantage over others in your marketplace.

This is the case for Freedom Wheels, a used car business in which top customer service is a key to success. In an industry with the reputation for providing possibly the poorest customer service of all, Freedom Wheels and its parent organization, Vehicles for Change, stand out, as the following case illustrates.

BUILDING A BUSINESS ON EXEMPLARY SERVICE

Vehicles for Change (VFC) opened in 1999 with a $30,000 grant and a goal of awarding cars to worthy families in one rural county in Maryland. VFC started with a staff of two individuals, a small office, a parts partner, and a dream of assisting low wage families attain their "American" dream by providing them with reliable transportation. Since then, VFC has grown, awarding over three thousand cars and changing the lives of more than six thousand individuals. Today VFC has twelve full-time team members, awards thirty to fifty cars per month in most of Maryland and Virginia, and operates a wholesale and used car business, Freedom Wheels, that generates as much as 30 percent of its total revenue. In 2007 alone, VFC awarded five hundred cars to worthy families, generated over $2 million in revenue and was highlighted in Public Television's Business Connection and Motor Week, *AAA Magazine*, the *Wall Street Journal*, the *Baltimore Sun*, the *Washington Post*, and appeared in a documentary created by the Casey Foundation called *Pursuit of the Dream*.

Vehicles for Change has attained this massive growth and success by providing a quality product and by creating the image of an organization that puts the customer first, will do whatever it takes to increase the number and quality of cars going to families in need, and communicating to the public that there is no better way to retire your old car than allowing Vehicles for Change to award it to a worthy family.

You have just survived some of the toughest economic times in history because you built an organization that provides a valuable service to the community and one that is most likely delivered with extreme passion. That is because you and your team believe in the mission and purpose of the organization. Your profit-making social venture is an extension of your mission. It is the funding arm of your organization and will most likely provide the funding for either current operating activities or expansion. In either case it is vital to achieving your mission. Take the same passion your team has for the mission and put it into the social venture.

Freedom Wheels was designed as a program of VFC in 2003 in response to the desire to expand VFC and to provide cars to more families. VFC had in essence built a used car business on the reputation of quality and service. Overall, the used car business has a very negative reputation. In designing Freedom Wheels, VFC set out to design a used car business that would directly address that trend. The great thing about starting a business from scratch is that it can be designed from the bottom up.

Freedom Wheels set out to attract customers interested in purchasing a low-cost (less than $6,000) car from an organization they could trust to provide them with the highest possible quality. Fortunately, Freedom Wheels had a head start in that VFC was built on this same reputation. Freedom Wheels has sold cars for the past three years in the price range of $2,500 to $6,000 and in 2007 generated over $400,000 in net income. This income was used to award four hundred cars to worthy families through Vehicles for Change.

Customer Service Starts with Strategy

Generating sales is the ultimate goal of an earned income venture. Price and quality will help bring your customers in the door. How you treat your customers will determine whether they buy your product and, more important, return for more and tell their friends.

In reality, sales actually begin long before you open your doors. This includes reviewing the competition, defining your customer base, understanding your own costs, understanding the market size and trends, and pricing your product to attract them. It is important to review the overall strategy to determine how you will offer your project. Let's look at some of the elements you should examine.

The Competition You must know how your competition is pricing their products. Are they higher, lower, or the same, and why? This can be done by shopping online or by going to their location and seeing what they offer. In the car business, the Internet makes this simple. Most car dealerships place their used cars on one of two car sales sites in our region. By reviewing similar cars on these sites, we can determine the selling points of the competition. Freedom Wheels cars are typically the least expensive by design.

Price Point How you determine the price of your product is a complicated process that has to take into account many factors. These include, but are not limited to, pricing strategy, the competition, cost of generating the product (cost of goods sold), the primary customers, and their ability to afford your product. A poorly priced product may not generate any sales if priced too high, and too low a selling price may not generate enough revenue to sustain your business.

Know Your Target Market The Freedom Wheels primary target market is the high school student population. This is a cost-conscious market looking to purchase a car for a short term—in most instances, during the last two years of high school. Freedom Wheels cars are priced at 10 to 20 percent below the competition and the marketing is kept to a minimum using Cars.com and creating a word-of-mouth network.

Cost of Goods Sold Your price point must take into account the costs incurred to produce one unit of product. That is how much it will cost to get one item on the sales floor, shelf, or Internet. At Freedom Wheels this cost includes towing, fuel, parts and labor for repairs, detailing, and direct marketing (Internet). The price must be greater than the total cost of these items plus the overhead and our desired net profit.

Market Size and Trends Customer service actually starts with knowing your market size and trends. You must determine whether there are enough customers in your region to support your sales projections. It is important to review the number of customers in your region, the competition for that customer, and how your product will penetrate that market. You will also need to review the market trends and how they affect your projections.

Freedom Wheels established their primary market as high school students and, in particular, student athletes. A review of the market trends revealed that parents were providing cars for high school student athletes. In fact, 92 percent of high school student athletes older than sixteen surveyed in the local region had cars for their personal use. But were there enough *potential* customers in this market to push the number of sales we projected? We discovered that within a ten-mile radius there was a total potential market of 5,100 students, with an annual market of 1,275 students turning sixteen each year. Sales projections were based on these numbers and a marketing plan outlining how Freedom Wheels would entice the customer to purchase from Freedom Wheels.

From Market Research to Customer Service   After looking at the market, Freedom Wheels decided to build its market based on five principles:

1. The Price Is Right   One of the key selling points in buying a used car, particularly for a young person, is price. Freedom Wheels cars are priced purposely 10 to 20 percent below market to ensure that our customers will chatter about the "great deal" they received.

2. Car Quality   Naturally, the quality of the car needs to be at a high level. Parents buying for their high school child want a reliable and safe car. Our research revealed that reliability and safety are important factors with this customer base.

3. No-Haggle Pricing   Most customers would prefer to have a set price and not have to negotiate. That way they know they are getting the same deal as anyone else. This is a growing trend in cars sales.

4. Warranty and Return Policy   Car buyers walk in the door of a used car business very skeptical. Freedom Wheels looked to alleviate this skepticism right from the start. Our goal was to make buyers feel certain that they were making a good purchase. So the thought was to provide them "peace of mind" with their purchase. Three elements assure peace of mind:

First, we want the customer to be sure that the car they purchase is all we say it is and that the price was in fact a bargain. We provide a CarFax report with every car and have an Internet browser available on a computer in the office where they can compare prices at car purchasing Internet sites. Customers are also allowed to take the car to their own mechanic for a full review. Often this mechanic recommends some repairs, which we take care of, whether this customer purchases the car or it winds up back on the lot.

Second, we provide a six-month/six-thousand-mile warranty. This is included with almost every car. Customers know that if there is a problem with their car, Freedom Wheels will stand behind it. We fix the car under warranty, no questions asked.

Third, Freedom Wheels customers have the option of returning their car within three days of purchase for a full refund, again no questions asked.

5. Make Sure You Always Know Your Customer When the Freedom Wheels business plan was first created, we did considerable research with our customer base. The desires of customers change. You need to adapt your offerings to their changing desires in style, in economy, or in technology.

Freedom Wheels surveys buyers on a bimonthly basis to find out what they like about Freedom Wheels and what they would change. We ask them for suggestions to help us make the business more customer friendly. This not only allows us to keep our finger on the pulse of our customer base, but they also feel like a part of our business—they will come back when they need another car, and they will tell others about us.

Freedom Wheels also tracks the source that brought every buyer to our front door. It might be an advertisement on Cars.com or someone who drove by and saw a car on the lot. In this way we can understand how best to invest our marketing funds. Currently 30 percent of our customers are recommended by a prior customer or are repeat customers. Great customer service does not usually cost any more than poor customer service. Except in future sales!

Tie It All Together with Great Customer Service

It is not that difficult to get customers to come into your place of business and, in some cases, to convince them to make a purchase. But ultimately you want that customer to become your top marketer. Consequently, your staff must go the extra mile. The effort is guaranteed to pay off.

Build the corporate culture of customer service. Let your team know that it is not only acceptable to go out of your way for a customer but it is encouraged!

The Freedom Wheels approach is to treat every customer as if he or she is our best friend, family member, or a guest in our home. Treat them as you want to be treated if you were on the customer side of the equation. Do the "right" thing. It is that simple. If you provide great customer service, the financial side of the ledger will take care of itself.

But what does this look like in practice? Following is the story of the "car that would not go away." It shows the lengths to which one should go when providing great customer service.

The Car That Would Not Go Away   At Freedom Wheels we have a particular customer who purchased a Jeep Cherokee for his high school–age son. He had had the car for two years and recently contacted us about trading in the Jeep for a smaller, more gas-efficient car. This customer had already recommended Freedom Wheels to several other high school parents.

The director of Freedom Wheels suggested that the customer come in and take a look at a Honda Civic that we had just placed on the sales lot. The customer had built such a trust in the director that he bought the car sight unseen. The car turned out to be nothing but trouble!

Within the first month a problem developed with the transmission. It took our mechanic three weeks to discover and finally correct the problem. During that time the director provided the customer with a loaner car at our expense and daily updates as to what was going on with the Honda. All the while he was offering the customer the opportunity to either receive a full refund or the opportunity to accept another car. The customer declined and the Honda was returned. The repairs were all covered under the six-month/six-thousand-mile warranty—something most used car businesses do not offer.

Within another month the customer called and the engine had overheated, destroying the engine. Though there was a good chance this problem was caused by driver error, the Freedom Wheels director did not even broach the subject. He had the car picked up that day, provided a loaner, replaced the engine and returned the vehicle to the customer in three days. Freedom Wheels absorbed the total costs, ultimately losing $250 on the total deal. This was all done because it was the "right" thing to do.

This customer had purchased a car and in the first three months of ownership had the transmission rebuilt and the engine replaced. He had the ability to drive the vehicle about sixty out of the ninety days he owned the car. Most customers would be calling their lawyer or at least the Better Business Bureau. This customer is telling everyone how Freedom Wheels is the most reliable and customer-friendly company he has ever encountered. That will generate more sales and bottom-line income than any advertising we could ever purchase. Freedom Wheels will recoup much more than the $250 lost in this transaction. AND we all sleep well every night!

TWO CUSTOMER SERVICE LESSONS

In our years operating Vehicles for Change and now Freedom Wheels, we've learned some important customer service lessons.

1. Treat Them "Right" and the Customer Will Sell Themselves and Others

Your customers are your most valued assets. If you treat them "right" they will generate more revenue than any other asset you own. There is no secret to understanding great customer service, but in many organizations this seems to be a hard thing to maintain. Companies lose track of what has made them successful—their customers. Instead they get greedy and focus on profits.

Freedom Wheels was designed and is operated with one person in mind and that is the customer. Unlike most car sales organizations, our sales team is not aware of how much money we have invested in a particular car. Our main goal is to find out what the customer wants and then to make sure we deliver it.

In the book *Positively Outrageous Service,* author T. Scott Gross states, "You cannot easily separate a product from the service experience. And, the service experience will have an even greater role in the purchase decision, especially when the products under consideration are similar."[2] Gross relates research showing that three elements influence the buying decision. First, that the product is effective—it performs as advertised. Second, that the seller is responsive—the product is delivered on time. And third, that the service is personal—the customer feels good about the purchase. And this last is actually the most important; research shows that customers weight it at 70 percent of the value of their experience.

It is our experience that this is never more true than in purchasing a used car. The total buying experience has been the reason our customers return. Treat them right and they will not only buy the first time, but you will also keep them coming back!

2. Convert Problems and Complaints into Your Best Sales Tools

Most organizations and people generally want to avoid confrontation. They think that if a problem is not addressed it might go away. This approach cannot be more destructive to your organization and sales when it comes to your customers. Complaints should be addressed immediately or as soon as possible. They should be addressed with complete satisfaction of the customer and whenever possible by the executive director of the organization.

Vehicles for Change and Freedom Wheels use problems or complaints as a means to better know our customers. If a customer has a complaint about the operation of a car, it is immediately reviewed and resolved.

For example, there was a particular customer who had a problem with a "check engine" light continually coming on in his car. Freedom Wheels attempted to repair the problem several times over the period of seven to eight months. The car ran fine but this light came on for many different reasons. In each situation the car was taken to a shop immediately, resolved, and returned to the customer. In a matter of several weeks the light would come back on. The customer and the salesperson were very discouraged and the customer had lost confidence in this car. The warranty had expired, and Freedom Wheels had no liability to continually correct the problem. It would have been easy to walk away. Instead the customer was provided with a full refund of his purchase price. He was so astonished that a used car business would do this he went back out on our lot and purchased another car. Since then he has recommended several of his friends to Freedom Wheels.

SALES MAKE THE WORLD GO ROUND

In the world of earned-income ventures, sales make the world go round. Pricing your product appropriately, identifying your market and customer, and then taking care of that customer at every opportunity will make your world go round.

Give your customers something to crow about. Provide them with service that goes beyond what they expect. Social organizations are born from a passion to make the world a better place, whether that organization is a domestic violence shelter or a recreation program. The passion should translate into an outstanding experience for the client.

That passion is your leg up on your competition. You understand what great customer service is all about. Take that same passion and implant it into your earned-income venture. Show your new customers the same love you show your current clients. Great success will follow!

Notes

1. Efraim Turban, *Electronic Commerce: A Managerial Perspective* (Prentice Hall, Upper Saddle River, NJ, 2002).
2. T. Scott Gross, *Positively Outrageous Service*, 2nd ed. (Dearborn Trading, Chicago, IL, 2004).

ABOUT THE AUTHOR

Martin Schwartz, president of Vehicles for Change, initiated more than five social ventures over the past twenty-eight years, starting with an adult education program in a private high school in 1981 and concluding with Freedom Wheels in 2005. In between, he directed the attendance record–setting NCAA Men's Lacrosse Championships in 2003, 2004, and 2007, received the Baltimore Area Visitors and Conventions Bureau "Salesperson of the Year" award and University of Baltimore's "Social Entrepreneur of the Year" award. Vehicles for Change is currently under a strategic plan to expand the number of cars awarded to worthy families from five hundred per year to two thousand per year by 2013.

Advocacy and Social Enterprise

By Charles King, *Founder and President of Housing Works, Inc.*

Too often, social enterprise is seen as just one more stream of revenue for organizations, particularly social service organizations, to carry out their social mission. I would argue that social enterprise is far more than that. At its core, social enterprise is about social change. First and foremost, it is about changing the organization so that it approaches its social mission from an entrepreneurial perspective. Second, in many, if not most, cases, it is about changing the people who are served by the organization, and about changing their roles in relation to the organization. Finally, it should be about changing the social structures that have compelled the organization into existence.

Most social service organizations are created because someone sees a serious social need that is not being addressed by the existing systems in the community. To meet that need, we respond by creating an organization that works to fill the gap. We see hungry people, so we decide to open a soup kitchen or a food bank. We see people sleeping on the street, so we open a shelter or supportive housing program. We see people without jobs, so we create employment programs. There are any number of other examples, but you get the idea.

Once we decide to develop an organized response, we start looking for funding. Here in the United States, the bulk of funding for these programs comes from the federal, state, and local governments, as it has at least since the War on Poverty programs of the Johnson era in the 1960s. Additional dollars come from the private and corporate philanthropic sectors, but these are rarely adequate to sustain a meaningful program without public moneys. So, responding to requests for proposals, we go on the government dole, taking tax dollars to fulfill our social mission, whether it is feeding the hungry, housing the homeless, or providing jobs.

The problem with this funding strategy is that our organizations quickly become a part of an industry that builds up around mitigating these social problems rather than serving the goal of *ending* the root causes of the problem.

Let's take, for example, hunger. At some point, you got tired of seeing hungry people in your community, and you decided that you had to do something about ending hunger. So you got a few grants and ultimately started receiving Federal Emergency Management Administration funds, and perhaps some state and local contracts as well. You set up a soup kitchen or a food pantry and you started giving away food. The problem with hunger is that you can't just fix it once. Those hungry people keep coming back. The lines get longer by the third week of the month. The complexion of the line changes as increasingly you see women coming with their children seeking food.

There is an odd thing about hunger here in North America. It doesn't particularly correlate with the overall economy. Even in expansive economic times over the last three decades, the demand for food by poor people has continued to increase. Meanwhile, if you look at the macro picture, it is hard to justify anyone going hungry anywhere on the planet. We produce more than enough food to feed every single person. As a matter of fact, between Western Europe, North America, and Japan, our governments spend over $65 billion in price supports and subsidies to agri-business. Essentially that dollar figure represents the food that we produce that we can't use. And because of government subsidies, that food is sold in developing countries at sometimes less than 20 percent of what it would cost that country to produce, thereby destroying those countries' agricultural economy and creating even more hunger. Yet we continue trying to serve one more meal or put out one more pantry bag, without ever focusing on the system that is causing the problem.

The same can be said for another example: homelessness. For the past twenty years, we've used the deinstitutionalization of the mentally ill and the scourge of chemical dependence as the rationale for increasing rates of homelessness. But if those are really the causes, why aren't we pouring money into community-based mental health programs? We would be pouring money into drug treatment programs instead of constantly investing in a prison-industrial complex that ruins the lives of so many young African American men.

The reality is that tonight in New York City, some seventeen thousand children will go to bed without a place to call home. The vast majority of these children aren't homeless because of mental illness or chemical dependence. In fact, the cofactor that probably causes more homelessness among children—more than chemical dependence and mental illness combined—is domestic violence.

But the reality is that the principal cause of homelessness in North America is none of the above. It's the lack of affordable housing, even in the midst of a mortgage crisis that is destroying the value of millions of homes. That is, in most parts of the country, there are poor people who simply cannot afford to pay the rent, much less make a down payment on home ownership. That is a fixable problem. We have the resources to be able to address it. We just lack the political will. So we in the homelessness industry keep scrounging for more money to build more shelters, because that's the way it is.

And of course there is another well-known example—in fact, it's the favorite of social entrepreneurs across the land, myself included: workforce development. I include myself in this class. It thrills me every time I see a Housing Works trainee graduate into a full-time job on our staff and watch someone who came through the doors homeless and despairing of hope move on to a full-time job with all the independence and autonomy that a full-time job affords. But deep down, each one of us knows that there are businesses in our communities that in the course of a single day can eliminate more jobs than we can collectively create in a lifetime.

My point here is not to be critical of folks who are feeding the hungry, housing the homeless, or giving job opportunities to those who are disadvantaged. My point is to acknowledge that what we are trying to do, metaphorically, at least, is to move a mountain. Instead of having a pick-axe and a shovel, we're armed with nothing but a teaspoon. And on the other side of the mountain, there's a steam shovel that piles up more tons of rocks and dirt every time we move away a few ounces. One of my fears for those of us who believe in social entrepreneurship is that we become self-satisfied that we have worked our way up from the teaspoon to the pick-axe and the shovel—that we never realize, if we really want to move the mountain, we have to find a way to turn off the engine on the steam shovel.

At Housing Works, we take that metaphor seriously. Like other nonprofit founders, the people who started Housing Works saw a critical unmet need. Very little was being done for homeless people in New York City who were living with AIDS and HIV. An overwhelming majority of these folk were chronically chemically dependent, chronically mentally ill, or both. What little housing was available required proof that residents had been "clean and sober" for at least 120 days. That didn't make a lot of sense when the average life span for a homeless person living with AIDS was six months from the time of diagnosis. With the slogan "Dead addicts don't recover," we started a housing program that served people who were still using illicit drugs. But from the very beginning, we knew that one little model program was never going to address the needs that we were seeing. So we committed ourselves to two things. First, at its core, Housing Works would be an advocacy organization, and we would maintain that commitment at whatever cost. The second was that we would do everything in our power to structure our programs so that the people we hoped to serve had opportunity for empowerment and participation in advocacy. It was actually those two commitments that turned us into an enterprising organization.

For us, empowerment meant structuring ourselves in a way that forced us to hear our constituents. Unlike most social service organizations, we structured ourselves as a membership corporation, in which consumers of our services directly elect one-third of our board and have to ratify outside directors. We also put in place an affirmative action policy around hiring people with HIV as well as histories of homelessness, mental illness, and chemical dependence so that our staff were reflective of the people we serve. It was our empowered consumers who demanded that we create jobs, and it was the need for funding for job training that first made us look for the right business venture...that plus the reality that there is very little funding for advocacy in the philanthropic arena. We quickly found earned-income strategies to be institutionally empowering, as well as empowering for our constituency. Not only did these strategies fund our job training and advocacy efforts, but they also allowed us to provide much needed services that no funding source was willing to underwrite. But it actually took an act of political retaliation for our advocacy to cause us to make a wholesale commitment to social enterprise.

Five years into Housing Works' development, we were still overwhelmingly dependent on government cost-reimbursement contracts. Only a third of our $18 million operating budget came from earned income. Then, in one fell swoop, we lost some $6.5 million in government contracts without reimbursement for $1.5 million in expenses incurred. Digging out of what would have probably put any other organization out of business, our board of directors made two important commitments: First, we would permanently restrict cost-reimbursement contracts to 20 percent of the organization's overall revenues, making us almost completely dependent on earned income strategies for our existence. Second, we would permanently commit 5 percent of our gross operating budget each year to advocacy irrespective of other demands on resources.

Now, 5 percent doesn't sound like a lot of money. But our budget is now $50 million. So just in terms of dollars, we spend more money on advocacy than any other organization in the nation. Not only that, but leveraging all of our clients, staff, and even customers, to make them activists for our cause, has made Housing Works a national and even international force shaping government and civil society response to the twin crises of homelessness and AIDS. Just an example of a victory we won early on in this effort is that no AIDS housing provider in New York City can decline housing or evict a tenant solely on the basis of illicit drug use, completely changing the nature of the structural problem that put us in business to start with.

Housing Works continues to help people very directly. Our commitment to help is what has led us to advocate as well. Following are six lessons we've learned about the role and importance of advocacy for social entrepreneurs.

Lesson 1: Advocacy Is a Mission Imperative

The vision statement of the Social Enterprise Alliance reads: "Strong, self-sustaining nonprofits lead to positive social change." Which is to say that if all social enterprise does is build a more self-sustaining not-for-profit sector, we will have failed. The measure of our success is whether, through social enterprise, we can build a sector that is strong enough and has the will to lead change to a more just and sustainable society.

So what's that mean in practical terms? *Flat out, it means having the courage and determination to commit your enterprise to advocacy on behalf of the people you serve.* The truth is that very few social service organizations in the United States and Canada engage in serious advocacy around the issues they were organized to address. If they engage in serious advocacy at all, it is almost exclusively around their institutional interests, primarily the continued funding of their own programs.

Lessons 2 and 3: Advocacy for Good Is Dangerous . . .

Most social service organizations will tell you they can't do advocacy because they aren't allowed to use their funds in that way. Obviously, if you are running a profitable social venture, that excuse immediately goes away. There is no reason why you can't use profits from your venture in any way that services the organization's mission—and that includes advocacy.

The real reason that most social service organizations don't engage in serious advocacy is because that would require them to confront the systems that sustain them. And, of course, that can be quite dangerous.

I know of this firsthand. When Rudy Giuliani was the mayor of New York City, he was not shy at all about developing a reputation for vindictiveness toward organizations that opposed his agenda. Housing

Works had initiated a number of advocacy campaigns in opposition to his policies that would have a negative impact on our constituency. This included several notable class action lawsuits that successfully thwarted his agenda.

Very quickly, we found it very difficult to do business with the City of New York. Contract negotiations stalled. Investigations began. Reimbursements were withheld, to the tune of over a million dollars. Ultimately, in 1998, the Mayor's Office issued a press release, announcing that the city was revoking contracts totaling over $6.5 million in annual operating dollars and would not reimburse any funds spent on these contracts because of "improprieties and malfeasance." At the time, Housing Works' operating budget was about $18 million. So the loss of over one-third of our funding was a serious hit. In addition, the city administration immediately set about depriving Housing Works of state and federal contracts as well.

. . . and Danger Can Be Good

To Housing Works' good fortune, we had already begun moving toward becoming self-sustaining. The Giuliani administration's actions simply accelerated the pace of the transition. Overnight, we went from being 60 percent funded by government contracts to receiving less than 20 percent of our revenue through government contracts. The year that followed was wrenching for the organization, but the result was that we became even more empowered, with 80 percent of our revenue coming through earned income. In fact, our entrepreneurial growth was such that—even though we ended the year with a significant deficit—we actually achieved net growth over our projected budget that same year. The icing on the cake came later when we won two lawsuits against the Giuliani administration for unlawful retaliation and settled a third for over $5 million, thereby creating our first endowment.

The institutional fallout from this experience was twofold. First, Housing Works' board of directors voted unanimously to implement a policy that no more than 20 percent of the organization's revenue could ever be derived from cost-reimbursement government contracts. Second, the board voted unanimously to implement a policy requiring that a minimum of 5 percent of the organization's total operating budget be dedicated each year to direct advocacy for social change.

Just imagine if every social service organization in the United States and Canada devoted a minimum of 5 percent of its budget toward advocacy toward progressive social change in accord with that organization's mission. Of course, most organizations can't do that because their government sources of funds can't be used for that purpose, and advocacy isn't what most private and corporate philanthropic sources want to fund. But organizations that are based on self-sustaining enterprise don't have that barrier. Setting aside a minimum of 5 percent of revenues for this purpose becomes just another discipline that is a part of the culture of the organization and a part of the bottom line by which it measures its performance.

Lesson 4: Advocacy Is Good Business

Truth be told, it isn't just the money that is the barrier to advocacy by most not-for-profit groups. The reality is that the kind of advocacy that is needed isn't always easy because, even if we have shed the folk who maintain the status quo as our funders, speaking truth to power always requires courage. But here's the flip side: It can also be very good for business!

Housing Works operates a chain of retail outlets including seven thrift stores, a used bookstore-café, and a rapidly growing online auction and "buy now" Internet program. We have learned that a good advocacy program is great for sales. We have branded ourselves as a cutting-edge, social change organization. So each time Housing Works is in the news for holding a demonstration, engaging in civil disobedience in the streets or filing a lawsuit, we actually build our brand, increasing our name recognition and popularity in exactly the market we want to cultivate.

Many a successful retailer has learned to capitalize on guerrilla marketing. We've learned that successfully publicized direct action is a great form of guerrilla marketing. Housing Works in the news means more hits to the Web site, more visits to the stores, more donations, and, above all, more sales.

Interestingly enough, great merchandising, great marketing, and great direct action have made the cause of homeless drug addicts living with HIV downright sexy. This approach has given Housing Works that special downtown New York edgy sex appeal that has attracted major corporate partners who want to co-brand with us. And what is better than a cause-related marketing campaign that promotes social change while selling your product?

The truth is that this kind of cause-related marketing has proven successful for corporations that are the furthest thing from social enterprise. Global energy companies that continue to make their fortunes off of gas and oil find it in their interests to promote "green" sustainable energy as the center piece of their marketing campaigns. There is no good reason why social enterprises working to tackle some of the most perverse problems facing our communities today can't capitalize on their social change agenda in the same way, and, in the process, recruit the support of larger corporate interests who would like to be co-branded with that enterprise's social capital.

Lesson 5: Make Advocacy Part of Your Brand

By making our advocacy and activism part of our brand, we have accomplished another thing. Our retail venues have now become a place where we can educate our customers and donors about the issues we are passionate about . . . and we use that opportunity to invite them to join in our efforts. This not only furthers our advocacy, but it also enlists brand loyalty. Anyone who engages in an advocacy action, whether it is signing a petition, writing a letter, or making a phone call, associates that affirmative act with our business.

Lesson 6: Advocacy Builds Ownership

Finally, engaging in advocacy and activism that involve the whole organization builds ownership and investment from your staff and the people your organization is serving. It creates a culture wherein people feel empowered. When our consumers go to the capitol and speak with a legislator, especially when the legislator actually listens, they come to appreciate their own ability to make change. When we engage in civil disobedience, so often I will find myself in jail with someone who has been in jail many times for other reasons. Inevitably, that person will say to me, "It feels so good to be in jail for the right reason!"

SOCIAL ENTERPRISE ADVOCACY: MORE THAN A FUNDING STREAM

Of course, empowered consumers can feel dangerous. Sometimes they use their advocacy skills on you. Twice since Housing Works' founding, I have had the experience of clients and staff feeling disgruntled enough with something going on in the organization to engage in a sit-in in my office. Our own tactic turned on us! Each time, I have listened to their complaints, shared ideas about how to address their concerns, and then joined their sit-in in solidarity. That hasn't made simple resolution of complex problems. But it has given people the belief that they could make change, not just in the larger world, but within our organization, and, most important, in their own lives.

In sum, social enterprise really does offer the possibility of progressive social change. But that doesn't happen inevitably. And then "social enterprise" is reduced to just another funding stream. Progressive social change as a function of social enterprise only happens if you make advocacy a fundamental part of your program and make social change one of the standards by which you measure your enterprise. When well executed, advocacy will not only create movement for change outside the organization, but it will change the organization as well, and make it a more successful social enterprise.

ABOUT THE AUTHOR

Charles King is one of the founders and the president of Housing Works, Inc., a minority-controlled, community-based, nonprofit organization that provides a full range of services including housing, health care, mental health services, chemical dependency services, legal advocacy, and job training and placement for homeless men, women, and children living with HIV/AIDS. Housing Works is the largest community-based AIDS services organization in the United States and currently services over five thousand people every year.

Housing Works pioneered housing for active drug users in the United States, and continues to use a nonjudgmental, harm reduction approach to serving New York's most marginalized communities. In addition, Housing

Works engages in advocacy and grassroots community organizing on issues impacting people living with HIV and AIDS throughout the United States, with advocacy offices in New York City; Albany, New York; Washington, D.C., and Jackson, Mississippi.

Charles has combined his background as a minister and lawyer to develop and articulate the vision of Housing Works as a self-sustaining, healing community based on aggressive advocacy, mutual aid, and collective empowerment. This has included the development of entrepreneurial ventures which consist of a chain of upscale thrift shops, a used book café, a food service business, a property management company, a consulting and lobbying firm, a management services company, and a health maintenance organization. Housing Works operational budget this year is $45 million, one-third of which is revenue from the organization's entrepreneurial ventures, and 80 percent of which is earned income.

Prior to the incorporation of Housing Works in June 1990, Charles served as staff attorney to the New York Coalition for the Homeless; as assistant pastor to Immanuel Baptist Church in New Haven, Connecticut; as director of an emergency center for abused children in Roundrock, Texas; and as Minister of Street Ministries at First Baptist Church in San Antonio, Texas. Charles holds both a law degree and a master of divinity from Yale University and is an ordained Baptist minister.

Innovation and Technology Strategies

By **Sean Milliken**, *Executive Director;*
Clam Lorenz, *Vice President, Operations;*
Oktay Dogramaci, *Chief Technology Officer; and*
Nancy Chen, *Product Director, all at MissionFish*

MissionFish was launched in October 2000 as a solution to the "in-kind donation" problem. Our experience had taught us that nonprofit organizations received endless offers of goods and services from well-intentioned donors, but few had the capacity to administer them. Moreover, these items held the potential to produce much-needed unrestricted funding, but there was not an efficient way to monetize them.

Inspired by the power of technology to address critical problems, we developed an online exchange where donors could offer in-kind goods and services to nonprofits. The organization could accept the item for use or sell it through our online auction marketplace without ever taking possession. The result was a way to keep in-kind gifts from becoming "un-kind gifts."

Since that time, we have reinvented MissionFish time and again—as new technologies became available, partnership opportunities presented themselves, and as market forces and users demanded it. In its current form, MissionFish powers eBay Giving Works, a program that enables eBay users to support causes when they buy and sell. The MissionFish-eBay collaboration has been active since 2003. As of late 2009 MissionFish has used the strategies described here to raise over $160 million for charities in the United States and United Kingdom, enlisted more than twenty-one thousand charities, and averaged an SROI of $14 raised for every $1 spent.

Any success that MissionFish has realized over the years can be traced to an ability to embrace change and an unwavering commitment to create new sources of unrestricted funding for nonprofits through technology. Along the way, we've learned five key strategies about innovation and technology: don't go it alone; make your service relevant and convenient; focus on "what" instead of "how"; ask your customers what they want; trust the data and make the change.

These concepts are not exclusive to MissionFish, and they aren't rocket science—but we certainly wish someone had shared them with us before we began our journey. We offer them to you now in the hope that they will add value in tackling the challenges facing your organization, regardless of whether those are technical, financial, or operational.

LESSON 1: DON'T GO IT ALONE

You don't have to do it yourself. There are plenty of best-in-class technology service providers and tools. They may have been built for other uses, but can be modified to meet your needs.

Maybe you are a small nonprofit that wants to begin accepting donations online. Network for Good is a leading provider of Web-based donation tools. They have already taken care of various solicitation registrations so you don't have to take on the administrative burden or cost. Better yet, they provide numerous tools and resources to help you build a strong community of givers. Or, maybe you are a larger organization that is looking for a better way to mobilize and engage your large community of constituents. You could spend millions of dollars and years of effort to develop a platform that has already been created by Convio, Blackbaud, and others based on the aggregated best practices of your peer organizations.

When we were searching for a customer service solution, we explored a range of expensive options—from building the tools ourselves to deploying software solutions that met our specific requirements. Fortunately for us, our research uncovered an altogether different kind of solution in Salesforce.com, an emerging Web-based CRM (Customer Relationship Management) application that was built primarily for businesses to manage their sales activities.

An initial review of the Salesforce.com functionality led us to believe that the company was focused on a different type of user and, therefore, would not meet our needs. Luckily, our initial concerns turned out to be unfounded. Exploratory conversations with Salesforce.com professionals introduced us to a platform that was extremely flexible and could be modified to meet our needs. Better yet, the company was forward thinking in their philanthropy. They were willing to donate perpetual licenses to us and give us training and support throughout the process of deployment. This is not an arrangement that is exclusive to MissionFish. Salesforce.com provides licenses free of charge to thousands of nonprofit organizations; several social entrepreneurs have developed applications designed to address a range of social needs on the Salesforce.com AppExchange platform.

This same rule applies to Web communities. Starting a new Web community can be done, but many enterprises have failed to build critical mass despite having a good idea and plentiful financial resources. There is so much "noise" on the Internet that it can be incredibly difficult to build a destination specific to your social enterprise. That said, there is tremendous opportunity to harness existing communities for the advancement of your purposes.

We learned this lesson—not to go it alone—the hard way. When we started MissionFish, we tried to do it all ourselves, often ignoring the incredible challenges that our approach presented. We chose to look past the significant burden that our model placed on the donor (take a picture of the item, list it in our exchange, and ship it to a nonprofit or buyer) and embarked on a strategy that required a great deal of money and a whole lot of luck to create a community of buyers big enough to ensure that items ultimately sold for a fair price.

Although there were many similarities between the MissionFish and eBay models, we never considered the possibility of partnership. If anything, we considered eBay to be a competitor.

Then, a fortunate thing happened—the Internet bubble burst and necessity brought clarity. If we could take our program built specifically for nonprofits and offer it within a community of buyers and sellers that had already embraced the auction model, our potential for good would be exponentially greater.

It was only natural then that we set our sites on a partnership with eBay, the world's largest online trading community. Little did we know that the relationship would offer so much more than its vibrant community of users. It has also provided us with expertise, tools, and resources that we could have never secured on our own.

A Powerful Partnership for Good

In 2003, eBay invited us to bring our experience to their global community. The combination of our technology and nonprofit expertise, plus eBay's active global community, forms eBay Giving Works—a powerful way for anyone to do good just by buying or selling online.

Sellers use the program to list items for sale on eBay and donate 10 to 100 percent of their proceeds to a nonprofit certified for participation in the program. Any nonprofit can register for free with MissionFish to participate in the eBay Giving Works program. The only requirements are that the organization meet our standards prohibiting violence, intolerance, and terrorism, and that donations to the organization be tax-deductible.

The eBay Giving Works listings stand out from regular eBay listings with a unique icon—and information about the nonprofit and the gift. When the item sells, MissionFish collects the donation, delivers it to the nonprofit, and provides a tax receipt to the seller. We also offer tools, training, and customer service to help organizations raise money by becoming eBay sellers themselves.

This practical and convenient giving solution—made possible by technology—provides:

- A way for anyone to do something good with the stuff they have
- A tool that lets nonprofits turn in-kind donations into money

- A platform for nonprofits of every size to maximize cause-marketing, without expensive setup costs or million-dollar commitments

MissionFish UK launched in 2005 and we recently expanded our offering to include "Donate Now"—a way nonprofits can receive donations through PayPal and "Give at Checkout"—a feature that enables buyers to add a contribution to their eBay purchases.

As of November 2009, our work with eBay had generated over $160 million for nonprofit organizations—and we are still writing our story today.

LESSON 2: MAKE YOUR SERVICE CONVENIENT AND RELEVANT

Much has been made about the transition of the Internet—from a web of destinations comprised of content generated *for* users to a web of destinations with content generated *by* users. Web 3.0 and beyond is unlikely to be about the destination at all. It will be about taking relevant content and tools to users—wherever they are—and making it convenient for them to learn, interact, and transact without disrupting their intended experience.

There was a great deal of controversy when Facebook launched Beacon, the company's advertising solution that shared the preferences of users with their "friends." Although Facebook has had to revisit its original plans for Beacon due to privacy issues, the company's foray into relevant advertising served as a strong indicator of where life and commerce online are headed.

Likewise, the future of online philanthropy will be less about bringing users to the nonprofit's site and more about making the interactions that happen online into philanthropic events.

"Make it more convenient" has been our product development mantra for the past six years. When eBay Giving Works launched in 2003, we made it convenient for the buyer to know that a purchase was supporting a nonprofit, but the seller still had to work too hard to give from those listings. Since then, we've made annual upgrades to the seller's experience: systematically removing barriers and infusing convenience for the seller throughout. The result has been steady growth in listings and donations, and spikes that follow our major new releases. Now we've moved on to offering more convenience for buyers too: a simple checkbox that appears when they complete a purchase on eBay. Want to give $1? Check a box. That's it.

Convenience ensures follow-through, but relevance spurs the user's desire to give, now. The next time you read a news story about a disaster on CNN.com, it is likely that you will be presented with an easy way to support a relief service. Send a "happy birthday" wish to a Facebook friend, and the Causes application invites you to send a donation "gift" in his or her honor.

For us, relevance is about introducing you to a nonprofit that we think you'd be interested in supporting while you're inside your normal buying or selling experience on eBay. Today we feature nonprofits that have seasonal relevance: children's causes during the holidays, breast cancer organizations in October, environmental nonprofits for Earth Day. We also pay attention to your behavior: if you donated to the Texas Rustlers Guinea Pig Rescue the last time you listed on eBay, we'll show them to you during your next listing too. Next we'll feature a charity based on your location, or on what you're buying. In every case we're trying to give you the most relevant cause we can and to make your decision to give as convenient as a checkbox.

Take the time to assess how convenience and relevance can be applied to your organization's efforts. Maybe you're a health-related organization that does an annual walk to raise funds to support your mission. If you have not already done so, partner with a local sporting goods store to promote the run. It can be good for the store and great for your cause. The store will become the place to buy gear for the big event, and your mission will resonate with their customers. And what better time to ask those customers to support your organization than when they are buying a new pair of running shoes in the store or online?

LESSON 3: FOCUS ON "WHAT," NOT "HOW"

Innovation for innovation's sake usually isn't worth it. Every day a business tackles dozens of problems, evaluating possible solutions for each one. As you go along, it's easy to fall in love with a great technical improvement, and lose sight of whether that's really the best answer to the problem at hand. If you're not careful, you can end up with a well-designed, highly functional technical fix, and a problem that still isn't resolved.

This trap can be especially easy for a mission-driven organization to fall into: where enthusiasm for the cause can lead to mistaking a particular way of doing something for an outcome to be achieved. "We need to be using Twitter!" may be a true statement, but only if you know what you're trying to use it to accomplish.

To avoid that trap, we try to keep ourselves focused on "what" we're trying to solve, and be as agnostic as possible about "how" we solve it. For us that means starting with a clearly stated definition of the problem. Sometimes it's just bullet points on a whiteboard. Other times it's a full-fledged "business requirements document"—a mini business plan for the issue at hand. As we evaluate potential solutions, we force ourselves to come back repeatedly to the question of whether or not the proposed solution fixes our "what." In turn, we end up refining the definition of our problem iteratively, as we gather new details.

After a few rounds of analysis we'll often realize that the details are trickier than originally thought, and that we don't know enough about the real problem yet. Instead of spending resources on a technical solution, we rely on a "GEFN"—a temporary solution that's "Good Enough, for Now."[1] GEFNs are a great way to get practical experience fast, which can be fed back into our ultimate solution design.

Usually our GEFNs are little more than a well-defined process: a person does steps 1 to 6, by hand. But by going through those steps, we learn about the true nuances of the problem and can build a longer-lasting solution that really solves it.

The eBay Giving Works program will always be a work in progress. Bringing together two technology platforms with distinct user needs has not been easy—we have had to constantly revisit our assumptions and make changes based on our experiences.

Shortly after the program launched, we struggled with a surprising number of sellers who wanted their donations back from us: they wanted refunds. They weren't asking because they were unhappy with the service, but because their eBay sale with the buyer had fallen through. The need was understandable—without the sale, the seller doesn't have money to give. The solution, however, was much more complex.

The refund process was an incredible drain on human resources, so we were motivated to automate a solution that was as quick as possible. We soon realized, however, that there were too many unknowns to build a tool for handling refunds (yet). So instead we created a 100 percent manual process that met our basic needs, and started learning. Soon we were able to categorize our refunds, and to sketch out tools to speed up steps for each. Eventually we were able to automate more and more of the process. Along the way we also learned why users were asking for refunds, and identified several changes to reduce the need in the first place.

Focusing on *what* rather than *how* can save your organization time and treasure. For example, two years ago Web-based "widgets" were the buzzword of Internet business. The conventional wisdom was that if you didn't have a widget strategy, you were in trouble (or at best, hopelessly Web 1.0). We loved the technology, but couldn't figure out how these really slick tools solved any of our biggest problems. In the end we opted to spend our resources elsewhere. Two years later, widgets are still great, but their limitations as a fund-raising tool have become much clearer. For our business at that time, building a widget would have been a fun but costly mistake. We would have invested ourselves in a *how* (cool technology) instead of a *what* (a solution to a problem).

The thing to remember is that a technology always has the potential to be a really great tool. Just make sure you fully understand the challenge you are trying to solve before utilizing it. Otherwise, it can quickly become part of the problem, rather than its solution.

LESSON 4: ASK YOUR CUSTOMERS WHAT THEY WANT

Real-time feedback on your business will provide valuable information that can keep you from making harmful missteps and, ultimately, save you time and resources. Feedback gained through message boards, online surveys, focus groups, and usability testing drives every decision we make at MissionFish—from business model changes to product enhancements.

Your organization should also use feedback tools that give you insight into what your customers are thinking: online surveys, focus group sessions, even something simple like tracking what your customers complain about the most, each month.

When developing the first MissionFish site back in 2000, we spent weeks huddled up in a room with our team, working feverishly to imagine how we might bring our idea to life. We had market research, of course, and our own experience as fund-raisers. But for the most part, we were sketching out what *we thought* our customers would want, and then building MissionFish to match that vision. It was a great experience, and we forged friendships we've counted on ever since. But boy, were we wrong about our customers!

In hindsight it seems obvious, but what we didn't realize at the time is that there is no substitute for direct customer input. Your team of smart people can create clever innovations, but without user input guiding what you build and how it behaves, you'll end up with more misses than hits and waste valuable resources in the process.

There are lots of ways to ask your customers what they want. Here are a few of the ones we use:

- **Performance metrics**: We regularly track data points on actual customer actions (listings posted, nonprofits selected, donations made, and so on), to understand what they are and are not doing. When we launch a new change, we define in advance the specific metrics to monitor.

- **Service inquiries**: When we want to know what's broken in our business, we count the complaints and confused questions we're getting. Issues are prioritized based on, in part, the volume of inquiries.

- **Focus groups and surveys**: The only way to know what someone thinks is to ask. This is especially helpful when refining a new product idea.

- **Usability testing**: If we're planning a really big change, it's great to sit beside customers and actually watch them use our service. This can be especially valuable since sometimes people say one thing in a survey, but do another in real life.

Some of these methods can get expensive: usability testing, for example, takes a lot of time and expert advice to do properly. However, others (such as tracking what your service inquiries are about) are practically free. The idea here isn't to break the bank, it's for you to find ways to emulate two time-honored business practices: offering customers a "comments box" to share their thoughts with you, and running your new ideas past some customers to get an honest appraisal of what you're thinking.

In a perfect world, you will design feedback into the heart of your service, so your customers can tell you what they want as part of their everyday activity. It's easy for you to maintain, it's routine for your customers, and, best of all, it's cheap to deploy!

LESSON 5: TRUST THE DATA—AND MAKE THE CHANGE!

To turn customer feedback into actionable change, you must establish key indicators of success and constantly measure, study, and refine based on what users are telling you.

Trusting user feedback often requires a leap of faith, however. There may be times when the data tells you something very different from what you believed to be true and, harder yet, it may test long-held positions that you believe are in the best interest of your enterprise. Decide what is most important for the business and make everything else negotiable. In general, the user is always right. Find out how you can give users what they want without compromising those things that are most important.

Start by accepting that innovation is iterative, and plan your resources accordingly. Hold back some of your budget for retooling and refining your offer as you learn more.

Deepening Audience Reach

In the fall of 2007 our business was as strong as ever. We had realized 40 percent growth in our key metrics—new listings and funds raised—in our most recent fiscal year. Plus, we had just closed our biggest donation ever: someone paid more than $2.1 million for a letter from a group of U.S. senators to radio personality Rush Limbaugh.

But despite our success, the data were pointing to a big problem. Our marketing programs were proving more effective than ever at attracting eBay sellers to try our program, but most of them were dropping out during their first attempt at listing an item. Only 25 percent of users who started our process were finishing it—and these were people who were already eBay users *and* motivated to sell for charity! There's no such thing as an unlimited audience, even on eBay. So it was immediately clear that we were not going to reach our potential without drastic changes to the user's experience.

We started an effort to get comprehensive feedback about the donor experience. We organized focus groups on our message and brand positioning within eBay. We set up usability tests with people who knew the program, and with those who didn't, to learn exactly what was tripping them up at the click-by-click level. We also studied the big picture "waterfall" of users who abandoned us at each step of our process, trying to understand which steps were having the biggest negative impact.

Through all of this research, we gathered a list of complaints large and small:

- "It's hard to find where I can donate to charity."
- "I'm selling on eBay—who is MissionFish and what are they doing here?"
- "But eBay already has my credit card on file—why do I need to give it to you again?"
- "I'm willing to give a little bit to charity, but you're asking me to do too much extra work."
- And many, many more.

This list made our challenge clear, but the solutions were not cut-and-dried. We had a few choices for addressing each complaint, ranging from "band-aids" to major reconstructive surgery. We decided on an incremental approach (see GEFN in Lesson 3): take the test results, make small decisions, and measure again along the way.

We started with a set of low-cost and quickly achievable changes. These made the feature easier to see on eBay, and tinkered with how we explained what it was and how it worked. The results were positive, but when we measured again it was clear we had to take more radical steps to achieve our goals.

So we went back to our list of possible changes and started to map the perfect user experience. Everything was on the table. As long as the change would result in more funds raised for our nonprofit partners and would not adversely affect MissionFish's sustainability, it was open for discussion.

In the end, it became clear to us that we needed to give up things that we once thought important (such as branding and credit) to give users what they wanted: an easy, seamless, and integrated process for donating. Specific changes we made included:

- Giving sellers a "one-click" option, in addition to the full flexibility to choose their nonprofit beneficiary and the amount to give
- Eliminating the MissionFish Donor Account by integrating the functionality within the seller's My eBay Account
- Eliminating the need to register separately with MissionFish
- Reusing the payment method the seller has on file with eBay, instead of requiring the user to give additional financial information to MissionFish
- Making the MissionFish brand almost invisible to sellers

Taken together, these changes would become the biggest development project we've ever undertaken. The team of contributors spanned three continents, and the project time line stretched to more than a year. Despite its risks, the impact has been overwhelmingly positive. Practically overnight, the number of items listed by members of the eBay community on behalf of a nonprofit rose an impressive 250 percent in the United States, and 700 percent in the United Kingdom.

CONCLUSION

Every business is unique, and the lessons you'll learn in growing your own social enterprise will certainly be different from the ones we've learned at MissionFish. However, our hope is that these general principles will prove beneficial as you embark on your own exciting journey as a social entrepreneur:

1. Don't go it alone.

2. Make it relevant and easy.

3. Focus on the "what," not the "how."

4. Ask your customers what they want: then give it to them.

5. Trust the data, and make the change.

Note

1. To give credit where it's due, GEFN is our interpretation of the "Genchi Genbutsu" principle ("go and see") from the famed Toyota Production System. The idea—which we've found to be true—is that you can't really understand something unless you go and see it yourself.

ABOUT THE AUTHORS

Sean Milliken is the founder and executive director of MissionFish. Under his leadership, the organization has raised over $110 million for over eighteen thousand nonprofits in the United States and the United Kingdom. Prior to starting MissionFish in 1999, Sean raised money and awareness for a variety of nonprofit organizations including Boys & Girls Clubs and Communities In Schools. He has traveled the southeastern United States building houses for Habitat for Humanity and helped create a business incubator and microloan program for young people in South Central Los Angeles. Sean is a member of the board of trustees for MissionFish UK and he frequently speaks at technology and nonprofit conferences about the importance of building nonprofit capacity, the power of the Internet in creating new forms of philanthropy, and the role of unrestricted funding in organizational effectiveness.

Clam Lorenz is the vice president of operations for MissionFish. Clam has held a variety of leadership positions since he joined the founding team in 1999. In his current role, Clam leads the organization's daily global business operations and is also responsible for the growth and financial performance of the U.S. business. Prior to MissionFish, Clam spent seven years with Boys & Girls Clubs in communications, resource development, and Club management.

Chief Technology Officer **Oktay Dogramaci** is responsible for Mission-Fish's technology efforts: bridging business requirements and technical capabilities. Prior to serving as the technical lead for the original MissionFish Web site, he was a consultant with PricewaterhouseCoopers, specializing in e-business services as well as an information technology analyst with NASA's Goddard Space Flight Center. In addition to his professional experience, Oktay is coauthor of a book on e-business, *Electronic Commerce: Technical, Business, and Legal Issues* (Prentice-Hall, 1999).

Nancy Chen is vice president of product for MissionFish, responsible for all product design, development, and platform maintenance. She began her career with MissionFish in 2000 as the lead developer for the original platform. Prior to MissionFish, Nancy demonstrated her skills in an array of programming languages, database design and administration for Synapsys, UUNET, and the U.S. Department of Labor.

MissionFish is an innovative social enterprise building technology, tools, and resources to harness the power of e-commerce for social good. Since 2003, MissionFish has enabled eBay users to support their favorite cause whenever they buy and sell. To date, more than $150 million have been raised by the eBay community for over nineteen thousand nonprofit organizations in the United States and United Kingdom.

Building a Performance Measurement System: Using Data to Accelerate Social Impact

*By **Andrew Wolk**, Founder, Root Cause*

In the private sector, performance measurement enables corporations to collect data that identify potential improvements to their business models. By acting on this data, a company can ultimately increase its financial performance. Performance measurement serves a similar purpose when applied to solving social problems. It provides vital information for assessing an organization's efficiency, sustainability, and progress toward achieving its mission.

Typically, an organization that has social impact as its primary mission measures at least some of its work, particularly in response to funder requirements. However, externally driven measurement does not necessarily serve internal performance assessment needs. Many organizations collect data relating to a few select programs and initiatives but have little understanding of their overall progress in achieving their missions. Alternatively, some organizations feel overwhelmed by a flood of potentially helpful data that they have not yet linked to management strategy and day-to-day operations. What all organizations dedicated to social

149

impact need is a customized internal *performance measurement system* that meets stakeholder requirements while also empowering the organization to make internal decisions. Ultimately, an effective performance measurement system serves as an essential tool for any organization seeking to:

- Select what to measure in order to obtain a clear picture of the organization's progress in achieving its mission, goals, and vision

- Develop dashboards for internal reporting and learn how to analyze performance data to gain insights into the organization's strengths and identify opportunities for improvement

- Create a culture of learning and continuous improvement that involves management, board, and staff in making strategic, data-driven decisions and ultimately accelerates the organization's progress toward enduring social impact

- Develop report cards to communicate performance and impact to external stakeholders

- Use data-based evidence to aid in building funder confidence and in securing new and returning investments

An effective performance measurement system offers a comprehensive, flexible framework for any organization dedicated to social impact. The system helps simplify an organization's existing measurement efforts—or it can be built from the ground up for organizations new to measurement. The approach to performance measurement described in this chapter draws on Root Cause's unique methodology developed through its consulting work with dozens of organizations throughout the United States, as well as a number of international organizations. Root Cause, a nonprofit organization, advances enduring solutions to social and economic problems by supporting social innovators—nonprofit organizations, government agencies, and businesses that offer innovative, results-driven solutions—and the social impact investors who invest in their work.

CASE STUDY: HOW PERFORMANCE MEASUREMENT INCREASED SOCIAL IMPACT

Our own experience at Root Cause illustrates how using performance measurement as a tool for internal learning and improvement is well worth the effort it requires. In 2004, we began an initiative called InnerCity Entrepreneurs (ICE), which provided us with powerful lessons on performance measurement. ICE helps a diverse group of urban entrepreneurs to strengthen and grow their existing businesses. The initiative promotes job creation, wealth generation, and community development.

Early on, ICE began collecting data as part of a performance measurement system that has proven instrumental in honing its approach to urban economic development—while also helping to attract and retain new investment. For example, during a review of its data in 2006, the organization identified a drop in applications to its nine-month certificate program for entrepreneurs. Further investigation indicated that its targeted businesses generally took more time to decide to commit to ICE's rigorous business-training program than the recruitment process allowed. Understanding that, the organization started its recruitment process for 2007 fully six months earlier than usual. As a result, ICE received 60 percent more applications to its Boston program that year than it did the previous year.

Making a commitment to tracking and communicating its results to external stakeholders through an annual report card also helped the organization retain its original social impact investors while attracting new ones. For example, in 2005, ICE found that its graduates in its first two years of operation had created seventy-seven new part- and full-time jobs in Boston. Of those jobs, 59 percent went to residents from the businesses' local neighborhoods. Reporting this performance data externally helped ICE secure several new funding sources, including a multiyear funder who helped to cover the salary of a CEO, a new position aimed at enabling the organization to scale nationally. By 2009, ICE had launched two more Massachusetts locations—in Worcester and the Merrimack Valley. The organization also secured a partnership with the Small Business Administration (SBA) through its Emerging 200 (e200) Initiative in order to bring the ICE's StreetWise Steps™ curriculum to fifteen cities across the United States.

As ICE's experience demonstrates, internal performance measurement systems enable organizations to make ongoing improvements to their models, while retaining existing investors and attracting new investments that can further propel their social impact.

THE ROLE OF THE PERFORMANCE MEASUREMENT SYSTEM

The performance measurement system constitutes a cycle that makes it possible to measure and adjust an organization's activities and operations in relation to its mission and its vision of success, by describing what the world would look like if the organization succeeded in achieving its mission (see Figure 11.1).

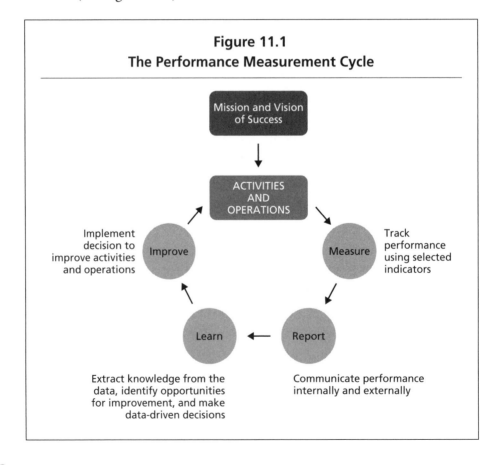

Figure 11.1
The Performance Measurement Cycle

Once it is up and running, the performance measurement cycle continually moves through the following phases:

- **Measure**: Organizations operating performance measurement systems use preselected indicators. Such metrics are tracked regularly to assess the results and scale of their activities and supporting operations.

- **Report**: To compile performance measurement data into a format that is easy to analyze, organizations use a management dashboard that compiles and compares data against standards in the field—and against the organization's past results and desired future results. Many organizations publish portions of their dashboards as public report cards to share with social impact investors and other stakeholders to establish accountability and demonstrate progress toward their missions and visions of success.

- **Learn**: From the management dashboard, an organization's management or performance review team draws conclusions and identifies opportunities for course corrections and improvements to the organization's model.

- **Improve**: The organization implements its decisions to improve its activities and operations. From there, the performance measurement cycle begins again.

MAKING A COMMITMENT: WHAT TO CONSIDER BEFORE STARTING TO MEASURE

Organizations that benefit most from performance measurement tend to have the following "commitments" in place before they begin to create their measurement approach. They should be committed to:

Use data to drive decision making. The organization, particularly senior leadership, commits to examine results critically and to learn from them. Building a performance measurement system will not be worth the effort unless a commitment is made to take action as improvement opportunities are identified.

Devote staff time to build the performance measurement system. Consider what resources are needed for planning and implementing the system. Depending on the size and complexity of the organization, the initial system development requires a few weeks to several months. One staff person will need to lead the effort, while a few others at different organizational levels will contribute to the overall design, develop measurement tools, and implement processes. Once the system is in place, assign responsibility to a senior staff member to ensure the system is maintained. Also ensure that a group of staff members, including leadership, have the responsibility for regularly reviewing data, drawing conclusions, and ensuring that the lessons learned inform future decision making.

Agree on the organization's mission and vision of success. Performance measurement is designed to help an organization assess its progress in carrying out its mission. Have a clear sense of mission before starting. To help guide the process of choosing what to measure, also consider articulating a vision of success if you do not already have one. For an organization in the middle of reevaluating its mission, it is best to wait until that process has ended before developing a measurement system. (For help clarifying an organization's mission and vision of success, we recommend the *Root Cause How-to Guide: Business Planning for Enduring Social Impact*.)

FIVE-STEP PROCESS TO BUILD A PERFORMANCE MEASUREMENT SYSTEM

In our own Root Cause experience, and in assisting organizations dedicated to social impact, we have evolved a five-step process to build or refine a performance measurement system (Figure 11.2). In considering this process, keep in mind your organization's unique mission and vision. They will have to inform every step of the process.

Step 1: Planning to Measure

Goals: Assemble a working group to develop the performance measurement system. Audit current measurement activities.

Form a Working Group   Typically, the performance measurement working group includes the organization's leader and key program staff—as

Figure 11.2
The Five-Step Process to Build a Performance Measurement System

● STEP 1	● STEP 2	● STEP 3	● STEP 4	● STEP 5
Planning to Measure	Choosing What to Measure	Determining How to Measure	Preparing to Use Your Data	Putting Your Performance Measurement System into Action

well as anyone who will be critical to get the system up and running once it is in place. The group generally includes one to five people, with one person designated as a leader.

Conduct a Performance Measurement Audit   A performance measurement audit will help the working group identify what is currently measured—so that the team can build on and strengthen what gets measured. The audit should answer questions like these:

What are you measuring? Compile a list of all the indicators that the organization currently tracks.

How and when are you measuring? In most organizations, multiple staff members on the activities and operational sides engage in data collection, using a variety of tools to capture data at different times. For all current measurement activities, list who is doing the measuring, and when and how.

Where and how are the data stored? Know where all of the data currently collected by the organization are stored. Take stock of all spreadsheets, databases, accounting systems, and other tools, and make a master list of data storage locations (if that list does not already exist).

How is the organization reviewing and using its data? Does it produce internal or external performance reports? Who creates and reviews those reports? Are performance review meetings held on a regular basis? How are data analyzed and interpreted? How does the organization incorporate conclusions drawn from data into the decision-making process?

In concluding Step 1, the answers to these audit questions will provide a helpful reference point as the organization moves on to build its performance measurement system in the steps that follow.

Step 2: Choosing What to Measure

Goals: *Develop a list of indicators that you will use to track your organization's progress toward carrying out its mission. Compile your selections in a master indicator list.*

In this critical step, the working group selects the most important indicators to help assess all areas of the organization's performance. The indicators are compiled in a master list that will serve as a starting point for developing additional elements of the performance measurement system later in the process.

Understanding the Indicators   Three categories of indicators are included in a performance measurement system:

1. **Organizational health indicators** provide critical insight into the organization's capacity to carry out its mission, including progress toward financial sustainability. Such indicators may include total revenue and expenses; the number of months for which the organization could operate using currently available cash; the distribution of your income between foundation funding, individual donors, earned income, and other sources; and the size and quality of your team.

2. **Program performance indicators** help an organization assess the outputs or short-term results generated directly by its programs and activities. Depending on the type of organization, program performance indicators could include the number of individuals enrolled in a given program, members in an association, partner organizations, or the size of an advocacy audience. These indicators might also cover client or stakeholder demographics and costs.

3. **Social and economic impact indicators** allow an organization to assess its outcomes, that is, its longer-term progress in meeting its mission and realizing its vision of success. For example, an organization aimed at getting high school students into college

would want to know what percent of the program graduates go on to enroll in a college or university. Depending on its mission and vision, the organization might decide to track how many of those students complete their degrees, what careers those graduates pursue, and their average salaries.

Select Indicators to Provide a Variety of Data   Various types of indicators can provide very different types of data. We recommend choosing from each of the following groups in selecting what indicators will best serve the organization.

Quantitative versus qualitative data: The tension between quantitative and qualitative data is the subject of a timeless debate. Today evaluation experts generally agree that these two data types support each other, and both are necessary to produce a complete picture of an organization. As the saying goes, "No numbers without stories, no stories without numbers."

Whole numbers versus ratio data: Quantitative data can take the form of whole numbers or ratios. Generally speaking, a mix of the two is necessary for generating meaningful data. For example, an organization placing high school students in colleges would likely want to look at the raw number of students who complete its program and also the ratio or percentage of participants who complete the program.

Select Indicators to Drive Effective Behaviors   Once performance measurement is integrated into the organizational culture, the chosen indicators will likely influence staff behaviors. Consider the experience of OASIS, a national nonprofit that provides lifelong learning classes and service opportunities for older adults. OASIS had determined that it needed to shift the focus of its measurement to align with the organization's renewed priority to expand participation in its programs, while increasing participation among low-income populations. OASIS had historically assessed growth by tracking the number of older adults who were registered members at each affiliate organization in its network. This created an incentive for each affiliate to sign up as many members as possible, even though those who signed up for OASIS's free membership did not necessarily participate in OASIS programs. Thus, focusing on membership levels encouraged behaviors that did not necessarily drive the growth that would truly help OASIS achieve its mission.

Shifting from measuring the number of members to measuring the number of active participants positioned the organization and its affiliates to assess growth more effectively. In addition, it incited a change in the organization's approach to driving that growth. OASIS staff members began to devote more attention to recruiting and retaining active participants rather than solely increasing membership numbers.

In concluding Step 2, the working group should compare the selected indicators with their investors' funding requirements. The underlying purpose of a performance measurement system is to empower the organization with information that will drive internal improvement. However, a coordinated approach will keep all measurement-related activities well organized under the same system. Ensure that the group has chosen indicators that will meet the social impact investors' reporting requirements. Some funders may consider changing a requirement if an organization feels it has found a more appropriate indicator. Compile the selected indicators into a master list before continuing to the next step.

Step 3: Determining How to Measure

Goal: *Determine how you will collect the data for each indicator, and select appropriate methods for storing your data. Specify when you will measure each indicator and who will be responsible for doing so.*

In this step, the working group will identify any measurement tools necessary to capture data, identify where to store collected data, and articulate the processes that will enable the organization to track data regularly once the performance measurement system is in place. In reality, an organization may already collect much of the data for its indicators from existing processes for accounting, human resources processes, and other assessments that measure organizational capacity. If so, Step 3 will provide an opportunity to audit and streamline the existing administrative systems. Having the measurement audit (from Step 1) at hand will help incorporate existing measurement practices into the new performance measurement system.

Prepare Measurement Tools Most organizations need to develop new measurement tools for some of their indicators. The measurement tools and processes an organization chooses greatly depend on the type of work it does. Options for tools include:

Intake forms and tracking spreadsheets: Intake forms, such as applications or informational forms completed by the organization's beneficiaries can help provide demographic and program-participation data. Some organizations may already receive this information through applications or inquiries. If so, a spreadsheet can be used for logging and tracking information.

Surveys via paper or Web-based questionnaires or phone surveys: Organizations generally decide how to collect survey data based on how to obtain the necessary information most reliably. For example, a questionnaire is the most cost-effective choice when the team believes that the survey participants will provide accurate data in a timely manner. Surveys are particularly useful for social and economic impact indicators, which often prove challenging to track.

Other common measurement tools include: Web analysis tools such as Google Analytics to track Web site traffic, usage, and e-mail, and Web messaging tools to track communications efforts.

Determine Where to Store Data Whatever method the working group chooses for storing and organizing data, the most important criterion is for the data to be centralized and easy to access and update on a regular basis. Ideally, the measurement processes will link directly to the data-storage tools so that data is compiled as it is captured. As a result, the ongoing data tracking can be integrated into daily operations and the organizational culture.

Most organizations have three main data-storage options (listed from least to most robust): (1) spreadsheet software; (2) standardized or packaged databases; (3) and custom-built databases or other software.

Choosing from these options depends on the size of the organization, available resources, and length of operation. Many small organizations use a simple Excel spreadsheet to track their indicators. Standardized databases offer a more robust way of collecting and organizing data. Larger organizations often create customized databases. OASIS, for example, developed a custom database that allows the national office and its twenty-one local centers to directly enter and access data relating to organizational health, program performance, and social and economic impact indicators. These data are instantly accessible via a range of custom reports that can be run by local centers or the national office.

Assign Responsibilities   Once an organization chooses how to collect and store its data, it can select team members to measure specific indicators and when. Some operational and program information will come in on an ongoing basis, whereas surveys and interviews to collect social and economic impact data might be conducted annually or several times per year. With this in mind, the working group should provide designated staff members with guidelines for when data should be collected.

In concluding Step 3, the working group should have a clear understanding about how to measure each indicator, where the data can be stored, and who will measure the data and when. Before proceeding to the next step, this is a good time to document the approach that will be used to collect and store data for each indicator.

Step 4: Preparing to Use the Data

Goal: Create your management dashboard and any additional program-level dashboards. Establish a team that will review the management dashboard and schedule regular dashboard reviews. Finalize measurement and reporting responsibilities and understand how to analyze your data.

Raw data are about as useful as no data at all. Thus, this step will prepare the organization to make use of the collected data. The team will create reporting tools—a management dashboard and possibly additional program-level dashboards—for reviewing data and drawing conclusions. Team members will also be named to review performance results regularly according to an established schedule. By the end of this step, the team members should have the necessary information to finalize their processes and further delegate responsibilities, if necessary. In addition, data-analysis techniques should help the team identify the right data to use when making continuous improvements to activities and operations.

Understanding Dashboards   The purpose of a dashboard is to provide a snapshot of the organization's progress on its way to its vision of success. It will include a selection of indicators from the master indicator list developed in Step 2. For each indicator, it shows current results in relation to a baseline or initial measurement and a target, which is the result that the organization will work to achieve within a certain period. Two main types of dashboards include a management dashboard and program-level dashboards. All performance measurement systems should include the management dashboard, and larger organizations will want to develop program-level dashboards to track the performance of individual programs, initiatives, operating areas, or departments on a more detailed level.

Figure 11.3 provides a sample management dashboard based on one recently created by the youth-mentoring organization Big Brothers Big Sisters of Bermuda, an affiliate of Big Brothers Big Sisters International. To place current and future quarterly results in context for quarterly reviews, the columns labeled "2008 Baseline" and "2009 Target" show past performance and end-of-year goals for each indicator chosen for the dashboard.

The way in which the indicators in Figure 11.3 have been organized provides insight into the process of selecting indicators for the management dashboard. Notice that within each of the three main categories of indicators (organizational health, program performance, and social and economic impact) the dashboard contains a number of subheadings. BBBS selected these subheadings based on its current management concerns and goals in order to ensure that the indicators selected from its master indicator list would address the organization's most pressing strategic questions. To provide a snapshot of organizational health, for example, BBBS's dashboard focuses on financial-health data (withheld here for privacy purposes) in addition to information on the size of its team.

Figure 11.3
Management Dashboard—An Example

Indicator	2008 Baseline	Q1	Q2	Q3	Q4	2009 Year to Date	2009 Target	Difference from 2009 Target to Date
Organizational Health								
Finacial Sustainability								
Revenue								
Expenses			Financial data withheld for privacy purposes					
Net Surplus/Loss								
Team Capacity								
Case Managers	3	3				3	tbd	tbd
Case Manager Hours per Week	40	40				40	50	(10)
Program Performance								
Recruitment of Big Brothers and Big Sisters (Mentors)								
Inquiries	74	28				28	60	(32)
Applications	44	7				7	49	(42)
Orientations	36	10				10	49	(39)
Application/Inquiry ratio (%)	59%	tbd				tbd	82%	tbd
Applications in Process	17	11				11	n/a	n/a
Recruitment of Little Brothers and Little Sisters (Mentees)								
Inquiries	82	20				20	115	(95)
Intakes	58	14				14	98	(84)
Intakes/Inquiry ratio (%)	71%	70%				70%	85%	(15%)
Matches								
Current Matches	119	125				125	147	(22)
Social and Economic Impact								
Success of BBBS Matches								
Mentees improving self-esteem (%)	n/a	tbd				tbd	tbd	tbd
Mentees improving values/responsibility (%)	n/a	tbd				tbd	tbd	tbd
Mentees improving academic performance (%)	n/a	tbd				tbd	tbd	tbd

The organization's program performance indicators focus on recruitment of mentors and mentees because these are the primary drivers of BBBS's core work of establishing and maintaining mentoring relationships. The social and economic impact category completes the story by showing the success of the mentoring process once mentors and mentees have been matched. (The spaces marked "tbd" in this section show areas that the organization has recently begun measuring and will begin to report later in the year.) As BBBS continues to fill in its management dashboard on a quarterly basis, it will be able to assess the core elements of its performance and how they change over time.

Build the Dashboards   The actions below outline the process the working group can follow to create the organization's dashboards. Start with the management dashboard. Then follow the same process for any additional program-level dashboards that the working group chooses.

Choose Subcategories   To aid in the selection of indicators to include in the dashboard, and to ensure that it is user friendly, define subheadings that will help guide reviewers of the dashboard. There are numerous ways to organize any dashboard. What is most important is that it presents information in a logical and intuitive format, which will help the individuals reviewing it to interpret the data presented in relation to key organizational goals.

Identify the Most Important Indicators from the Master List   Think about which indicators will provide the best sense of the organization's overall capacity, its progress toward its mission, and any current strategic priorities that require management attention. Keep in mind that the management dashboard may end up being weighted toward certain categories of indicators—as shown above in BBBS's focus on program performance indicators that tracked its mentor recruitment process.

Determine Preliminary Baselines and Targets   To define baselines, start by referring to the performance measurement audit to locate any currently stored data that pertains to your indicators. If the working group could easily collect baseline data for any of the remaining spaces in this column, do so at this point. Because the group likely selected a variety of new indicators that are not yet being tracked, there will be some cases in which baseline data will not be available until the performance measurement system has gone through a few cycles.

Next, for each indicator on the dashboard, identify the target that you will be aiming for and when you hope to reach it. Based on past performance and any current plans and goals, what results does the organization aim to achieve for each indicator? Also consider standards in your field. Remember that targets can be moving or fixed. For example, you may set a target for client satisfaction at 95 percent, which may remain constant over time, whereas the target for program participants may be raised each year.

Repeat the Process for Program-Level Dashboards For organizations with multiple programs or initiatives, we highly recommend creating additional dashboards to aid managing staff in monitoring those areas on a more detailed level. Many organizations also choose to create dashboards to help internal departments, such as marketing and operations, set and monitor progress toward their own targets. Make sure the management dashboard includes a few indicators for each program-level dashboard, in order to help the management team stay connected to what program level managers are tracking.

Plan for Regular Performance Reviews Start by identifying the group that will review the management dashboard. This team will hold primary responsibility for drawing lessons from the performance measurement system and employing those lessons to inform organizational decision making. If the organization already has a management team, that team should play this role. Otherwise, choose a group of staff members who provide a range of perspectives to help interpret the data and determine how to adjust activities and operations as needed.

Next, create a regular meeting schedule to review the dashboard. Meetings should take place often enough to ensure that your organizational learning becomes integrated into the culture of the organization. Quarterly reviews are a popular choice among many organizations. Whenever possible, incorporate the review of performance data into existing meetings so that it becomes an integral part of the management function and can directly inform management decisions.

Finally, remember to determine which staff members will hold the responsibility for compiling data and preparing the management dashboard and any program-level dashboards in time for scheduled review meetings. These individuals may be the same staff members who were assigned to the various measurement tasks in Step 3. Also make sure that program managers establish their own schedules for reviewing any program-level dashboards.

Prepare to Learn From and Act On Data   Reviews of the dashboards should spark and inform deeper interpretation and analysis of why performance turns out the way it does and how it can be strengthened.

Key Questions to Guide the Analysis   Start with these basic questions for each indicator:

- How have results changed over time, either positively or negatively?
- How do results compare to the baseline and targets?
- For indicators being tracked for the first time, what do the results show?

Also, look across all indicators to see relationships and patterns, analyze and interpret the results, and begin to ask probing questions and look for answers. In particular, consider:

- Why have results exceeded or missed the targets?
- What are the underlying drivers?
- How do the data align (or not) with intuitive expectations regarding activities and operations?
- What areas require further research?

Finally, look for linkages between organizational performance, program performance, and social and economic impact. Ultimately, the review team will be looking to answer:

- What is working and what is not?
- What opportunities for improvement exist?

- What challenges need to be addressed and how?

- Where should the organization focus its attention and resources?

- Which decisions regarding activities and operations should ultimately be made based on this knowledge?

In concluding Step 4, the groundwork will be in place for the organization to report, review, and learn from its performance data and, ultimately, to apply that learning to make more strategic decisions. Management will understand what questions to ask and how to answer them.

Step 5: Putting the Performance Measurement System into Action

Goal: *Launch your performance measurement system. Prepare to update your baselines and targets, refine your performance measurement system, and publish a report card for external stakeholders.*

Now return to the performance measurement framework (Figure 11.1) to envision what tasks to carry out on a regular basis throughout the cycle.

- **Measure**: Designated staff members will collect data for the indicators selected in Step 2 by the measurement processes and the tools developed in Step 3.

- **Report**: Designated staff members complete and send the management dashboard and any program-level dashboards to the appropriate review teams. After a few cycles, a report card summarizing key performance data goes out to external stakeholders.

- **Learn**: Following the established review schedule, the management and any program-level review teams meet regularly to interpret and analyze the reported data, ask probing questions, and conduct necessary research to learn, generate insights, and draw conclusions.

- **Improve**: Based on the insights and conclusions drawn from the reported data, the review teams assign responsibilities for implementing improvements regarding the organization's strategy, activities, and operations.

As an organization progresses through its first few performance measurement cycles, the team will want to revisit the system components. An additional or different indicator may be needed, and measuring that indicator may require refining an existing measurement tool or developing a new tool. Further, as discussed in Step 2 in relation to OASIS's experience with finding the right indicator to track program participation, an organization can discover that an indicator has ended up reinforcing the wrong practices and may decide to make necessary adjustments. Though minimal revisions are common, the measurement system will prove most useful when the team collects consistent data over a period of time.

REPORT CARDS: MAKING AN EXTERNAL COMMITMENT TO SELF-IMPROVEMENT

Once the leadership team is confident that they are getting reliable data from the performance measurement cycle, they can begin to share with external stakeholders what they have learned and are working to improve. This can be done via publications, such as an annual report, or with a report card presenting selected data from the dashboard. Thus, the organization will hold itself accountable to social impact investors and partners. Although the report card should unquestionably include positive results, being transparent about negative results and potential solutions will help build trust with external stakeholders.

In concluding Step 5, the organization's new or refined performance measurement system should be up and running. The team will also have an understanding of what work needs to happen in upcoming measurement cycles to update baselines and targets, make additional refinements to the system, and begin reporting performance data to external stakeholders.

CONCLUSION: PERFORMANCE MEASUREMENT AS AN ESSENTIAL TOOL FOR ACCELERATING SOCIAL IMPACT

At Root Cause we believe that there is no better way for an organization to learn from its successes and failures, and thus drive organizational improvement, than from an effective performance measurement system. Ultimately, we envision a day when all organizations measure their performance and put their results to use to accelerate the advancement of enduring solutions to our most pressing social problems.

ABOUT THE AUTHOR

Widely recognized as a leading social innovator and a pioneering teacher of social entrepreneurship, **Andrew Wolk** founded Root Cause in 2004 and continues to lead its strategic direction. He consults to organizations across the nonprofit, for-profit, and government sectors that are seeking to advance effective solutions to pressing social problems. In addition, he has authored a number of publications on social innovation. They include a report for the Aspen Institute on policy recommendations for advancing social innovation, a chapter on social entrepreneurship and government in the Small Business Administration's 2007 annual report to the president of the United States, and Root Cause's first how-to guide, *Business Planning for Enduring Social Impact*. In 1999, Andrew designed and taught one of the first courses on social entrepreneurship in the country. For the past five years, Andrew has taught social innovation and entrepreneurship at MIT. He is also a Gleitsman Visiting Practitioner in Social Innovation at the Center for Public Leadership at Harvard University's Kennedy School of Government.

Root Cause is a nonprofit organization dedicated to advancing innovative, proven solutions to our most pressing social and economic problems. We support social innovators and educate social impact investors through advisory and consulting services, knowledge sharing, and community building.

Value Versus Waste

Leaning the Enterprise

*By **Kevin Lynch**, President, Rebuild Resources,
and **Julius Walls, Jr.**, Chief of Staff at Greater
Centennial A.M.E. Zion Church,
former Chief Executive Officer, Greyston Bakery*

W e define a social enterprise as a business whose purpose is to change the world for the common good.

In our view, all social enterprises have in common two distinct characteristics. First, they are real, live *businesses*: organizations whose primary activities and means of revenue are the profitable trading of products and services, whether incorporated under a for-profit, a nonprofit, or some other legal structure. And second, they are driven by a social purpose; their driving force—created by charter, form, bylaws, mission statement, governance structure, or shareholder fiat—is to reform current conditions (not to maximize financial returns for ownership, although owners, too, may benefit) so that the social systems, institutions, and environments on which we all depend work in a manner that best benefits all people.

But every social enterprise exists and competes in the world of *traditional* businesses—in our parlance, the world of Non-Social Enterprises, or NSEs. Much as we'd like it to not be so, you and we recognize that social enterprises, at least at this point in the evolution of economic systems,

Reprinted with permission of the publisher. From *Mission Inc*, copyright © 2009 by Kevin Lynch and Julius Walls, Jr., Berrett-Koehler Publishers, Inc., San Francisco, CA. All rights reserved. www.bkconnection.com

represent but a rounding error in the sum of all the commerce that is done in the United States, much less globally.

Even when we accept for the moment the unfortunate fact that not every business is out to change the world for the common good, it's still fair to ask, Why aren't more NSEs at least modestly socially responsible? The simple answer is that most businesses think it costs too much.

In purely rational economic terms, traditional businesses are right. The cost of the common good is real. As the traditional wisdom goes, doing the right thing squeezes your bottom line. Do you want to use environmentally safe, fairly traded, humanely produced raw materials? *Your cost of goods sold will go up.* Pay your employees a living wage, provide first-class benefits, work reasonable hours? *There goes your labor budget.* Produce in America, or closely monitor human-rights policies of offshore manufacturers? *Too expensive; say good-bye to shelf space at Walmart.* Give money to the community and encourage employee volunteerism? *Less profit to reinvest in growth.* Operate from green, built-to-last facilities? *More up-front costs.*

So yes, most NSEs are inherently averse to socially responsible business practices for a "good" reason. This reason is baked right into the DNA of the underlying double-entry accounting method, which demands that every possible cost, especially the cost of doing the right thing, be externalized. Keep the environmental cost off the books by pushing it onto future generations or indigenous peoples. Keep the labor cost down by pushing it onto the families of workers. And so on. You get the picture.

It doesn't have to be this way, of course. Great minds have been hard at work devising entirely new methods of corporate reporting that give credit for internalizing the cost of social good, thereby giving companies the incentive to do the right thing or, at least, to not do the wrong thing. This point is made by Marjorie Kelly and David Korten:[1]

> In any socially efficient market, [wrote David Korten in *Business Ethics* magazine], "producers must bear the full cost of the products they sell," because when costs are not internalized, "a firm's profits represent not an addition to societal wealth,

but an expropriation of the community's existing wealth." Externalized costs would include items like public subsidies, costs borne by injured workers, the depletion of the earth's natural capital, or the $54 billion annual cost of the health consequences of cigarettes.

We take great hope in this kind of thinking. If for no other reason than its own survival, society is finally waking up to the realization that the real cost of business can't be pushed off of the corporate financial statement forever. When this is finally and inevitably understood, it will be a good day for the planet and all the peoples and species that populate it.

Even within the limitations of the existing rules for financial reporting, there is a considerable and growing realization that the cost of doing the right thing is eventually, and often very quickly, returned to the company with the foresight and vision to do so. This is why, quite independent of the social enterprise movement, more and more NSE companies even without a common good purpose, understand that *being good* is good for shareholder value. These companies have noticed that ethically produced, environmentally respectable products command better pricing, that humanely treated employees are more effective, that corporate citizenship creates more loyal customers, and that doing the right thing mitigates risk.

ENTER LEAN

It is against this backdrop that we now turn our attention to the subject of the actual day-to-day operations of a social enterprise and how you can (and must) aspire toward a world-class level of operational excellence. Our inspiration for this topic is the concept of Lean manufacturing, a name that is usually traced to a description of the Toyota Production System in a 1990 book by James P. Womack, Daniel T. Jones, and Daniel Roos, *The Machine That Changed the World: The Story of Lean Production,* and further developed in Womack and Jones's landmark 1996 work, *Lean Thinking.*[2]

"Lean manufacturing" is a slightly misleading phrase in that it applies equally well to nonmanufacturing environments, for example, retail and service businesses. For our purposes, we prefer to simply call the entire idea Lean. It's one of those words that works as an adjective (as in "That's a great Lean technique!"), as a verb ("Now that we're Leaning the shipping and receiving department, we need to start Leaning the office"), and as a noun ("Wow, this place could really use some Lean!").

At the heart of Lean thinking is a simple core principle:

> Anything that does not add value is waste. Waste is undesirable and makes you uncompetitive and socially irresponsible. Therefore, you must relentlessly seek out and eliminate waste.

Since Womack, Jones, and Roos first popularized the notion of Lean, millions of words have been written about it, hundreds of thousands of hours of training conducted, and thousands of miles of production lines transformed. What is beautiful about it as an operating philosophy is that it is simple enough to be understood by every person in every organization and simultaneously complex enough that there is no limit to how Lean an organization can get.

To understand Lean, let's use the living example of Greyston Bakery. The core of Greyston's business is making the chocolate fudge brownies that go into Ben & Jerry's ice cream. An ice cream this amazing can only be made with amazing brownies. To make a brownie worthy of the ice cream it goes into, Greyston purchases the best all-natural ingredients, which include flour, sugar, cocoa, soybean oil, and vanilla. Greyston employees check the ingredients for quality. They meticulously measure each ingredient and in a specified manner, blend all the ingredients just so. Then they deposit a certain amount of the mixture on a tray at a certain temperature, with the same amount on each tray, and bake it at a specific temperature for a specific amount of time. They cool the baked product under controlled temperatures and then cut it to a certain size and pack it at certain temperatures.

Everything we just described makes the brownie better, which makes the ice cream better. Ben & Jerry's is happy to pay for it. But Greyston needs to do a great deal more along the way in order to make its brownies. The cocoa, flour, sugar, soybean oil, and vanilla need to come into the plant. They need to be received, weighed, counted, and stored. They need to be moved from storage to the bakery floor. They need to be unpacked. Something needs to be done with the bags and cartons that these ingredients came in. Once everything is mixed together, the mix needs to find its way to the baking pans. The baking pans need to go into the ovens. They need to come out of the ovens.

None of these activities contribute to a better brownie. Ben & Jerry's has no reason to want to pay for them. If Greyston could eliminate them altogether without hurting the product or slowing the production line—and with proper Lean attention, it *almost* could—it would get no complaint whatsoever from the customer.

Other activities happen at Greyston as well. Someone sells. Someone receives the receivables and pays the payables. The furnace filters get changed, and the bathrooms get cleaned. The payroll taxes get filed, and the health plan enrollment forms stay up to date. None of these activities make a better brownie either. But if they don't get done, no brownies can be made at all.

Through Lean eyes, Greyston's operations, like those of any enterprise, are easily classified into three groups:

Value-added activities: Activities that tangibly add "form, fit, or function" for the customer. These are activities for which customers are ready and willing to pay.

Non-value-added activities: Activities that add nothing to the customer's experience of the product or service. Customers have no interest in paying for such activities.

Non-value-added but business-essential activities: Activities in which customers have little interest but that are necessary parts of doing business for you and your competitors.

Remember, anything that does not add value is waste, which must be eliminated. In the Greyston example, as in any Lean company, the non-value-added activities must be attacked and driven out, and the non-value-added but business-essential activities must, at the very least, be minimized.

In most of the core literature about Lean you'll find variations on a simple list of seven types of waste that were first identified in the

Table 12.1
The Seven Kinds of Waste

Type of Waste	Cause
1. Transportation Waste	Moving stuff around
2. Waiting-around Waste	Queuing stuff up
3. Overproduction Waste	Making too much stuff or too soon
4. Defect Waste	Looking for bad stuff and throwing it away
5. Inventory Waste	Letting stuff sit around
6. Motion Waste	Moving people around
7. Overprocessing	Doing more to the product than the customer wants

Toyota Production System, documented by Womack, Jones, and Roos, and restated by dozens of others since then. These forms of waste and their causes are shown in the table above.

Over a long enough period, and all other things being equal, eliminating waste is a matter of life and death. The Lean company puts more energy into value-added activities—creating better products that lead to happier customers. The Lean company puts less money into non-value-added activities—saving money that can lead to better prices, a better bottom line, growth capital, or all three. The non-Lean company gradually loses ground to the Lean rival and eventually doesn't make it.

Ultimately, the Lean company will (at least at the level of its operational approach) have the potential to be a much more responsible company than its non-Lean counterpart. True Lean disciples won't settle for conveniently externalizing waste nor the cost thereof. Lean is about eliminating it altogether. Waste is waste, no matter its form. Wasted raw materials, wasted energy costs, wasted square footage, wasted transport cost, wasted human potential, toxic leftover waste—they all have to go.

If that isn't a beautiful, socially responsible idea, we don't know what is.

It's not that Lean, as widely practiced today, evolved from any advanced sense of social responsibility or anything resembling such. No, it came about simply as a means of improving quality, raising margins, reducing capital costs, and enhancing customer satisfaction—altogether, as a tool for gaining and maintaining a competitive advantage and, ultimately, for improving shareholder value. But the law of unintended consequences sometimes turns to the advantage of the common good, and this is such a case. Imagine a world where every business is completely Lean, and you'll be imagining a world where no excess costs are being dumped off the corporate financial statement onto the planet, people, and community.

Lean will contribute to *any* company's well-being. For your social enterprise, we would argue that it is even more essential. You have a high calling. At the level of the marketplace in which your enterprise operates, Lean will help you compete. And unlike your competitors, Lean or not, you cannot even consider the option of externalizing the true costs of doing business, at least if you intend to remain true to your commitment to the common good.

As the leader of a social enterprise, you are shooting for a different value proposition altogether. You must deliver value for your customers or else they will go somewhere else. Anything that's not adding to that value is waste, from a customer perspective, and must be eliminated. But you are simultaneously delivering value to the common good as a whole, and anything that's not creating *that* kind of value is also waste and must also be eliminated. Complicating matters further, waste of the first kind might actually be value of the second kind and vice versa.

For social enterprise, anything that detracts from mission is *also* waste. You'd better be able to sort out what's waste (and what's not) and drive it from the system. You've got your work cut out for you, so you'll need some tools.

THE LEAN TOOL BELT

The actual set of Lean tools that will help you drive both business waste and mission waste from your enterprise has yet to be invented. Your enterprise must invent them for itself because your enterprise is different from any other. Any Lean technique that is not invented inside your enterprise will not stick.

Anything that we or anyone else might offer is a set of approximations. Lean is a very specific philosophy that is carried out by a very generalized set of tools that each company must customize for itself. Some tools focus on increasing speed, others on reducing cost, and others on improving quality, while all of them seek out and eliminate waste. Rebuild Resources, the enterprise led by coauthor Kevin Lynch, has immersed itself in Lean training over the last few years. Its working definition of Lean (lifted from so many different sources that no one remembers which ones) is "Getting the right things to the right place at the right time in the right quantity, while minimizing waste and being flexible and open to change."

We must warn you that Lean will succeed only with a complete top-down commitment from the leader of the enterprise. It is not a shortcut, a trend, or a silver bullet. For a social enterprise, Lean represents a total commitment to not externalizing waste and to eliminating it altogether. It means placing customer value and mission value at the center of everything that the enterprise does. And it means constant, relentless change that will energize some people and scare the daylights out of others. So remember to hire the kind that it will energize!

Lean is simple. But first, it's complicated. To simplify the complicated part of Lean, go out and spend a few dollars on some of the resources that are readily available. Lean is a workbook lover's, diagram-and-flow-chart junkie's dream. Google "Lean manufacturing" to find dozens of quick and easy hands-on tools to help you turn our generalizations into tools you can work with.

A handful of Lean tools exist from which any social enterprise will benefit, whether manufacturing, retail, or service businesses. (We'll use the language of manufacturing companies, because that's what Rebuild and Greyston are, but the concepts are universal.) They are:

Value-stream mapping: Diagramming the value-added and non-value-added flow of all that you do

Kaizen: Gaining wisdom from change

5S: Removing the clutter under which waste hides, by sorting, stabilizing, shining, standardizing, and sustaining

Learn to use these Lean tools and you'll make great strides.

Value-Stream Mapping

Value-stream mapping is the core Lean process that precedes all the others. For a traditional business, it is a matter of identifying, measuring, diagramming, and flowing all of the tasks, both value-added and non-value-added, that bring the product all the way from raw material to the customer's hands. For a social enterprise, value-stream mapping also involves every activity that adds to or detracts from mission delivery. The process uses a simple but specific language and set of symbols to represent various aspects of the value stream. It places equal emphasis on identifying where value is created and identifying where it is not. It starts with a description of how things are now (often called the "current-state map") and then progresses to a description of how things should be in a world where waste has been eliminated (the "future-state map"). The gaps between current and future state become the focus of a continuous series of Lean projects.

Value-stream mapping can be done at the macro level of an organization as a whole or at the micro level of a division, a department, a product line, or even a single manufacturing line. Consider using it at a micro level first to produce immediate gains that will create belief and buy-in. Then roll it back to a macro view to identify priority targets. And then start knocking off the priority targets at a midview level for the long haul.

Some key concepts will come up time and time again in value-stream mapping. They are stated here from the perspective of a manufacturing environment but, with minimal modification, apply equally well to service and retail enterprises as well:

- Avoiding batch and queue production (which inevitably creates over-production) in favor of continuous flow

- Using cellular thinking, which shortens production lines and sequences and replaces them with discrete, interchangeable, movable production functions

- Reducing changeover time by rethinking design and machine sequence issues

- Taking on the discipline of a FIFO (first in, first out) system to avoid obsolescence, waste, and deterioration

Kaizen

Lean is full of wonderful Japanese words like *hejunka, muda,* and our personal favorite, *poka-yoke.* Let's concentrate on perhaps the most important, *Kaizen.* This is a combination of two terms: *kai,* which means "to change," and *zen,* "to gain wisdom from doing." Put them together, and you're talking about *gaining wisdom from change.*

Kaizen picks up where your value-stream mapping left off. In the mapping process you identify the gaps between the current state and the idealized future state. Those gaps become grist for the mill of an endless series of incremental, worker-led improvements. What makes this process Kaiz*en,* not just *kai,* is the emphasis on constancy that is implied by continual wisdom gaining. In other words, the process that was just improved is now exposed as something that can and should be improved again, and what is learned in improving it can also be used to improve dozens of other processes.

As the leader of a social enterprise, you may particularly appreciate the democratic, grassroots nature of Kaizen. To carry it off, you must respect your workers' abilities to spot problems and be willing to release their innate capacity to fix them. Your emphasis is on making small improvements all the time, which will accumulate to become large systemic changes. You must focus on the improvement, not the source. A good idea for a small change recognizes neither rank nor hierarchy. All that matters is the change, the waste it drives out, and the further wisdom it produces.

Lean companies reject the traditional thinking of "if it ain't broke, don't fix it" and replace it with the Kaizen philosophy of "do it better, make it better, improve it even if it ain't broken, because if we don't, we can't compete with those who do."[3]

Only a company with a healthy culture can produce a bountiful Kaizen harvest. If you are unwilling to be the kind of leader who creates an atmosphere of honesty and humility where everyone can freely admit problems, if your ego precludes a collaborative environment where value is placed not on the source of an idea but only on the idea itself, or if you are not personally passionate about producing value for the customer and the common good, Kaizen cannot succeed.

If you embrace Kaizen, it will help you create the healthy culture you crave.

5S

5S derives from a Japanese concept of housekeeping. The fundamental idea is that waste hides beneath clutter and can be eliminated only when the clutter is removed. 5S is a systematic way to remove clutter and keep it from reappearing so that inconspicuous waste becomes exposed to the light of day. Here are the steps you will take in that process, whether for an area, a department, or a whole plant:

1. *Sort* everything out into three groups: what you will retain, what you will return elsewhere, and what you will get rid of.

2. *Stabilize* whatever you will retain so that, in the words of your mother, there is a place for everything, and everything in its place.

3. *Shine* the entire area with a deep clean. You'll be amazed what it does for attitudes, for your ability to spot malfunctioning gear, and for worker safety.

4. *Standardize/systematize* schedules and systems of regulation to maintain the stable and shiny state you've created.

5. *Sustain* the culture through enforcements, consequences, and reinforcement.

THE LEAN SOCIAL ENTERPRISE

Remember, you're not just a manufacturing, retailing, or service company in the widget business. You're in the business of widgets *and the common good.*

Your mission delivery might be harder to Lean than your core business processes if for no other reason than that your mission is probably more subtle, qualitative, and difficult to measure. It may even be counterintuitive to *want* to Lean it. For example, many social enterprises deliver their missions by employing people. You might worry that Lean will make you so efficient as to require fewer workers, thereby reducing your mission delivery.

That's a terrible trap you must avoid. Your enterprise cannot succeed without relentlessly focusing on customer value. If creating that value conflicts with mission, then the answer is not to reduce customer value, but to increase mission delivery.

Consider the case of Rebuild Resources, a social enterprise whose core process is to take in the raw material of recovering people who want to put their lives back together and produce sober people who are capable of holding a job and becoming self-sufficient. For Rebuild, success means that someone gets a job elsewhere and leaves Rebuild. It also means that Rebuild loses a good worker, which wreaks havoc with production.

A few years back, Rebuild reviewed its mission delivery results and noticed that, over the course of time, people were getting stuck and not leaving the Rebuild program long after they were ready because it was too comfortable for them to stay. Rebuild set out to Lean its program side. It set a limit on the program length, which gave people a firm deadline by which they had to find a job. It added all sorts of coaching and job-search training to give people the tools with which to move on. It created an evaluation process that let them see their progress at every step. And most important, it created an orientation process at the front end so that they would understand from day one that their main job was to leave.

It was no coincidence that Rebuild was doing all of this at the same time that it was getting deeply into Lean work on the production floor. And a funny thing happened. Despite higher turnover, Rebuild created more value for its customers because the workforce became more vital, engaged, and committed. And it created more value for the community because Rebuild placed many more graduates.

Scaling the Lean Enterprise

Together, we need to take our social enterprises to scale so that we can collectively create the common good at the massive level these times require. If we cannot get our "little" social enterprises to operate at the highest possible levels of quality, productivity, efficiency, and customer value, they will remain just that: little social enterprises, spread all across the land, tapping little markets of sympathizers and fighting merely to sustain themselves.

That's not what the authors signed up for. We're pretty sure it's not what our readers signed up for either. Scale enterprises require scale thinking, and that means competing with the best traditional businesses in our industries.

Darell Hammond, CEO of KaBOOM!, one of the most meteorically successful social enterprises of recent times, sums it up with this anecdote:

> I remember in the early days of KaBOOM!! we were working with Home Depot. There was a problem in a project in Vancouver, and the head of community relations called me and told me about the problem. I jumped on a plane. We solved the problem, and I can still remember Saturday night after the playground was built, leaving her a message saying, "Problem solved. I was there. No problem." She called me on Monday morning and said, "You know, you don't get it. The issue is, if you have to jump on a plane, there must be something wrong with your processes or checks and balances. It's not scalable because it needs to be dependent on you." And it was a humbling moment in time to say that the systems and the processes have to be as great and as significant as the people, that if anything ever happens to you it can outlive and scale beyond what one person is capable of doing.

Scale thinking requires a fierce commitment to operational excellence.

Notes

1. Marjorie Kelly, *The Divine Right of Capital: Dethroning the Corporate Aristocracy* (San Francisco: Berrett-Koehler, 2001), 5, quoting David C. Korten, "A New Focus: Corporate Cost Internalization," *Business Ethics* (July–Aug. 1997): 16.
2. James P. Womack and Daniel T. Jones, *Lean Thinking* (New York: Simon & Schuster, 1996).
3. Masaaki Imai, *Kaizen: The Key to Japan's Competitive Success* (New York: McGraw Hill, 1986).

ABOUT THE AUTHORS

Kevin Lynch is president of Rebuild Resources, Inc., a $2.2 million nonprofit social-purpose business in St. Paul, Minnesota, that helps chronic addicts and alcoholics find a path to sobriety through a program of spiritual recovery and work. Rebuild's business operations include a custom apparel and promotional-items business and a contract manufacturer. These businesses provide the recovery environment for Rebuild's student-employees and serve as the economic engines that fuel the enterprise.

Lynch is currently a board member of the Social Enterprise Alliance and has served on several national and local boards, including those of Social Venture Network, Headwaters Foundation for Justice, Twin Cities Community Gospel Choir, and (as the cofounder) Responsible Minnesota Business. Lynch has started several successful businesses, including a direct-mail business (while in college) and Lynch Jarvis Jones, a social enterprise ad agency whose mission was to create positive social change through the power of advertising and marketing.

Julius Walls, Jr., is chief of staff for Greater Centennial A.M.E. Zion Church, a five-thousand-member church in Mount Vernon, New York, as of July 2009. Walls supports the pastor, Rev. Dr. W. Darin Moore, in overseeing their more than fifteen ministers and over one hundred ministries. As CEO of the Greyston Bakery, Walls grew the bakery to a $7 million social enterprise. Walls is a professor at the business graduate schools at NYU and Bainbridge Graduate Institute, the coauthor of *MISSION, INC., The Practitioners Guide to Social Enterprise*, 2008, and participates in Harvard University's Executive Session on Transforming Cities through

Civic Entrepreneurs. Born in Brooklyn, New York, Walls attended college seminary before receiving his B.S. from Concordia College. Walls served as vice president of operations for a chocolate manufacturing company and founded his own chocolate company, Sweet Roots, Inc. Core ingredients in Walls' life are his spiritual practice, family, and service. Walls serves on several local and national nonprofit and government boards.

PART THREE

Leadership

Good Board Governance Is a Good Business Practice

*By **Sonia Pouyat**, M.S.W., kidsLINK*

Nonprofit organizations, including charities, operate under the guidance and oversight of boards of directors or trustees that are typically populated by volunteers. As traditional nonprofits have successfully launched social enterprises, or as new social enterprise organizations have been created, their leaders have grappled with enabling a culture and business model that is entrepreneurial, market driven, and open to making profit—while remaining committed to their mission. In this context, it seems logical that one of the first questions to be addressed would be what this means for the board of directors. Does a board operate differently when governing a social enterprise? Does its role change as the social enterprise moves through different stages?

Chief executives of nonprofit organizations have wrestled for decades with the question of how to work most productively with boards. In recent years, government and foundations have become aware of the impact of boards and are paying more attention to how boards are governing and meeting their obligations. Effective board governance is important for all corporate entities, whether for-profit or nonprofit. In the third sector, where these bodies are comprised of community volunteers who are collectively responsible for the use of "public" funds for public benefit, the accountability of the board is theoretically more subject to scrutiny. There is a general expectation that boards capably fulfill their fiduciary and trusteeship responsibilities and do so at a reasonable cost to the organization and public.

However, with social enterprises, most funders and investors are exercising their due diligence by scrutinizing business plans rather than governance. I suggest that failure to attend to board governance by funders, executive leaders, or the boards themselves, puts each party and the organization or enterprise at risk. Minimizing risk is especially crucial for a social enterprise that is expanding or making a significant change in business direction. It is wise that in addressing potential threats to the business, plans include ensuring sound leadership with effective and efficient board governance.

Historically, however, board effectiveness has for the most part been examined only when serious trouble occurred within organizations. If attention to a board's effectiveness is rare and reactive in the nonprofit sector, attention to governance of a social enterprise that is largely dependent on earned income is even less likely. In any kind of business with a board of directors, good management and oversight to minimize risk require diligence in setting and meeting standards for governance. Good governance requires diligence in setting and meeting standards for operations and risk management. Entrepreneurial nonprofits may be even more vulnerable to the consequences of neglecting this diligence.

When I first became the executive director of a nonprofit agency twenty-five years ago, working with boards was the biggest and most persistent focus of meetings with my seasoned peers, locally, provincially, nationally, and in the United States. It dominated networking meetings and conference agendas. Why? Because we were all running mature agencies but were suffering under the strain of unproductive, costly, or downright hazardous board processes. It was easy to point to what was wrong but hard to fix it. We sought to identify models for governance that actually worked well, and to find training for board members that would make a difference. We saw evidence of the immense cost of boards that were not doing their governance job when agencies ended up in crisis. In most cases, the CEOs took the fall, closely followed by board members. As we discovered models and tools that raised the standard for boards, I decided that demanding good governance by the boards with which I am involved was to be my personal risk-management strategy to protect myself as a chief executive.

A CAUTIONARY TALE

Governance can make or break an organization. The story of CivSoc (fictional name) is a cautionary tale for those of us working in social enterprise. CivSoc had tremendous growth and success, followed by devastating failure. And as this story shows, governance played a critical role.

Just over ten years ago, CivSoc was born through the efforts of three creative individuals. One founder became the chief executive, the other two inaugural board members. At its inception, CivSoc came together with everything it takes to launch a dynamic and successful social enterprise that quickly develops an excellent reputation for its work:

- An entrepreneur with vision, drive, and a good idea
- An effective salesperson
- An effective fund-raiser
- A network of good contacts and connections
- A recognized leader with visibility and a good reputation
- An audience of people interested in the vision

CivSoc was a Canadian charitable organization committed to strengthening charities in their work toward a civil society. It provided a range of services to nonprofit organizations in Canada and internationally. This established social enterprise declared voluntary bankruptcy after ten years of filling a unique niche with excellence and delivering on its mission through well-respected and much-needed activities.

Two of CivSoc's services generated earned income and supported, with the substantial help of foundation grants, its advocacy work for charities. Just prior to its demise, CivSoc had its biggest share of business to date.

It had an operating budget of $6 million, a staff of seven, a nine-member board of directors, many of whom had been on the board since its inception, and an executive director who had joined the organization only six months before it shut down.

CivSoc was a growing, admirable social enterprise. On the surface and officially, the reason for CivSoc's failure was financial. The enterprise was in financial trouble, which the board ascribed to a lack of "core funding" (that is, revenue sources from operating or grants from governments or foundations that can sustain what is even the modest central management function at the heart of any organization). It could not see its way out of the crisis due to emerging government policy that was having a negative impact on its market.

Lack of money was, no doubt, a problem. But was that really *the* root cause of CivSoc's closure? Was it weak business planning or deficits in financial management? Whenever there is a crisis in a nonprofit organization, especially one that results in its demise, the first action is to examine what kind of leadership was in place by the board and the chief executive. As is to be expected, the CivSoc's board members did a lot of soul-searching in the final days and beyond. What did they discover?

The chair of the board of directors retrospectively points to a number of factors that contributed to CivSoc's downfall, many of which can be summarized as lack of effective oversight and management. When distilled down, the core factors point to failure by the board to fulfill its governance responsibilities. Yet, CivSoc seemed to have very capable leadership—board members with considerable governance and executive management experience who came well prepared to meetings and were fully engaged in the work and an outstanding chief executive with impressive credentials in management, community leadership, and the core business.

So, how did the board fail? The board came to see that it had not kept its sights on its governance responsibilities. It did not define the board to chief executive relationship objectively; did not assess and monitor business risk adequately; did not respond to signs of operational shortcomings when they arose, such as unavailable financial reports, excessive turnover of finance staff, and anxiety at the manager level; nor did it get the information it needed, as it was deficient in processes for obtaining critical information or addressing issues.

Why did the board fail? With the clarity of hindsight that comes after much introspection, the chair admits that:

- The board was well aware of its responsibilities but did not focus on executing them. Instead, it focused on discussing, reflecting, and advising on program activity that attracted them to the organization in the first place—a common occurrence with nonprofit board volunteers.

- Board members were recruited to be champions for the cause, not overseers, thus it did not provide management oversight.

- The board saw its role as assisting and supporting the chief executive. With that person having been a founder of the organization, his drive and vision were outstanding—the business was "his show." The board did not monitor his work. It did not explore the reasons for his desire to resign a few years earlier; instead it encouraged him to continue in his position.

- The board did not oversee business planning decisions to ensure organizational capacity matched the amount of business and that its structure limited liability and financial risk. The board's financial monitoring lacked rigor.

- Relationships lacked boundaries between personal and professional sides, blurring business accountabilities. Expectations between employer (board) and employee (chief executive) were not well articulated.

The failure of CivSoc boils down to one main reason: **the board as a whole did not stay focused on, assume, or execute its unique governance job.** It could be said that board members were dazzled by the vision, ideas, and dynamism of the entrepreneurial leader and blinded by their own investment in the business—they had donned rose-colored glasses.

CivSoc was a flourishing social enterprise with ten years of successful operations. It had bright and capable leadership and an engaging mission.

Its vision was compelling and its customers were happy. The true Achilles heel of the enterprise was growth on a foundation that was not strong enough to sustain the challenges. What happened to CivSoc can happen to any social enterprise that mistakes serious gaps in governance oversight for everyday business challenges. It can happen to any organization that does not attend to governing properly and maintaining a transparent, productive, and accountable way of working between the board and the chief executive.

The lessons to be learned from CivSoc have significance to any social enterprise, especially those expanding and taking on more business risk. We would do well to recognize that:

- Governance is not something most volunteers joining boards are well informed about or interested in. Therefore, boards have to learn how to govern. They have to put processes in place and sustain them consciously in order to ensure that they will meet their basic but critical responsibilities.

- Boards are responsible for the performance of their employee, the chief executive, yet this employee guides and facilitates the board's work. This complex and somewhat codependent relationship is best managed through objective definition of both roles and the board-CEO relationship, especially where a founder or founders are involved.

- Good governance does not preclude board members from being able to contribute in other ways to the enterprise. Efficiency and clarity in governance practices leave time and space for desired secondary roles.

- Unconscious, blind, or deluded leaders comprise a significant risk to a social enterprise. This risk must be managed for both board and chief executive. Attending to how the board governs, through regular monitoring of both the board's effectiveness and the chief executive's results and compliance with requirements, mitigates that risk.

- Individual attention of board members and chief executives to their personal governance responsibility, by challenging the group and identifying its omissions on record, serves to protect the organization, its stakeholders, and themselves from risk.

A TALE OF RECOVERY AND SUCCESS

Just as inattentive governance can allow a social enterprise to slip into chaos, good governance can help it grow. The story of kidsLINK, shows how the transition from a leadership crisis to good board governance laid the groundwork for it to evolve into a successful social enterprise.

KidsLINK is a 151-year-old organization that works with eleven thousand children and youth who have or are at risk of developing serious social, emotional, and mental health problems. In 1999, though 100 percent funded by government, kidsLINK adopted a social enterprise strategy. It has since then tripled its budget and mission impact. Today kidsLINK delivers a wide range of treatment and early intervention services with a budget of over $7 million and 150 staff. Over $1.5 million is earned income from selling specialized treatment services that generate an annual profit in the range of 8 to 10 percent. It has recently developed a new product line based on service experience that, once launched, will extend its reach nationally and internationally.

When I became CEO of kidsLINK, with the mandate to transform the then 136-year-old organization into a social enterprise, my first priority was the immediate implementation of a transparent board model. This meant taking time to ensure that solid governance practices were in place. Two key practices were regular and careful monitoring of the CEO's accomplishments by the board, and the board engaging in regular self-evaluation. The board engaged fully to this end, largely because it was just recovering from an organizational crisis related to its own governance.

The organization was then facing the serious and high cost of not having had an oversight system in place for monitoring the actions of previous chief executives. The board also had not had a clear approach to its governance role or agreed-on, clearly articulated expectations of the chief executive. Thus, it was unable to determine from reports received whether the organization was being run to a desired standard or not. When it was notified of serious irregularities, there were no documented guiding principles in place to assist the board in dealing with them. And board members did not have consensus on how to deal with the issues.

Through the difficult time that ensued, and the subsequent fallout, the board lost some members and the respect of management. The organization lost employees, and others became ill from the stress. The organization paid the price financially. Thus, my new employer had recently learned the hard way that the absence of good governance can be destructive to an organization. For me, this was an appealing aspect of the new job— I would not have to overcome resistance to demonstrate the importance of maintaining effective board governance. Within a year, the same board meticulously developed a system of doing its job that was designed to address all worries and minimize risk. It established clear, value-based expectations with a comprehensive and specific executive accountability and monitoring system. It began the practice of evaluating its own process for continual improvement.

Since 1995, kidsLINK has had an engaged and supportive board of directors that has exercised its governance responsibilities and organized its work with deliberation and prudence, delegating clear responsibility to the CEO, and monitoring outcomes closely. It ensures that its individual members will understand and contribute to key board decisions through its recruitment and board training practices. It requires that the CEO provide evidence of due diligence in her decisions and does not act on recommendations without exercising its own decision-making deliberations.

The board engages with executive and senior staff in generative discussions that inform mission focus, long-term direction, and enterprise development. It is careful to respect the CEO's role and authority while checking to ensure that the CEO operates within the limits of its expectations; it tracks business results and holds the CEO responsible for them. The board evaluates itself in the execution of its governance role, identifies weaknesses, and strives to get better. The outcome of proven and continually improving board governance processes has been a board that contributes positively to the organization, rather than creating risk for the organization. There have been no significant issues with the board's execution of its job due to defined governance processes and clear policies. In this way, the board has provided governance stability throughout twelve years of dynamic social enterprise business development.

BOARD EFFECTIVENESS ADDS VALUE

Looking closely at these tales of woe and joy, you can begin to see what makes a board effective—and what may cause it to fail. The issues central to boards working productively cluster around three key obligations that are especially crucial to complex and growing social enterprises. A board is obliged to:

1. Fulfill its unique and unassignable role and work in a way that adds value

2. Establish an accountable and complementary shared leadership relationship with the chief executive

3. Bring rigor and its collective wisdom to deliberations for reasonable, timely decision making

Fulfilling a unique role while adding value. First, if boards are to be effective, efficient, and add value beyond their minimum responsibilities, they need to be clear about the work that is uniquely theirs, understand and meet their obligations, differentiate between their job and that of staff, articulate expectations and aims of the organization, monitor to ensure compliance with and achievement of their expectations, and do their part in risk management through oversight of the work and leadership of the organization by the chief executive. What gets in the way of achieving this?

There are four common reasons boards fail to focus adequately on doing their core job:

- *People either don't know what it takes or simply do not care about investing in governance.* Organizations are vulnerable to the governance intelligence of their board members and their willingness to invest in the quality of their board process. Ignorance or apathy cannot be allowed.

- *With the proliferation of nonprofits seeking board members, it is difficult to recruit volunteers with a best-practice-informed understanding of and solid experience with quality governance practices.* Thus, training is required on an ongoing basis.

- *Board members are too often recruited to fill the secondary roles boards choose to assume, such as fund-raising or networking, which does not always expedite good governance.* They are more interested in the secondary activities than in their primary responsibilities as board members. Governance is seen as just too boring or tedious by many. Hence, disciplined implementation of governance practices is required.

- *Most volunteers who join nonprofit boards do so because they are attracted to or passionate about the mission. They naturally gravitate toward attending to programs or services, rather than governance.* Meticulously communicating the role of the board when recruiting, and focusing board member orientation on governance rather than programs or operations, ensures that people join boards for the right reasons.

Establishing an accountable and complementary shared leadership relationship with the chief executive. Creating and maintaining a shared leadership approach with accountability between board and a chief executive is complex and prone to imbalances. Chief executives' personal styles or agendas may contribute to board troubles. Strong CEOs who are inclined to direct the organization rather than empower the board to provide direction can be a challenge to boards. This inclination comes easily, as the CEO is often the only consistent leader over the years and is usually strongly invested in the organization. Some give up on their boards, others regretfully still consider boards to be a necessary evil to be tolerated and managed for minimum interference. This is the unfortunate consequence of boards that waste organizations' resources, the CEOs' time, and do not add value. Regardless, no one person, either board member or staff, should drive a board's decisions. A trusting but mutually accountable relationship between board and chief executive provides a reliable base for quality decision making.

Situations in which founders of the business are involved, either on the board or as the chief executive, present unique dynamics that create potential pitfalls. The status of founder or their sense of ownership can interfere with the appropriate execution of roles. Respect and admiration or interpersonal tension caused by evolving differences of opinion can lead to abdication of responsibilities or to conflict and risk.

Bringing rigor and collective wisdom to deliberations for reasonable, timely decisions. Quality of decision making is often correlated with effective governance. My observation over the years is that organized boards with clear governance policies, methods, and tools are more likely to apply their skills and wisdom to making the best decisions. Broken governance systems drain resources and energy and divert focus, which can contribute to flawed decisions.

The role of boards and complications of not practicing good governance apply to both traditional nonprofits and social enterprises, regardless of their size or stage of development. However, social enterprises may be more vulnerable to certain pitfalls because of the demands of entrepreneurism and the traits of their entrepreneurial leaders. In particular, advanced-stage enterprises and those scaling up or moving in a new direction need to be able to count on their boards to be clear about and to reliably expedite their governance functions.

GOOD GOVERNANCE AND SOCIAL ENTERPRISE

A well-established nonprofit social enterprise typically has a board aligned behind the mission and the venture. Without this alignment, growth of the venture would have been unlikely. Regardless, the questions that historically plagued traditional nonprofits definitely continue to have relevance for social enterprises.

- Does the board know and execute its governance job deliberately and effectively?
- Is it efficient, not draining resources from the enterprise?
- Does it add value to the enterprise?
- Do the board and CEO work well together, aligned toward a shared vision?

A social enterprise with capable leadership by board and CEO will test positively for all four. Such an enterprise will have a solid foundation for growth.

Successful social enterprises, of course, typically have strong entrepreneurial leaders at the helm. They have the capacity to be nimble and respond to market opportunities, take and limit risk, overcome obstacles, have the right people, secure venture financing, invest in their own development, make money, balance mission with money in decision making, and so on.

Particular challenges for a social enterprise board are to provide appropriate and clear direction for this often charismatic leader. The board must adequately monitor and ensure that expectations are met and risk appropriately managed, and contribute to and be invested in key business decisions—all while not getting in the way of the entrepreneur's efforts or impeding the venture's ability to develop successfully.

A clear distinction between the work and authority of the board and of the entrepreneurial CEO is critical to the enterprise's capacity for responsiveness, just as collaboration and buy-in by both board and CEO are crucial when taking risks and making big decisions. Lack of clarity can hinder decision making and result in significant cost to an enterprise. In social enterprises with founders still in leadership roles, there is the possibility that accountabilities may become fuzzy or the accountability process may become tension-ridden due to feelings of ownership, a struggle for power, or desire for control. Again, clear definition of relationships, roles, and expectations, combined with commitment and follow-through, can bring a degree of objectivity to the accountabilities and enable the work to be done with minimal stress. Without this clarity and commitment, avoidance behavior may occur and result in crucial responsibilities not being met, thus putting the enterprise at risk.

As social enterprise companies expand and operate with multiple divisions for multiple products or services, differences in leaders' styles or division cultures can be a challenge to boards. Complexity in operations can create challenges in balancing double or triple bottom lines when making decisions. Capable boards establish values, clear expectations, and authority about such decisions, and they recognize that they cannot provide good oversight equally to a number of diverse and competing parts of the business. In those companies, trusting and accountable relationships are essential. The dialogue from routine monitoring by the board is the substance of that trust and accountability.

As we saw in the case of CivSoc, blindness and delusion are common afflictions of nonprofit leaders when it comes to good governance. Too often they genuinely believe things are going well and just do not see what is lacking. In fact, they may see success everywhere. But governance is partly about protecting the business—it requires consideration and putting processes and preventive practices in place *before* trouble strikes; and it often takes trouble to reveal the weak spots in the plan.

Investing for Success

Good governance by volunteer boards of directors has long been a challenge to achieve within nonprofit organizations. Limited interest in that very necessary function often results in substandard board accountability. However, well-functioning boards can add significant value to nonprofit businesses.

Social enterprises that are about to scale up, launch a new product or service, or change direction need boards that are engaged in the deliberations, exercising proper oversight, monitoring vulnerability, and adding value to decisions as a governing body. Regretfully, there are still examples of well-established social enterprises that collapse due to what, in hindsight, proves to be a board simply not doing its job. The story of CivSoc demonstrates that neglect of the governance role can create risk. As we see in the case of kidsLINK and as we know as entrepreneurs, failure is fraught with learning and can be the basis of future success. Investing in good board governance will contribute to your organization's success.

ABOUT THE AUTHOR

Sonia Pouyat, M.S.W., has been CEO of Notre Dame of St. Agatha (NDSA), operating as kidsLINK, since 1994. She has more than twenty-six years' experience as chief executive with nonprofits. Her interest in nonprofit governance was born of her experience as executive director working previously for a large and floundering board, which would not change. Disillusionment led her to the brink of relinquishing her career path. Instead, Pouyat decided that she would only be an employee or member of boards that endeavor to govern productively toward a set of standards, and that she would develop and bring that expertise to them. Since that decision eighteen years ago, Pouyat has led her several boards through a process to become conscious and conscientious in carrying out their governance mandate. On a volunteer basis, Sonia Pouyat has helped community agencies, memberships associations, and an elected school authority with their governance structure and board development. She has been a leader in the social enterprise movement in the United States and Canada for more than a decade and is very committed to enabling effective and sustainable entrepreneurial nonprofit businesses. Pouyat lives and works in Kitchener-Waterloo, Ontario, Canada.

Leading Change

*By **Deborah Alvarez-Rodriguez**, President
and CEO, Goodwill Industries of San Francisco,
San Mateo, and Marin Counties*

S urvival requires adaptation. As social entrepreneurs, we must be
sure that our mission and vision are constantly relevant to the
real world. Increasingly, we are called upon to change, sometimes
on a quarterly basis and sometimes yearly. Those who cannot lead
change are gambling with core community assets.

Leading change varies in different settings. Newer organizations may
be more fluid but struggle to achieve scale. At venerable organizations,
with long-established cultures, change can be painful, but momentum can
gather quickly once transformation begins. Size and complexity do matter.

But the fundamentals of all social enterprises are the same. Certain
principles apply across the board. The CEO must always play three essential
roles: facilitator of change, promoter of teamwork, and agent of disruption.

As leader, it is my job to facilitate change, but it is not my job to impose
it. I create the vision of where we need to go and I am the caretaker of the
culture and values that will bring us there. Although I set the direction,
when it comes down to the specifics of how we will be heading out, it is up
to the management team and key staff. In fact, the CEO should make the
fewest decisions of anyone in the organization. It is my job to provide
the framework and the resources for others to get the job done.

Leading change through teamwork is harder than simply moving ahead to implement your vision. It is slower in the short run and it costs more. It is a challenge for people to step outside their comfort zones, where they feel most competent, and think about the organization as a whole. I am utterly convinced, however, that in the long run teamwork by empowered staff not only produces the best solution but also brings out the best in everyone. The CEO needs to invest time and effort in creating a culture of support for risk taking, so that the organization ends up with the optimal conditions under which one plus one equals three.

Finally, another key responsibility of the change leader is to create disruption. As the work moves forward to establish systems and processes, the CEO must step in on occasion, challenge assumptions, and even overturn things. The creative tension between chaos and stability is essential to innovation and sustainability. If you want an organization that remains relevant, you need to build one that can tolerate disruption.

CASE STUDY: CONVERTING COSTS TO PROFITS

A little less than five years ago, we faced a challenge at Goodwill Industries of San Francisco, San Mateo, and Marin. Even though we kept telling the public that we did not want their computers, people continued to dump computers at our donation sites and we were spending a lot of money to dispose of them properly. We asked ourselves how we could turn this operation from a cost center into a profit center.

A few other Goodwills had achieved some success with computer recycling, so we sent some members of our staff on a fact-finding mission to Austin, Los Angeles, and Pittsburgh. They were charged with finding out what others were doing and what might make sense for us. When they returned and shared their knowledge, it was soon clear that we had a real opportunity to take something that was costing us a lot of money and turn it into a powerful tool for transformation. Other people were already doing wonderful things, so we didn't need to invent anything new. We just needed to put various parts together in a slightly different way. And so the management team began to build a business that would not only make money but also meet the other demands of our triple bottom line, to transform lives and care for the environment. Our process to develop the business plan for a new enterprise illustrates the principles I mentioned earlier.

Knowing nothing about computers and very little about e-waste recycling, I found it easy to stick to the role of facilitator and visionary. Clearly, there was an opportunity out there for us, but I had no idea how we could best capitalize on it. We established a goal: to responsibly recycle electronics while creating meaningful career development for our difficult-to-employ participants and at the same time make money. I created a task force and provided the platform and the environment for the group to work together. But then I stood aside and let the team loose to figure out how we'd reach the goal and what our new enterprise would look like.

Building a structure for the project was a big challenge. We knew that we had to bite the bullet and figure out once and for all how to create a business that would manage risk, create efficiencies, and accomplish our environmental and social goals—while making money for us. So we had to involve four groups within our organization that up until this point had very little to do with each other: salvage operations, retail stores, training programs, and risk management. We also brought in outside collaborators: Dell has been a strategic partner from the beginning; Goodwill Industries of Central Texas shared their expertise; and Hunter Lovins from the Rocky Mountain Institute, along with the Origo consultancy, generously helped design the new business model. Because we had a group of such disparate thinkers all working together, we put together a model that no one person was capable of imagining alone. Collaboration enabled innovation.

Disruption became necessary, too. Things were not going so well at one point. We were struggling with our corporate partner, Dell. Their double-bottom-line priorities were to protect the environment by responsibly disposing of as many computers as possible through the most cost-effective method available. So they thought that we should collect unwanted computers and turn them over to licensed recyclers. But that simple an operation, although much less expensive and much easier to expand quickly, would have provided the low-income, on-the-job trainees working in it with only the most rudimentary job skills that would qualify them for minimum-wage positions at best. We wanted to handle the computer recycling and refurbishing ourselves, so that our trainees would gain more complex skills and ultimately obtain higher-paying jobs with potential for genuine career advancement.

Things were pretty tense. We got to a place where people were starting to think that maybe it was just too hard, that we should just admit that we could not do it all and should simply recycle computers the way Dell wanted us to, the way everybody else did. I stepped in and issued a challenge: either we'd do it the right way or we wouldn't do it at all. If it was impossible for us to build this venture according to the values we espouse, in line with our triple bottom line, we were going to walk away. This was a difficult thing for some people to accept. We lost a key staff member, a bright and talented man who'd put a lot into building this business. But we gained some new employees who said, "Yes, we can do this. I know we can."

The result of this collaboration was ReCompute, our electronics recycling and refurbishing program, launched in 2005. It is currently on track to train ninety-four low-income, difficult-to-employ participants every year in either basic office technology skills or as computer technicians. Thus far, ReCompute has diverted more than six million pounds of electronic waste from landfills and operates at significantly better than breakeven, generating $606,000 in revenue and a 20 percent profit margin during its latest fiscal year (as compared to a slight deficit in its first year of operation).

If we had approached the design of ReCompute in a more traditional way, we would have ended up with more traditional results. We would have a good recycling business capable of generating a little bit of profit and supporting a job-training program administered by others, but the size and the scale of both would be limited. By putting all of our assets into play to create social value, we can support a robust training program as well as a successful enterprise.

> **Goodwill Industries of San Francisco, San Mateo, and Marin Counties, Inc.**
>
> *Mission*: Goodwill creates solutions to poverty through the businesses we operate.
>
> *Vision*: We envision a world free of poverty where people have the power to support themselves and their families, live in safe and thriving communities, and actively care for the environment
>
> Goodwill Industries of San Francisco, San Mateo, and Marin Counties, Inc., is a ninety-three-year-old social enterprise that operates seventeen retails stores, an online business, and a recycling-reuse enterprise, which cover 85 percent of the organization's $32 million operating budget; it has 450 employees.

LESSONS LEARNED

We live more and more in Internet time; things happen in much shorter cycles than in ordinary life. So we tend to think that the pace of change must have sped up as well. But it hasn't. People change slowly, and what is an organization, after all, but a collection of individuals bound by a culture and a mission?

Change is uncomfortable and it takes time. Each change process has its own character, but I think I've learned a few lessons that will be useful to apply in most situations.

Lesson Number 1: Budget Enough Time and Mental Space

For-profit institutions sometimes shortchange the front end of a change process, but nonprofits are notorious for thinking, "Who can afford the luxury of setting aside time to think about these things? We have people to serve, programs to run!" In reality, of course, they cannot afford not to plan.

Early on in the reorganization of Goodwill San Francisco, I was calling six-hour meetings to have people just think, not do. My management team was acutely uncomfortable, feeling as if the meetings were a colossal waste of time. But we needed that time to raise our discourse from the level of how many clients we were placing in jobs to a meaningful conversation about poverty and how to end it. We had to create a sufficiently open-ended psychic space and get over how uncomfortable it was to inhabit it before we could begin to fully consider what we would dare to take on.

Our results-oriented culture is constantly tempting us to short-circuit exploration and move quickly toward solutions. We had to struggle with ourselves, to make sure that we were not taking any shortcuts. We had to start at the beginning and ask ourselves whether our mission was still relevant to the world. We had to push ourselves to be sure that we had what Collins and Porras so compellingly defined as a BHAG—a Big, Hairy, Audacious Goal.

Because we had set aside the time and created the mental space to consider these fundamental issues so deeply, we were able to discern profound truths about ourselves. And we decided that our mission "to train, support, and challenge individuals to overcome employment barriers and achieve self-sufficiency through work" was no longer enough. We had built enough scale that we could solve a larger social issue. Our revised mission, adopted by our board in November 2005, more accurately conveys the sense of what we want to do: "We create solutions to poverty through the businesses we operate."

Lesson Number 2: Make Internal Communications a Priority

In leading change, internal communications are all-important. You need to have consistent messages and tailor them to different audiences. And you need to create multiple feedback loops, so that communication is not one-way.

We put the mission of Goodwill San Francisco front and center in our internal communications. It is a filter through which every choice is evaluated. As any organization does, we occasionally hit a financial bump in the road. At one such time in the past, I thought that the expedient and seemingly logical decision was to retain what was driving the revenue and eliminate what was not. I announced my intention to cut some things. But people in the room used that lens of our mission and spoke up to question my choice, pointing out that using the single metric of expense-to-revenue ratio was not true to our triple bottom line of social and environmental as well as financial returns. Because we had built those feedback loops into our communications system, they were able to bring that point forward. I was able to step back and see that they were right: productivity had gone up since we'd started investing more intensively in our staff and it was appropriate to reconsider the weight that we gave our financial metrics.

If you have built a culture that supports risk taking and have created opportunities for your staff to push back, you can change your mind and not lose face. With permission to make mistakes and lots of help to recover from them, everyone can work more effectively.

Be honest in your communications. Acknowledge that change is scary, even for the CEO. If you really believe in change, then you have to demonstrate that you are willing to be transformed. Transformation is a significant personal challenge. It is scary, and it doesn't do any good to pretend otherwise.

Personal interaction is essential for internal communications. If you want to facilitate innovative conversations, then you have to spend a fair amount of time with people. There is a delicate balance between demands from the outside (raising money and awareness), and those from the inside. Yet in your role as "chief culture officer," you need to be in on some of those messy internal conversations. When we first began our change process at Goodwill San Francisco, we held seventeen town hall meetings over two years. I met every employee and many of the participants in our training programs. More than one person asked why we didn't just use an online service like Survey Monkey to solicit the feedback we wanted. We knew, though, that a computer-based platform would not be comfortable for everyone we wanted to hear from. You need to include a mix of high tech and high touch in your communications system.

Lesson Number 3: Pay Attention to How Much Space You Take up

The biggest mistake that I have made, and continue to make, is to get impatient with the pace of change. It just happens too slowly for me. But when I show that impatience, people around me interpret it very differently from any way that I expect them to. They think that they are doing something wrong, or they are in trouble, or they've disappointed me because they're not smart enough. And the reality is that my reaction had nothing to do with them, it has only to do with me and my unfortunate tendency to occasionally be impatient.

Along those same lines, I will come up with what I think is a great idea and cheerfully offer it up during a brainstorming session. I think of myself as a collaborator on a par with everyone else in the room and expect that my rough idea will be subjected to the same scrutiny as all the others are. In the past, though, people have run off and started to work on a concept that I thought would be kicked around for half an hour and then probably killed. Now when I'm putting out an idea so that other people can chew on it, I make a practice of announcing that I'm sharing my "first-draft thinking." This makes it clear that the idea is not baked enough to warrant much attention yet.

You must be aware of the power that you have as a leader, even in a situation where you have no interest in wielding it. I have strong opinions; most CEOs do. But I've learned that I sometimes need to just shut up and listen. I need to pay attention to the space that I take up, by virtue of my job title, and sometimes try to make myself a little smaller so that someone else has room to blossom.

Lesson Number 4: Never Compromise on Vision or Values, but Tactics Are Always Up for Grabs

I think of myself as being responsible for holding up the compass so that everyone can see where the needle is pointing, but I must leave it to my management team and senior staff to decide whether they should make a left here or a right there. They are much better informed than I of what's going on down on the ground. As long as the overall progress is adequate and we are heading in the right direction, it would be a mistake to dictate the exact path we take.

Lesson Number 5: Have a Point of View (and Stick to It)

If you are leading change, you must have a good reason. You need to have a point of view. New research may come out that seems, at first glance, to challenge your point of view. The debate of the month among colleagues in your field may center on the pros and cons of your point of view. Don't abandon it. Stick with it long enough to see whether it bears fruit.

At Goodwill San Francisco, our point of view is that in order to bring about the change we want to see, we must become an embedded social venture—that is, an organization in which programs and enterprises operate as one integrated whole rather than as independent silos. Many people are telling us that we need to make a choice between accomplishing social change and running successful businesses; we don't think that we should have to make this choice. We not only refuse to accept that there is a dichotomy between mission and margin—we have torn down the wall between them.

With this point of view, we have achieved one of the lowest rates of recidivism in the state with our Back on Track criminal justice intervention program, because we have tapped every asset we have for it: our retail stores, our IT infrastructure, our transportation academy, everything.

With this point of view, we have increased our environmental impact to the point that the energy saved in 2008 through our store sales was equal to four thousand households turning off their electricity for an entire year.

With this point of view, we have in less than four years tripled the number of participants we serve annually, almost doubled the number of our employees, and significantly increased the volume of material we divert from the waste stream. And although our budget has grown in this time, it hasn't even doubled. And that's because we have put all the assets of our enterprise truly into play to advance our mission.

LEADING CHANGE FROM THE INSIDE OUT

In the early decades of the twentieth century, corporate greed ran rampant. Many business owners across the country abandoned their obligations to their employees and communities so that a small number of men could amass vast stores of wealth. America's first social enterprises, Goodwill among them, sprang into existence in response to this injustice. A number of these legacy organizations continue to thrive today. They offer some valuable lessons to the social innovators of our time.

Perhaps the most important lesson is also the simplest. Creating change is hard work. Every morning as I prepare myself for my workday, I look at my schedule and try to anticipate what will change. At the end of a ten- or twelve-hour day I return home to my family, review my mistakes and accomplishments, and realize that it is I who have changed. Whether in the arena of healing the world and or in the realm of keeping your organization relevant, lasting results are personal and hard won.

For one thing, you must always build for the future while continuing to maintain current operations. This dual focus is an especially heavy responsibility for the CEO at the beginning of a change process, but the load lightens over time. During the reengineering of Goodwill San Francisco, we developed leadership throughout our divisions and departments. So there came a time when I could feel that the organization as a whole had moved into alignment with our new strategy. There are still pockets of people holding on to what was, but now that we have achieved a certain momentum I no longer feel personally responsible for every inch of movement forward.

Then there is the constant challenge of disruptions, both external and internal. Among nonprofits, social enterprises will always be most affected by market forces, for instance. But if you have been leading a successful change process, you will have built an organization that has the capacity to ride out disruptions, whatever their origins. Your group will be able to respond to the disruption of a market downturn with hard decisions that meet the demands of the day without derailing the plans for the future.

And teamwork needs to be constantly nurtured. You cannot think that once you have created a culture of teamwork your work is done. The reality is that you are always introducing new players into the mix, and new drivers and conditions force themselves in as well. Effective teamwork requires intentionality and it requires resources: perhaps you will need to bring in an outside facilitator from time to time; the staff involved need to have the space in their schedules for meetings, which may mean that something else on their plates needs to be reassigned.

The demands of the job may sometimes seem unrelenting, but leading change is nonetheless the work of joy and hope. As social enterprises, we have much to offer in meeting the great challenges of our day.

The hope of a secure and livable world lies with disciplined nonconformists who are dedicated to justice, peace, and brotherhood.

—Martin Luther King, Jr.

ABOUT THE AUTHOR

Deborah Alvarez-Rodriguez joined Goodwill San Francisco as president and CEO in March 2004. Known for her dynamic leadership style, Ms. Alvarez-Rodriguez has a track record of catalyzing change within organizations and leading them toward greater innovation, accountability, and responsiveness. Previously, she was vice president of Silicon Valley's Omidyar Foundation and was director of San Francisco's Department of Children, Youth, and their Families. She chairs the boards of the East Bay Community Foundation and the advisory board of John Gardner Center at Stanford University, and she serves on the boards of the Harwood Institute and the Employment Opportunities for People with Prior Convictions at the Berkeley Center for Criminal Justice, U.C. Berkeley School of Law.

Leadership Succession

By Jim Schorr, *Clinical Professor of Management, Vanderbilt University Owen School of Management, and Founding Director, Vanderbilt Center for Business & Society*

Periods of leadership succession—from the point when the existing leader or board initiates plans to move on to the point when a new leader is in place—are especially important times for every organization. Seemingly at once, everything is in a state of flux. Key relationships, particularly those between the exiting leader and important stakeholders, are vulnerable. Employee productivity suffers. Board engagement necessarily intensifies. In large organizations, there is often sufficient capital and other resources to insulate an organization through a succession period. Smaller organizations usually aren't so fortunate. Well-managed successions propel organizations to greater heights, whereas mismanaged successions cause organizations to stagnate or decline. Succession periods are inherently times of great risk for organizations, but they are also potentially times of great opportunity.

In most social enterprises, these risks and opportunities are magnified by their lack of a resource cushion to bridge a leadership gap, and their over-reliance on dynamic founders and CEOs to secure the resources needed for ongoing operations and future growth. All social entrepreneurs—until they reach a point of financial self-sufficiency—are familiar with the reality of managing a funding pipeline that must be regularly filled to keep the doors open and the lights on. During succession periods, these pipelines can and do go dry, and the result is financial havoc for an organization and the incoming CEO. Perhaps even more alarming is the reality that so many social enterprise CEOs are young, high-profile founders who have become inextricably linked with their organizations. What happens when the current social entrepreneurs have had enough—they are entrepreneurs, after all, so they won't stay forever—and move on to new pursuits? All succession processes present challenges, but founder successions are recognized as among the most crucial—a study by the Center for Non-profit Management observed that the average tenure for CEOs succeeding founders was less than two years, which suggests that the average founder succession fails, often miserably. My experience is that social enterprises share this succession challenge with their nonprofit brethren.

This chapter on leadership succession begins with a case study on one of the United States' most prominent social enterprises—Juma Ventures in San Francisco. During my tenure there from 2000 to 2007, I had the opportunity to be on the front lines of two leadership succession processes—the first when I succeeded the founder, the second when I transitioned out of the CEO role several years later. During these experiences, I learned a number of valuable lessons, which I've described both at a general level and as they relate specifically to my experience at Juma Ventures. I'm somewhat biased, but I think the case of leadership succession at Juma Ventures is rich with lessons for social entrepreneurs, their organizations, and boards. Enjoy.

CASE STUDY: LEADERSHIP SUCCESSION AT JUMA VENTURES

In December of 2002, I was named CEO of Juma Ventures (Juma, pronounced Jew-ma), a prominent social enterprise located in San Francisco. Since opening its first social enterprise in 1994—a Ben & Jerry's ice cream shop employing high-risk youth—Juma had been one of the pioneers in the emerging social enterprise landscape. More than a thousand low-income teens had found employment, job training, and other support services through Juma's social enterprises, and many were leaving Juma and successfully transitioning to college and mainstream employment.

I joined Juma in 2000 as an MBA-toting, thirty-three-year-old entrepreneur with no nonprofit experience. My role was to develop and grow its portfolio of social enterprises and the consequent number of opportunities for youth engagement. By 2002, the deflation of the Internet bubble, and its impact on the local economy in the Bay Area, had put the organization in a vulnerable position. The social enterprises weren't yet profitable and continued to require significant funding subsidies. The senior management team was depleted, and four of six executives reporting to the CEO moved on to new opportunities. The board was small—six members—and didn't have the capacity to provide significant levels of assistance and support. The staff was divided—torn apart by the maddening tension of Juma's "social mission meets business model" approach. A failed strategic planning process that year had left the organization's future direction uncertain.

By the fall of 2002, the founder and CEO—a visionary woman who had devoted nearly ten years of her life to building Juma—informed the board and two remaining executives that she intended to move on as well. In a brief search process, the board considered both of the remaining executives—the CFO and yours truly—and ultimately chose me to succeed the founder. The CFO then let me know that he too would be leaving. Within six months, four of the six board members were exiting as well. As if all that weren't enough, our leading funder (and the source of nearly all of our social enterprise subsidy funding) went through a major strategic shift and announced plans for a gradual phaseout of funding for their portfolio of grantees. My task as Juma's new leader seemed to grow more daunting by the day.

My first year as CEO was anything but dull and was replete with big decisions that I'd soon regret. Optimistic that I could get the enterprise portfolio profitable in short order, I resisted thoughts of an immediate and major restructuring. Sensitive to the founder's legacy and wanting to maintain some sense of continuity with the staff, I promoted several talented but inexperienced staff members into the key leadership roles reporting to me. Seeking experience to complement others on my new leadership team, I rehired a former star employee who had a lot of history with and knowledge of the organization. Almost immediately, I launched my new leadership team into a strategic planning process to consider and resolve our future direction.

A year into my tenure, we had a bold, visionary new strategic plan, and none of the conditions needed to implement it successfully. My leadership team, stretched to the limit of their experience and abilities, was fried. The financial situation with our enterprises had improved a bit, but continued to represent a major near-term financial challenge. The board was growing and glad to have some direction, but was not much more prepared to help make it happen. The staff felt relatively disengaged with the planning effort, and resented the implication that Juma's future was more important than their daily work with the youth. Shortly thereafter, amid major challenges with the implementation of the "Juma 2.0" plan, I came to terms with the reality that significant changes would need to be made in order to create the context for future success. Enterprises would need to be sold or closed. People would need to leave.

The decision to sell or close our Ben & Jerry's shops and lay off nearly half our staff was among the most difficult I've had to make. Those ice cream shops were absolutely central to Juma's history and personality. I hated the idea that we couldn't make these enterprises viable, and I felt a great sense of responsibility for having created a situation for my leadership team and staff that hadn't been conducive to their success. Three of four of my leadership team members moved on during this downsizing. But a major restructuring was exactly what we needed—both to stabilize the organization financially and to clear the air for my vision of a new future that could be even brighter than the past.

Two years into this restructuring it was clear that we'd finally turned the corner on our strategic, financial, and personnel challenges. Our vision and direction were clear, and the organization was aligned accordingly. The social enterprises had stabilized and were moving swiftly toward profitability. With greater strategic clarity and focus, fund-raising success came much more easily, and we began to secure the resources needed for future growth and heightened impact. Staff, management, and board conditions were improving, with less attrition, more effective recruiting, and improved productivity levels. Juma 2.0 was still a work in progress, but we had successfully weathered the restructuring storm and saw blue skies ahead.

Having accomplished much of what I'd hoped to do, I began to think about my own transition. Now intimately familiar with the issues and challenges of leadership succession, I made two decisions: (1) to hire and develop a second-in-command chief operating officer (COO) who would have the capability to succeed me when the time was right and (2) to give the board ample lead time for managing a succession process and ensuring that Juma's progress and momentum would not be negatively affected by my eventual departure. In early 2006, we recruited an exceptionally talented and qualified individual with CEO ambitions to fill the COO position. After a nearly year-long succession process in 2007, the COO replaced me as CEO and I joined Juma's board of directors.

Fortunately, this story has a happy ending: Today, Juma is thriving. The annual budget size has more than tripled since the 2004 restructuring. Juma's primary social enterprise is scaling across California. Enterprise revenues are growing 20 to 30 percent annually, and it's been profitable since 2006. We work with many more youth each year, and 97 percent—a record number—of our graduates made successful transitions to college in 2009. The leadership team is solid and highly capable. Staff are more aligned than ever before, integrating social and financial goals in their work better than I could have dreamed just a few years ago. The board has fifteen highly engaged members who provide great support and governance. Last but not least, the new CEO is flourishing in the leadership role. Of course, this thrills me for him and for Juma, and it is gratifying for me personally as well. While he and others deserve the credit for Juma's success today, I suppose there is some truth to the notion that one's success as a leader is defined as much by what happens after you move on as by what happens while you're in charge.

LESSONS LEARNED

To say that the leadership succession process is critical is a major understatement—social enterprises often thrive or struggle based on successful or failed leadership transitions. Particularly in small, entrepreneurial social enterprises—which describes most of them—turbulent transitions can seriously destabilize an organization. Social enterprises usually are forced to "bootstrap it," operating with such meager financial reserves that even a relatively brief disruption in funding can create significant financial problems that ripple throughout the organization. During my tenure at Juma, I was a part of both sides of the leadership succession process—first replacing the founder and then transitioning executive leadership to the COO five years later.

Many of the moving parts of a social enterprise—funder relationships, staff engagement and productivity, board engagement, plans for the future, and so forth—are subject to disruption during periods of leadership transition. For example, even successful social enterprises rely on a constant stream of incoming revenue from a pipeline of grant proposals and other donations to fund related programs and initiatives or subsidize social enterprise revenue or cost deficits. So even a short-term disruption in fund-raising efforts can be seriously debilitating. Simply put, there is no room for error with leadership transitions. Social enterprise CEOs and boards must strive to ensure that their organizations remain healthy and high functioning during these periods.

From my experience, the key continuity-related issues to consider and plan around include: (1) the length of time that the board has to design and manage the succession process, (2) the opportunity to develop and consider internal candidates, and (3) the role of the exiting CEO during and post-transition. From these three considerations and my experiences with Juma's leadership transitions, I've extracted the following lessons for social enterprise practitioners.

Lesson 1: Timing Is Everything

When it comes to the time line for successfully managing a leadership succession process, it's pretty simple: the more time, the better. An ample amount of time enables the board to fully engage in managing the succession planning process, and no board responsibility is more important. In my experience at Juma, one year of notice was sufficient to allow the board to design a succession process, conduct a search, interview candidates, and hire someone, and it provided an opportunity for the outgoing and incoming CEOs to work together to transition important relationships and other matters. This time line assumes that finding great candidates, internally or externally, can be accomplished in about six months; in some cases, particularly in organizations where no internal candidate is a likely successor, additional time may be required for a search to produce the right person. Executive search processes in social enterprises can take longer than in other organizations, as individuals with the right mix of mission-related experience and business expertise can be difficult to find.

Although it might be ideal if all social enterprise CEOs would willingly agree to provide a year's notice in advance of any plans to leave the organization, it's also not a bad idea for social enterprise boards to create incentives that encourage a well-planned exit. Boards can, for example, choose to create employment agreements with the CEO and stipulate that a certain amount of notice be given in advance of a planned transition in order to receive a modest "service bonus" upon exit. Trust me, money that buys the board some time to manage a leadership succession process is money well spent. My employment contract at Juma did not stipulate any such time line—but I gave the board a year's notice because I knew from experience that a short transition window was not ideal. My successor now has a contract that gives him incentives (albeit modest ones—this is a social enterprise after all) to give the board plenty of notice when the day comes when it's time for him to move on.

Lesson 2: Transition Creates Opportunity

More often than not, leadership successions do more harm than good to a social enterprise's bottom line. Communication between the organization and its funders can become a secondary priority in the midst of a litany of new succession issues and to-do items. Relationships of trust that took years to develop begin to fray, as funders grow concerned that their investments won't be well managed during a period of disruption. New contacts, proposals, and prospective relationships get put on hold pending some clarity about future direction. Juma's founder once taught me the truism that "people invest money in people," not in impersonal proposals, and succession is all about people. Unless an organization is well capitalized and can weather a revenue drought, even a short-term disruption in the funding pipeline can result in financial chaos for a social enterprise.

But it doesn't have to be that way. With the time to manage a planned succession process, my exit from Juma actually become a fundraising *opportunity*. As the CEO, I developed most of our funder relationships, and many of them had invested in Juma in part because they believed in me as its leader. Some had made major grants only months before I initiated my transition. It was clear to me that a succession process that enabled me to personally introduce each of them to my successor was the way I wanted to honor these organizations and people who had been my partners in building Juma over the years. So, once the new CEO selection had been made, we used the transition as an opportunity to set up meetings with all of Juma's current and several former funders. I used these meetings to introduce the new CEO, update these key partners on the organization's direction, and communicate my enthusiasm for the CEO-elect and Juma's future. These efforts, and those that followed thereafter, produced significant increases in fund-raising revenue in the year following my transition.

Lesson 3: Continuity Is Crucial

Whether or not to consider an internal candidate to replace a departing CEO is a key question that a board must resolve early in the succession process. Boards and CEOs should assess the opportunity for new leadership to come from within at the outset of a leadership succession process, because the process design will be significantly affected by this issue. If there is a qualified candidate, by all means consider him or her. At the same time, boards should be clear that an internal hire is more aligned with a desire to continue moving in a similar strategic direction, whereas a CEO from outside the organization is likely better suited to a direction that involves significant change. In some cases, some dose of organizational upheaval will be the right prescription to create the context for change. In part, my early struggles as Juma's CEO were a result of my attachment to the people and programs I had worked with for two years, and my sensitivity to the history and the founder's legacy. Someone needed to make wholesale changes, and it took a while for me to come around to that necessity. Ideally, though, things won't have reached a point where a fresh start is necessary, and a social enterprise can achieve a level of continuity in a leadership succession that maintains, and sometimes even propels, organizational momentum.

In my experience, the goal of continuity is so well served by having a qualified internal CEO candidate that boards and CEOs should prioritize the development of peer-level, CEO-ready "bench strength" long before any leadership transition is anticipated. Developing a shared leadership approach among CEOs and peer-level COOs is a characteristic of many of the most impressive nonprofits that have successfully scaled their organizations, and it should be a more common strategy for social enterprises trying to scale their impact as well. At Juma, we created the COO position and hired someone more than two-and-a-half years before I moved on, in part as a long-term succession planning strategy. By no means did my plans proceed flawlessly: the first COO we hired left after a year, when he was recruited away for a CEO role in an organization that was the perfect fit for him. Even with well-crafted plans, that sort of thing happens sometimes. Fortunately, shortly thereafter we hired another high-caliber COO for whom Juma was an ideal fit, and he's been successfully leading the organization since my departure. Our ability to manage my transition so gracefully enabled Juma to continue—and even accelerate—the growth and mission impact gains we'd made since the difficult days of restructuring.

Lesson 4: Let Leaders Lead

As the outgoing CEO prepares to depart, the question of whether he or she should join the board of directors is likely to come up, assuming the exit doesn't relate to CEO underperformance. This is a delicate matter that should be treated thoughtfully by all key parties involved—the board, the outgoing CEO, and the successor. On the plus side, it can be very helpful for the ex-CEO to join the board to support continuity through the transition to new leadership. Funders and other stakeholders will appreciate knowing that the outgoing leader will continue to be an available resource to the board and new CEO. Without well-developed systems for knowledge and relationship management—which social enterprises rarely have the time or resources to develop—it can take some time for the outgoing CEO to transition everything, and a board role for the exiting leader can provide more time to get this done properly. The downside to a CEO-to-board transition is that it potentially inhibits the new CEO from fully assuming the leadership role and taking charge of the organization. In those initial board meetings post-transition, if the ex-CEO is at the table, out of habit the board will continue to seek his or her input and leadership as if nothing has changed. It takes a measure of wisdom on the part of the ex-CEO and courage on the part of his or her successor to manage this dynamic in a way that helps the transition take root.

One of the many important lessons I learned from Juma's founder was how to manage this issue and the related dynamics appropriately. At the board's request, she joined Juma's board after stepping down as CEO, and her participation during my initial year as her successor was invaluable to me. We interacted regularly, and I tapped her knowledge and counsel on many issues, always in a one-on-one manner, outside of regular board meetings. During board meetings, she kept quiet and let me take the lead, no doubt having to bite her tongue regularly as I bumbled through issues that she had expertise with. She knew that Juma needed me to step up and lead, and that her presence could make it more difficult for me to do so. Eventually, the time came for her to move on completely, but her involvement in my initial year as CEO was her parting gift to Juma and one that I was grateful for. Years later, I carried this experience into my own succession plans. When Juma's board requested that I transition to the board upon completing my term as CEO, I agreed to do it for a one-year term to enhance succession continuity. In doing so, I made it clear to the board that my role was simply to be a resource to support the new CEO's development and success, and not to play an active role in other organizational matters. I did a lot of tongue biting too during the board meetings that year.

Communication Is Key

Though stakeholder communication should always be a priority, it is especially important and an essential component of a well-orchestrated leadership succession process. A thoughtful process will include personal engagement and communication with all key stakeholders—staff, funders, donors, partners, former board members, and others. Internally, an open, ongoing dialogue between the board and staff will prevent people from making up their own answers to questions that aren't being addressed. Some level of active staff involvement in the succession process, such as a staff representative on the search committee, will make people feel included in the process and not like bystanders. Depending on the board size, the board may need to form a succession planning committee to manage the process on an ongoing basis, but it is important that the full board be informed and engaged as well. Externally, the goal of stakeholder communication is straightforward: to preserve the organizational relationships that are the lifeblood of a social enterprise. To accomplish this, stakeholders need to get the news firsthand, not through the grapevine. Relationships and partnerships that have developed over years deserve such treatment and must be prioritized during a leadership succession process.

If I had to summarize the communication plan in six words, they'd be: make it timely, make it personal. As I mentioned earlier, we used the transition period to set up meetings with all of Juma's key stakeholders—funders, donors, business partners, government agencies, and others. We're talking about a lot of meetings, so these took place over a period of a few months. But long before those meetings, we managed the succession announcement through a pair of well-timed letters—one from the CEO and board chair announcing the exiting CEO's departure plans and the upcoming search process, and another from the board chair and CEO announcing the decision and timing around the incoming CEO—to keep key constituencies apprised, communicate that the transition has been an orderly one, and set the table for the new CEO to assume these relationships. Both of these letters were in the mail to hundreds of stakeholders the same week that the transition and succession news was announced to the staff, so there wasn't much time for things to travel the grapevine. And before these letters ever hit the mail, I'd had personal communication with the full board, the COO, the full staff, and a dozen or so of our most important stakeholders. The board chair and vice chair were the first to know, and they partnered with me to design and lead the board through the process that followed. In the end, we got rave reviews from stakeholders for how successful the succession process had been, and the new CEO was well prepared to assume the leadership role.

CONCLUSION

Periods of leadership succession in social enterprises are critical times. Seemingly at once, everything is up in the air—strategy and plans for the future, staff job security, board commitments, and, of course, the question of who will replace the leader—and organizations can quickly stagnate or decline. Unless there are significant resources to support a period when the organization languishes, the risk involved with failed successions is significant. Simply put, social enterprises thrive or struggle depending on how successfully leadership transitions are managed. At some point, given high burnout levels and a relatively short lifespan for most social enterprise CEOs, most organizations face this challenge, and their futures hinge on a successful succession process.

The case of Juma Ventures and my experience there is by no means reflective of and instructive for all leadership successions, but I do think it's an illustrative example for many social enterprises. In particular, those that face issues related to founder succession and internal CEO development should find this experience useful. The five lessons learned herein—summarized as *Timing Is Everything, Transition Creates Opportunity, Continuity Is Crucial, Let Leaders Lead,* and *Communication Is Key*—provide some of the highlights of this experience. In writing this chapter, my hope is that Juma's story and these lessons will help social enterprise CEOs and boards more effectively manage their own successions and assist them in building vibrant social enterprises that make an impact on the social and environmental issues of our time.

ABOUT THE AUTHOR

Jim Schorr is currently a clinical professor of management at Vanderbilt University's Owen School of Management in Nashville, Tennessee, and the founding director of the Vanderbilt Center for Business & Society. His work and teaching at Vanderbilt are focused on social and environmental issues and opportunities in business and include courses on social enterprise and innovation and on corporate responsibility and sustainability. Near the end of his tenure at Juma Ventures in 2007, Schorr received a teaching appointment from U.C. Berkeley's Haas School of Business, where he developed the Social Enterprise and Entrepreneurship course and initiated his transition into a full-time academic role.

As an MBA student in 1993, Professor Schorr was a part of a student group that founded Net Impact, an organization dedicated to inspiring, educating, and equipping students to use the power of business to create a more socially and environmentally sustainable world. He continues to be actively involved in Net Impact's work, and he currently is the organization's board chairman. Schorr is also actively involved in the work of several related organizations, serving on the boards of the Social Enterprise Alliance, The Nature Conservancy (TN), Global Social Venture Competition, and Oasis Center. By weekend, he is an avid traveler, a music lover, a scratch golfer, and a rabid college football fan.

Scaling Back or Shutting Down the Venture

*By **Gerry Higgins**, Chief Executive Officer, CEiS, and **James Finnie**, Senior Business Adviser, CEiS*

Many businesses will fail and close in their first three years, and we need to expect that, despite high-quality planning, mentoring, and support, social enterprises will also fail. In deciding to create social value through the social enterprise business model, business factors such as cash flow and market competition become significant to the sustainability of the venture. Social enterprises aren't immune to recession and, although for some social enterprises high unemployment is good for business, many others will close due to shortage of money or lack of demand for products or services.

As social enterprise grows as a worldwide movement, we need to anticipate and prepare for regular crises. Those who promote social enterprise as a worthwhile business model will need to deal with the failure of businesses, including some of the high-profile ventures that are held up as exemplars for others to follow. Our ability to build a robust movement of enterprises will be significantly influenced by our ability to learn from failures and ensure that mistakes aren't repeated.

Formed in 1984, Community Enterprise in Scotland (CEiS, www.ceis .org.uk/) is the largest and oldest social enterprise business support agency in the United Kingdom. Based in Glasgow, Scotland, with a team of ten business advisers and eight associate consultants dedicated to social enterprise support, CEiS engages with over one hundred businesses annually. Working primarily in Scotland, CEiS delivers a wide range of business development services to grow and strengthen its clients' businesses. CEiS is also called upon to deliver crisis management support, scaling back or shutting down enterprises that haven't worked. The authors of this chapter, Gerry Higgins and James Finnie, are, respectively, CEO and business adviser at CEiS. They form the initial CEiS crisis management response team and have firsthand experience of shutting ventures, reprovisioning services, and, happily, on many occasions preventing closure through early intervention.

The case study featured in this chapter, is that of One Plus: One Parent Families ("One Plus"), the largest social enterprise in the United Kingdom to have gone into liquidation in recent years. The closure of this business led to a review of governance among charities by the Office of the Scottish Charity Regulator (OSCR, www.oscr.org.uk/). CEiS was initially commissioned once the business identified itself as in crisis, and over a six-month period our advisers determined the options for One Plus, worked with the insolvency practitioners, and led a program of work aimed at transferring the portfolio of One Plus services to new service providers.

The content in this chapter reflects the company law and employment law situation in the United Kingdom. This can be a complex area, as the legal status of a business and the relevant national laws will heavily influence the options open to a business when it identifies itself as "in crisis." We intend to reflect on experiences, lessons, and principles that apply to social enterprise businesses internationally.

CASE STUDY: CLOSING A RESPECTED SOCIAL ENTERPRISE

One Plus was a key participant in Scotland's social economy, creating employment and training opportunities and delivering services that helped support the government's agenda around child poverty, Welfare to Work, and sustainable communities. One Plus had over twenty-five corporate customers, over forty funding streams valued at over £9 million, 104 individual projects, and over ten thousand end users. One Plus was a major employer in the West of Scotland, with around 858 full-time, part-time, and seasonal staff.

One Plus provided:

- A diverse range of services that benefited one-parent families and other low-income groups
- Local projects and initiatives, which contributed to the economic regeneration of the communities where single parents live
- Campaigning and policy work to promote positive policies for single parents and children
- Training places for over two thousand people per year, primarily single parents
- Twenty-nine out-of-school care centers, pre-five provision in eight child and family centers
- Over five thousand enquiry responses a year to single parents, and a project that employed eighty "intermediate labor market" workers
- Eight thousand hours of social care to 195 clients
- Employment to over 150 people in social care

Figure 16.1 demonstrates the revenue growth of One Plus, growth that led to widespread perception of a successful, dynamic organization.

At the end of 2006 CEiS was called in to assist One Plus address its financial difficulties. In a very short period of time, it became clear that the organization was in crisis. The founding CEO had recently retired and, once the new CEO and the crisis management team from CEiS had opportunity to examine the business, it was evident that the organization had significant financial problems and was possibly insolvent. The board had not been made aware of the extent of the financial difficulties, funders had not been informed of the problems, and there was quite a high risk that the December wages would not be paid due to lack of cash.

At this point CEiS added an insolvency specialist to our team and within a number of weeks confirmed that there was a black hole in the organization's finances of between £5 and 7 million. The main creditors were its bankers

Figure 16.1
One Plus Key Financial Indicators

One Plus—Group Revenue and Expenditure

	1996	1997	1998	1999	2000	2001	2002	2003
Group Turnover	£1,329,135	£1,963,825	£2,367,362	£3,326,431	£4,632,222	£5,438,492	£6,348,793	£7,897,584
Group Total Expenditure	£1,959,156	£1,959,156	£2,355,499	£3,327,459	£4,643,826	£5,219,552	£6,348,700	£7,915,261

One Plus—Debtor and Creditor Summary

	1996	1997	1998	1999	2000	2001	2002	2003
Group Debtors	£271,715	£322,342	£536,440	£674,502	£601,563	£1,142,722	£1,558,376	£2,321,465
Group Creditors	£229,242	£322,531	£525,415	£661,320	£607,935	£1,071,736	£1,567,835	£2,383,056
Group Net Debt	£0	£0	£0	-£200,168	-£181,395	£27,834	-£804,886	-£1,290,541

One Plus—Staffing Levels

	1997	1998	1999	2000	2001	2002	2003
Group Staff	153	191	239	274	375	420	576

One Plus—Cash, Reserves, and Borrowings

	1996	1997	1998	1999	2000	2001	2002	2003
Group Secured Bank Loans & Overdraft (<1yr)						£299,152	£300,254	£287,205
Group Cash at bank/In Hand							-£748,867	-£1,266,673
Group Reserves								

Source: One Plus Annual Audited Accounts

and the Inland Revenue as outstanding National Insurance payments exceeded £1 million. The scale of the problem would have taken some time to bottom out, as the financial systems were completely inadequate for an organization of this size. With our team in daily contact with government and local authorities, a meeting was arranged to outline the situation and to examine options. There was no economic basis for financially supporting an organization with this level of debt through a refinancing package. When broader political considerations were discussed, it became apparent that, although there was goodwill toward One Plus and its staff, the scale of a rescue package was far greater than the benefit that would accrue. A key factor here was that One Plus had not acted in a manner that gave confidence that it could operate sustainably in the future. The funding difficulties were not discussed with funders and partners until the organization was deeply in crisis, leaving an expensive rescue or insolvency as the only options to be considered. The scale of the "black hole" and the inadequacy of the organization's management capacity meant that regretfully, insolvency was the only option.

With the decision taken to liquidate the company, a two-pronged process was initiated. Auditors were appointed to deal with the formal liquidation process. In parallel, CEiS was requested by the Scottish government to lead the process to transfer as many as possible of the One Plus services to new providers. The key aim for CEiS was to minimize the risk and impact of One Plus's closure on service users, beneficiaries, staff, and trainees.

In any such activity, both information and communication are vital. Our short-term goals were twofold, namely (1) to identify all active services, programs, and projects being delivered by One Plus and (2) to identify, engage, and communicate with all key stakeholders, funders, delivery partners, and staff contacts in order to facilitate as full, timely, and successful a transfer process as possible.

To this effect our team of two experienced business advisers kicked in. The main focus of activity centered on a number of key areas, namely:

1. A master electronic project plan and contact database were developed to capture as much information as possible, including service

location, staffing, funders, service specifics, and potential new service providers

2. Stakeholders and existing networks were engaged to work in proactive partnership by volunteering and sharing their knowledge, expertise, and resources and to identify and progress potential new service providers

3. Key partners—auditors, government agencies, legal professionals—were engaged to ensure that all statutory and legal requirements were met

4. A communication strategy—face-to-face meetings, telephone updates, weekly e-mails with project plan updates—was developed to ensure that all stakeholders were briefed and had the opportunity to contribute and that service users had a new interim point of contact

Over a six-week period of intense activity, we made significant progress, and the process that was put in place yielded positive results. By the end of this time, the service transfer activity involving CEiS and other key partners saw:

- 163 staff reemployed by new service providers covering forty-seven services and ranging across the childcare, social care, and family support sectors

- 133 Intermediate Labour Market (ILM) child care and social care placements transferred to other providers

- Four social enterprises, one further education establishment, one private sector organization, and six public sector agency delivery partners established themselves as new service providers covering five local authority geographic areas

- Positive discussions ongoing with new potential delivery partners covering nine further services and totaling over forty-eight staff positions

Many of the services formerly delivered by One Plus have been re-commissioned and are being delivered by other service providers. In some cases the new owners have scaled back or substantially altered services, but for those who commissioned the contracts for the services, the end result supports the decision not to put a financial rescue package into an organization that had a flawed infrastructure and limited capacity to continue sustainable service delivery. At the end of the day the public profile of the company, the number of people who used its services, its proud history from its roots as a campaigning organization, and the level of public and political support for its activity, could not prevent the business reality that resulted in closure.

Lessons Learned—Business Failure

Looking back at the main lessons learned from this business failure, a number of key issues emerge. These relate to two internal issues—governance and capacity—and one external issue—the role of funders and government.

Lesson 1: Governance (Internal)

- **The board of directors did not hold the management to account.** Social enterprise boards are often selected by the lead officer, and in this case priority was given to board members supportive of the organization's mission rather than to identifying skill sets required for the governance of a business of this size. Financial reporting to the board was poor; the board had little idea that the organization was in difficulty until it was too late to do something about this.

- **Delivery of mission overrode good business practice.** When one chooses a business model to deliver social outcomes, the rules of business still apply. The fact that an enterprise is working with deserving communities and vulnerable clients does not absolve it from living within its means and endeavoring to operate sustainably. In some cases this may mean scaling back activity to avoid losses that will affect the entire organization.

Lesson 2: Organizational Capacity and Capability (Internal)

- **The capacity of the organization did not keep pace with the demands of rapid growth.** If an enterprise knew that within six years its revenue was going to increase from £2 million to £7 million, it would build infrastructure that was fit for purpose at each stage. One Plus kept winning contracts and grants, and the infrastructure constantly struggled to keep pace with the new shape and size of the organization. The more activity the organization generated, the more people it assisted, and this constant growth was regarded by many as a sign of success. It ultimately led to its downfall.

- **Management and board did not have sufficient financial expertise to run a multimillion-pound business.** How many times do we hear social enterprise leaders admit that they have brought their business as far as they can and it's now time to let more experienced people lead the enterprise to the next stage? This is uncommon but often unnecessary if the skills and experience are kept in line with the organization's requirements through training and external recruitment. In this case, one key appointment of a chartered accountant to the senior finance post a number of years into the operation of the business would have resulted in different practices and outcomes. It may even have prevented the organization from declining into a terminal crisis, as the four key financial issues were

  - The financial systems were inadequate to manage a complex business of this scale

  - Aged debts were not effectively controlled, managed, or communicated

  - There were unaddressed, long-term issues of project costs exceeding project revenue

  - The funding structure of the organization was inadequate, with an overdependence on credit from suppliers and a large overdraft predicated on the level of receivables

Lesson 3: Commissioners and Funders (External)

- **External funders and service commissioners did not pick up on, or act on, warning signs that might have prevented this crisis.** There was a diverse range of funders, each with their own contracts and relationships. Many of the projects were well delivered, but in the later years of the business, some funders did not apply their own rules of engagement in respect of contract management. Some did not ensure compliance to agreed terms and conditions, and some commissioners were not capable of interpreting the financial information available. Some recognized problems but realized that action may have detrimental consequences on their own service or on the organization, and they chose not to act. In spite of warning signs, funders continued to commission new and additional activity while there was inadequate monitoring of current activity.

- **In this case the early warning signs that were visible, but not acted upon, included:**
  - Severe and protracted cash-flow difficulties
  - Failure to accurately report on a timely basis
  - Increasingly poor evaluation results
  - Increasingly combative relationships with commissioners
  - Board known to be pliant and lacking in business experience
  - Poor and inadequate management accounting
  - Lack of openness about business performance
  - Not being prepared to take business advice
  - Public profile not matching experience of key personnel
  - The mission taking precedence over good business practice

Lessons Learned—Shutdown and Service Transfer

The closure of such a prominent and sizable social enterprise reverberated throughout the sector and gained national media attention and debate.

That said, although One Plus did close its doors in early 2007, ultimately this did not mean that all services and jobs were lost. Swift action by the Scottish government in engaging a trusted and experienced partner such as CEiS allowed for action to be taken in order to mitigate the impact of the closure on services, staff, and end users.

Looking back at the main lessons learned from the shutdown and service transfer process, a number of key factors emerge. As a whole these relate to two main areas—conservation and communication; individually they form six key lessons about the process of orderly analysis and shut down of a failed enterprise in order to ensure the preservation of developed resources crucial to the sector as a whole.

Lesson 1: Services Can Be Preserved (Conservation)   The time needed to come to a decision on closure can, and should, take a period of months in order to ensure that this is the best available option for all involved. Once the decision is taken, however, and professionals are engaged to enact the closure, things will move swiftly. The key to ensuring that services can be preserved and transferred to new providers is timely, decisive, and focused action by experienced professionals, coupled with communication with all professional advisers engaged in the process to ensure that they are working together. Such an approach allowed CEiS to coordinate the transfer of forty-seven services, ranging across the child care, social care, and family support sectors to new providers in a two-month time period.

Lesson 2: New Providers Can Be Engaged (Conservation)   Although One Plus as a group entity was unable to continue trading, a number of its services were innovative, respected, in demand, and thus—in their own right—sustainable. This made them attractive to other service providers—be they from the social enterprise, public sector agency, further education, or private sectors, as in this case. With One Plus, a number of providers initiated the discussion re possible service transfer, and this was aided by the extensive networks established by CEiS in over twenty-five years of operation. Whatever the source, new service providers should be targeted and engaged, and disclosure agreements need to be signed to allow detailed transfer of information and the progression of discussions in as swift a time frame as possible.

Lesson 3: Jobs Can Be Preserved (Conservation)   At the peak of its powers, One Plus had 858 full-time, part-time, and seasonal staff and trainees employed in the delivery of their services. Swift action was required in order to sustain employment of as many of those affected individuals as possible. The key driver toward enabling this, however, was not to ensure employment for all previous employees but to ensure that sustainable services were transferred to new providers—with the new providers making the decision on recruitment. This approach put control where it needed to be, resulting in the employment of 163 former One Plus staff and the placement of 133 ILM trainees with further actions in place to secure a further forty-eight staff positions.

Lesson 4: Stakeholders Are Key to Ensuring Ongoing Provision (Communication)   An organization the size of One Plus had many tentacles—reaching services, funders, stakeholders, and the like. Each of these had an interest—large or small, direct or indirect—in the decision to close One Plus. Stakeholder communication was therefore key in the closure and transfer process to ensure that all interests were accounted for. The formation of a core team represented by the main stakeholders, funders, and professional advisers was crucial to achieving this, with communication enabled by regular meetings, daily telephone updates, and a weekly e-mail status update—owned by the central coordinating partner CEiS—issued to all stakeholders and new service providers.

Lesson 5: Staff and End Users Need to Be Engaged (Communication) At the heart of any closure, the people most affected are those employed by the organization and those who benefited from the services provided. Communication is required to ensure that staff do not seek new employment too readily or that end users do not seek new provisions elsewhere. Both can have an impact on the ongoing sustainability of any service once transferred to a new provider. In the One Plus example, communication was enabled by a cascade process. Key decisions and actions were taken by the core team of CEiS, professional advisers, key stakeholders, and new targeted providers—then cascaded down to staff and end users at each service location by the new targeted providers.

Lesson 6: Financial Crisis Does Not Necessarily Mean Failure (Communication)   The financial crisis that enveloped One Plus could have led to failure on all levels, services being lost for good, jobs being lost, and end users being affected for a prolonged period. This did not happen. Swift decision making and intervention by experienced professionals and stakeholders ensured that many services were preserved, jobs were sustained, and end user impacts minimized. The key lesson here is not to wallow in the hows and whys of the past but to take action to ensure success for the future. This way failure will be minimized and limited.

Lessons Learned—Actionable Advice

With a business failure of the scale of One Plus there are hundreds of major and minor learning points for those starting out on social enterprise, those who commission services, those with a governance role, or those who are responsible for leadership and strategic planning. Here are a few pointers for the future emanating from our experience of the past:

Lesson 1: Never Assume   Stakeholders, investors, and funders need to look out for the early warning signs and act upon them. If your gut feeling tells you that something is wrong, it normally is. Doing nothing should never be an option.

Lesson 2: Grow and Plateau   Growth is good, but constant growth that continually outstrips the capacity and capability of the organization is not. A plateau period to allow for the consolidation of the organization's activities, capacity, and capabilities is, at the right times, just as beneficial to the long-term success of the organisation.

Lesson 3: Good Governance Is Good   Good governance comes from good people. Good governors must be qualified and must challenge the officers on strategy, developments, and governance issues. Investors and stakeholders should insist on the appointment of their own co-opted board member. For organizations of a certain revenue, consider organizing and arranging funding of an independent review covering capacity of the board, senior executives, management systems, and current financial position.

Lesson 4: In MAE We Trust Monitoring and evaluation (MAE) is key. Institute a program of supervisions at which Key Performance Indicators (KPIs) are reviewed together internally and externally. There should be an agreed set of Key Performance Indicators with agreed reporting lines, content, and timetable. These should be taken in conjunction with audited annual and management accounts, ongoing evaluations, and recent regulators' reports. Ongoing failure to meet KPIs should create a warning sign to be acted on. For external investors, stakeholders, and funders, ensure that compliance is a condition of payment and that compliance failure is a trigger to cancel the contract or Service Level Agreement.

Lesson 5: Have Contingency Plans It's business and it's not always going to work as planned. Identify the major risks, and work out the actions to be taken if these risks materialize. Even when it looks grim, there will invariably be a range of options open to a business, but these might not immediately be apparent. Ask for assistance to help your team to consider all options objectively and to ensure that the best decisions are taken.

Lesson 6: Act Early It's OK to be an optimist, but an ostrich shouldn't run a business. If your enterprise is having problems or is in crisis, the earlier you act, the more likely you are to achieve a solution. Get your head out of the sand.

Lesson 7: Don't Believe Your Own PR Social enterprises can talk a good game. They convince others about their social value and economic impact, and on occasion they convince themselves that all is well, when in fact it isn't. We recognize that the enterprises with the highest public profile often find it the most difficult to shatter illusions as their staff, customers, and stakeholders may all be wedded to a vision that has been continually positive. This isn't the reality for most businesses; think of a responsible and appropriate message when times are tough.

CONCLUSION

One of the critical issues for social enterprise leaders, as the movement grows in number and businesses get larger, is whether the prevailing culture will support responsible and tough decision making. In Scotland one of our leading social enterprises, McSense, has shown that they aren't shy in starting new ventures, but if they can't pay their way after a development period, they shut, lessons are learned, and the company moves on. Any negative effects of shutting an unprofitable venture need to be contrasted with the impact of placing a wider organization, its staff, and service users at risk.

In 2008 one of the leading social enterprises in England, the recycling firm ECT Group, hit serious liquidity problems and sold the business to a private company. Once the furor over "selling out" to the private sector had died down, it became clear that this decision was made early when options were open. Ultimately the decision preserved hundreds of jobs and, given the impact of the 2008–2009 recession, it now appears to have been a very good business choice. Enterprises in difficulty will have a range of options open to them, including scaling back and discontinuing unprofitable activity, merging with another social enterprise, renegotiating contracts and payment terms, and so forth. It is important to act early and be open with the stakeholders involved; the fate of One Plus shows that late action reduces the viable options.

Those responsible for promoting the social enterprise business model also have a role to play in creating a culture where failure is regarded as a learning and improving experience. One of your authors has learned far more from developing two social enterprises that failed as businesses than having established or supported six social enterprises that reached a sustainable trading level. This is a new movement, and success stories are used to inspire and motivate others to explore the possibilities of social enterprise. In a culture that is hungry for knowledge and encouragement, it's difficult to deliver the hard message that an enterprise is not working well, that it's fragile, that it might not be sustainable—but this is what people really need to hear. We hope social enterprisers will learn from what hasn't worked, and that they will be inspired by and encouraged by best practice, innovation, and success.

ABOUT THE AUTHORS

Gerry Higgins has been chief executive officer at CEiS for over three years. Gerry was the founding chief executive of Social Firms UK in 1999 and has assisted the UK and Scottish governments to develop their policies and support structures for social enterprise. Gerry was also responsible for the creation of the Social Enterprise World Forum, the annual international gathering of social enterprise practitioners and support agencies.

James Finnie is thirty-eight years old and lives in the Scottish Borders. He is a senior business adviser with CEiS and has worked with the organization for four years, providing business consultancy support to social enterprises across Scotland. Prior to joining CEiS, James worked with Motorola Semiconductors for thirteen years.

CEiS's Vision is for communities and individuals who are economically disadvantaged to realize their potential. Our mission is to build and maintain a reputation for excellence in our support to enterprises and in our services to communities and individuals.

INDEX

Page references followed by *fig* indicate an illustrated figure; followed by *t* indicate a table.

A

AAA Magazine, 100, 112

Action while planning: description of, 43–44; PYD's example of successful, 44

Actions: finalizing plan and putting it into, 43; social impact implementation strategy on needed, 37–43; to take while planning, 43–44

Advertising: Canon commercials, 99; description and function of, 99–100; image as driving messages of, 101–102; knowing your donor base to focus, 102–103; lessons learned on effective, 101–108; VFC (Vehicles for Change) approach to, 102. *See also* Marketing

Advertising lessons: advantageous use of news media, 104–105; creating the optimum advertising campaign, 103–104; employ constant creativity, 105–107; using people power, 107–108

Advocacy: expenses related to investing in, 127–128; guiding principles on, 20*t*; lessons learned about, 128–131; public perception shaped through, 10–11; social enterprise need for, 123–126, 132

Advocacy lessons: 1: advocacy is mission imperative, 128; 2: advocacy for good is dangerous, 128–129; 3: and danger from advocacy can be good, 129–130; 4: advocacy is good business,

130–131; 5: make advocacy part of your brand, 131; 6: advocacy builds ownership, 131

Agassi, A., 99, 108

AIDS housing providers, 127–128, 132–133

Alvarez-Rodriquez, D., 201, 211

Amazon.com, 87

Annie E. Casey Foundation, 100, 112

Artin, K., 3, 15–16

Aspen Institute, 45

The Association of Enterprise Opportunity, 64

The Atlantic Philanthropies, 29

B

Baltimore Sun, 100

Baumann, W. K., 47, 64

Beacon, 139

Beecher, H. W., 50

Ben & Jerry's, 172, 173, 214, 216

Berenbach, S., 17

BHAG (Big, Hairy, Audacious Goal), 206

Blackbaud, 136

Boards: aligning staff and, 50–56, 61–64; CEO effective work relationship with, 187–188; CivSoc (fictional name) example of failed, 190–192; good governance by aligning CEO and, 197–199; KidsLINK example of effective governance, 193–194; lessons on reducing risk by effective governance, 192; product/service development tied to needs of, 93–94; shared leadership by CEO and, 196; social venture failures related to, 233, 234; value added by effectiveness of, 195–197. *See also* CEOs; Governance; Leadership

"Bootstrapping," 72

Boys & Girls Clubs, 147

Brand, 131. *See also* Image

"Burn rate," 71

Business ethics principles, 20*t*

Business failures. *See* Social venture closure

Business planning: action to take during the, 43–44; conducting gap analysis, 32; differences between for-profit and nonprofit, 88–89; illustrated overview of, 31*fig*; ITN*America's* experience with, 29; multiple roles played by, 28; outline of an effective, 32–33; process of, 30–43; service and product development using, 91–97; small business development as part of, 52–53; social impact accelerated by effective, 44–45; social impact created through, 27–29; working group and work plan for, 30–31

Business planning steps: 1: planning to plan, 30–32; 2: articulating social impact model, 33–37; 3: developing an implementation strategy, 37–43; 4: finalizing the plan and putting it into action, 43

Business purpose, 88

C

Calvert Foundation, 17, 84

Canon commercials, 99

Capital: collateral issue of, 80–81; distinctions between nonprofit and for-profit sources of, 73, 88; early warning signs related to, 235; growth stage needs and sources of, 76–78; mature stage need for working, 82; problem of mismatched, 67; start-up stage need for equity, 71–73*fig*; survival stage needs and sources of, 74–75. *See also* Financial issues

Casey Foundation, 100, 112

Cash flow issue, 80

CDFIs (Community Development Financial Institutions), 83, 84

CEiS (Community Enterprise in Scotland): lessons on preventing venture failures, 238–239; One Plus's closure supervised by, 231–233; origins and development of, 227–228; social venture closure lessons learned by, 233–238; vision and mission of, 241

Center for Public Leadership (Harvard University), 45

CEOs: as change leader, 201–202, 210–211; CivSoc (fictional name) governance failure by board and, 189–192; effective work relationship between boards and, 187–188; good governance by aligning board and, 197–199; KidsLINK example of effective governance, 193–194; leadership succession of, 213–225; lessons on reducing risk to effective governance, 192; risk-management strategy by, 189; value added by shared leadership of board and, 196. *See also* Boards; Governance; Leadership

Champions: characteristics of, 60; staff-board alignment and role of, 58–60

Change: CEO leadership role in, 201–202; customer feedback driving, 144–146; Goodwill Industries case study on, 202–205; leading from the inside out, 210–211; lessons learned on, 205–209

Change lessons: 1: budget enough time and mental space, 205–206;

2: make internal communications a priority, 206–207; 3: pay attention to how much space you take up, 208; 4: never compromise on vision or values/tactics are OK, 208–209; 5: have a point of view, 209

Chen, N., 135, 148

The Chicago Federal Home Loan Advisory Board, 64

Chrysalis Enterprises case study: background information on, 89–90; expanding and developing services, 90–91

Chrysalis Green, 91, 94

Chrysalis Works, 90

Chrysalist Staffing, 90

CivSoc (fictional name): background information on, 189–190; governance failure by, 190–192, 199

Collateral issue, 80–81

Communication: image as driving advertising, 101–102; leadership succession and role of, 223–224; priority of internal, 206–207; during venture closure process, 237–238. *See also* Feedback

Communities In Schools, 147

Community Enterprise in Scotland. *See* CEiS (Community Enterprise in Scotland)

Community guiding principle, 20*t*

Competitive advantage criteria, 13

Consumer Federation of America-America Saves, 64

Convio, 136

COOs (chief operating officers), 217, 221, 224

Customer Relationship Management (CRM), 137

Customer service: building corporate culture of, 117–118; definition of, 111; importance of providing good, 111–112; strategic development of, 113–114; two important lessons of, 118–120. *See also* Service development

Customer service lessons: 1. treating customers "right" creates assets, 118–119; 2. convert problems/complaints into sales tools, 119–120

Customers: advertising driving behavior of, 99–100; distinctions between nonprofit and for-profit, 89; feedback from, 142–146; identifying what is valued by your, 9; impact of social venture on your, 14; knowing your, 116; marketing to your target market of, 114; "tipping point" generated by satisfied, 107

CWAC (Coffee With A Conscience): adventurous approach of, 63–64; champions at, 58–60; introduction to, 47–48; lessons learned from staff-board alignment at, 50–63; origins and early development of, 49–50; WWBIC parent organization of, 48–49. *See also* WWBIC (Wisconsin Women's Business Initiative Corporation)

D

Dashboards. *See* Performance dashboards

Decision making: effective governance and, 197; guiding principles on, 20*t*; using performance data to drive, 153. *See also* Leadership

Dell Computers, 203

Diversity guiding principle, 20*t*

Dogramaci, O., 135, 148

Donor base study (2005), 102–103

Dorten, D., 170–171

Durham Herald-Sun, 10

E

eBay Giving Works program: continuous search for improving, 141–142; description of, 135–136; GEFN (Good Enough, for Now) approach of, 141, 145, 147; how it works, 138–139; improvements in convenience of, 139–140; making changes based on customer feedback, 144–146

Economic impact indicators, 156–157

ECT Group, 240

Electronic Commerce: Technical, Business, and Legal Issues (Dogramaci), 148

Emerging 200 (e200) Initiative, 151–152

Employees. *See* Staff

Enterprises. *See* Social enterprises

The Enterprising Kitchen, 22

Entrepreneurial Culture Pop Quiz, 53, 54*e*–55*e*

Environment guiding principle, 20*t*

Equity capital: description and sources of, 71–73; spectrum of social capital market finance tools for, 73*fig*

Ethics principles, 20*t*

Expected outcomes, 36

F

Facebook, 139

Feedback: making changes based on customer, 144–146; value of customer, 142–143; ways of gathering customer, 143–144. *See also* Communication

Financial issues: advocacy expenses, 127–128, 130; case flow, 80; collateral, 80–81; controlling "burn rate," 71; distinctions between nonprofit and for-profit, 73, 88; early warning signs related to, 235; five Cs of credit, 78; four distinct stages of enterprise development, 68–82; limitation criteria, 13; organizational capacity for sustainability, 39–40, 79–80; self-sustaining funding approach, 127–128, 129–130; shifting revenue to predictable funding sources, 40–41*fig. See also* Capital

Finnie, J., 227, 228, 241

Five Cs of credit, 78

501c3 corporation, 5

Focus groups, 143

For-profit sector: differences in planning nonprofit and, 88–89; financial distinctions between nonprofit and, 73, 88. *See also* Non-Social Enterprises (NSEs)

Freedom Wheels: building business on exemplary service, 112–118; important customer service lessons learned by, 118–120; marketing approach used by, 115–118; origins and development of, 100–101, 113; using people power to market, 107–108.

See also Vehicles for Change (VFC)

Freund, K., 29

Fruchterman, J., 27

G

Gap analysis, 32

GEFN (Good Enough, for Now), 141, 145, 147

Genchi Genbutsu (go and see) principle, 147

Giuliani, R., 128–129

Gladwell, M., 107

Gleitsman Visiting Practitioner in Social Innovation, 45

Good Capital Fund, 72–73

Goodwill Industries: converting costs to profits, 202–204; mission and vision of, 205; staying true to mission, 209

Governance: CivSoc (fictional name) example of failed, 190–192, 199; decision making role in effective, 197; guiding principles on, 20*t*; KidsLINK example of effective, 193–194, 199; lesson learned on good, 238–239; lessons on reducing risk by effective, 192; minimizing risk by due diligence of, 188; organizational capacity for, 39; social enterprise and CEO-board aligned, 197–199; social venture failures related to, 233; value added by effective, 195–197. *See also* Boards; CEOs

Governor's Council on Financial Literacy, 64

Grameen Bank, 27

Great Bay Foundation for Social Entrepreneurs, 29

Greater Centennial A.M.E. Zion Church (Mount Vernon), 25, 182

Greyston Bakery: guiding principles of, 21; Lean manufacturing approach of, 172–175; origins and growth of, 26, 182

Gross, T. S., 119

Growth/expansion stage: capital needs and sources during, 76–81; challenges during, 75–76; description of, 69; funding to financing continuum during, 70*fig*

Guiding principles: description of, 19; Greyston Bakery's, 21; mission versus margin balance through, 19, 21–22; sample elements of, 20*t*

H

Habitat for Humanity, 25, 147

Hammond, D., 181

Harvard University, 45

Headwaters Foundation for Justice, 25

Higgins, G., 227, 228, 241

HIV/AIDS housing providers, 127–128, 132–133

Hollender, J., 23

Home Depot, 181

Homelessness: Housing Works advocacy approach to, 126–132; serious social problem of, 125

Hopper, G., 56

Housing Works: advocacy approach taken by, 126–132; advocacy investment made by, 127–128, 130; advocacy lessons learned by, 128–131; HIV/AIDS housing advocacy of, 127–128, 132–133; self-sustaining funding approach of, 127–128, 129–130; structured as membership corporation, 126–127

How-to Guide: Business Planning for Enduring Social Impact (Root Cause), 45, 154, 168

Hunger problem, 124–125

I

ICE (InnerCity Entrepreneurs), 151–152

Image: advertising messages driven by, 101–102; continual process of building your, 108–109; grounded in reality criteria of effective, 100–101; importance of your, 99; making advocacy part of your brand and, 131;

VFC (Vehicles for Change), 100–101. *See also* Reputation

Impact. *See* Social impact

Independent Transportation Network, 29

Intake forms, 159

Internal Revenue Service: 501c3 regulation of, 5; nonprofit regulations by, 72

ITN*America,* 29, 41–42

ITNRides, 41–42

J

Jacokes, J., 67, 83–84

Jatczak, J., 47, 64–65

Johnson Bank New Markets Tax Credit Advisory Board, 64

Jones, D. T., 171, 172, 174

Juma Ventures: communication with stakeholders during succession at, 223–224; leadership succession in, 214–217; previous CEOs' role in leadership succession, 222–223

K

KaBOOM!, 181

Kaizen: description of, 176; process of using, 178–179

Kelly, M., 170–171

Key Performance Indicators (KPIs), 239

KidsLINK, 193–194, 199

King, B. J., 58

King, C., 123, 132–133

King, M. L., Jr., 211

Kopp, W., 27

L

Leadership: change, 201–211; product/service development and issue of, 96–97; social venture failures related to poor, 234. *See also* Boards; CEOs; Decision making

Leadership succession: communication as key during, 223–224; importance of, 213–214; Juma Ventures case study on, 214–217; lessons learned from, 218–223

Leadership succession lessons: 1: timing is everything, 218–219; 2: transition creates opportunity, 219–220; 3: continuity is crucial, 220–221; 4: let leaders lead, 221–223

Lean manufacturing: description of, 171–172; Greyston Bakery approach of, 172–175; seven kinds of waste to avoid with, 174*t*; tool belt of, 175–179; waste not as core principle of, 172

Lean social enterprise: mission delivery of, 180; scaling the, 181

Lean Thinking (Womack and Jones), 171

Lean tool belt: inventing your enterprise's, 175–176; Kaizen as, 176, 178–179; SS as, 177, 179; value-stream mapping as, 176, 177–178

Limbaugh, R., 144

Loranger, M. J., 87, 98

Lorenz, C., 135, 147–148

Lovins, H., 203

Lynch, K., 17, 24, 25, 169, 182

M

MacArthur Foundation, 27

McDonald, K., 4, 7

The Machine That Changed the World: The Story of Lean Production (Womack, Jones, and Roos), 171

McSense, 240

Marketing: creativity approach to, 105–107; distinctions between nonprofit and for-profit, 89; Freedom Wheels' approach to, 115–117; organizational capacity for, 41; people power approach to, 107–108; of staff-board alignment around venture, 61–63; targeting your primary market for, 112. *See also* Advertising

Markets: knowing the size and trends of your, 114–115; targeting your primary, 112

Mature stage: capital needs and sources during, 82; challenges during, 81; description of, 69; funding to financing continuum during, 70*fig*

Milliken, S., 135, 147

Milwaukee Art Museum, 59

Mission: aligning social venture with your organizational, 3–4; allowing social enterprise to be driven by, 97; of CEiS (Community Enterprise in Scotland), 241; connecting product or service development to, 87, 92–93, 94–96; criteria for aligning social venture with, 12–14; definition of, 3; financial leverage of your, 23–25; Lean social enterprise delivery of the, 180; performance measurement linked to, 154; social venture failures related to ignoring, 233; staying true to the, 209. *See also* Vision

MISSION, INC., The Practitioners Guide to Social Enterprise (Lynch and Walls), 26, 182

Mission statement, 36

Mission versus margin balance: description of the issue, 17–18; guiding principles of balancing, 19–22; leveraging mission to reach, 23–25; practicalities beyond principles for, 22–23. *See also* Profitability

MissionFish: eBay Giving Works program of, 135, 138–146; GEFN (Good Enough, for Now) approach of, 141, 145, 147; specific improved changes made by, 146; technological advances embraced by, 135–136; technological lessons learned by, 136–146

MissionFish technology lessons: 1: don't go it alone, 136–139; 2: make your service convenient and relevant, 39–140; 3: focus on "what" and not "how," 140–142; 4: ask your customers what they want, 142–144; 5: trust the data and make the change, 144–146

MissionFish UK, 139

Monitoring and evaluation (MAE), 239

Moore, Rev. Dr. W. D., 25, 182

Morgan Stanley, 84

N

Napoleon Bonaparte, 61

Need and opportunity analysis, 35

Net Impact, 225

Network for Good, 136

Neuberger & Berman, 84

New media, 104–105

Nike, 107

Non-Social Enterprises (NSEs), 169–171. *See also* For-profit sector

Nonfinancial resources, 40

Nonprofit sector: capital markets for, 72–73; differences in planning for-profit and, 88–89; financial distinctions between for-profit and, 73; four stages of development/financing in, 68–82. *See also* Social enterprises

NxLevel Education Foundation, 64

O

OASIS Institute: indicators driving performance at, 157–158; social impact strategic goals of, 38–39

Office of the Scottish Charity Regulator (OSCR), 228

One Plus case study: background information on, 228–229; CEiS's supervision of One Plus closure, 231–233; financial difficulties of, 229–231; key financial indicators of, 230*fig*; lessons learned from, 233–238, 240; services provided by, 229

Operating model: continual progress of, 37; distinctions between nonprofit and for-profit, 89; shaping your, 36

Organizational capacity: determining available, 38–43; financial sustainability, 39–41*fig*, 79–80; marketing, 41; performance and social impact measurement, 28, 42; public policy, 20*t*, 42; risk mitigation, 42–43; social venture failures related to, 234; for staff-board alignment, 51–56; team and governance, 20*t*, 39; technology, 41–42

Organizational health indicators, 156

P

Partners for Youth with Disabilities (PYD), 44

Partnerships: business planning to establish, 28; VFC's creative marketing through, 106–107

PayPal "Give at checkout" feature, 139

PCG (Partners for the Common Good), 83

Performance: business planning to measure/monitor, 28; indicators of, 156–158; making external commitment to self-improve, 167; organizational capacity for, 42

Performance dashboards: building, 163–164; determining baselines and targets, 163–164; example of management, 162*fig*; overview of, 161, 163; program-level, 164; purpose of, 161;

regular performance reviews using, 164–165; review and analysis of, 165–166. *See also* Report cards

Performance data: determining how to measure, 158–159; determining where to store, 159–160; preparing to use the, 160–166; quantitative versus qualitative, 157; tools used to collect, 159; whole numbers versus ratio, 157

Performance indicators: data provided by, 157; driving effective behaviors, 157–158; identifying the most important, 163; One Plus key financial, 230*fig*; organizational health, 156; program performance, 156; social and economic impact, 156–157

Performance measurement audit, 155–156

Performance measurement process: 1: planning to measure, 154–156; 2: choosing what to measure, 156–158; 3: determining how to measure, 158–160; 4: preparing to use the data, 160–166; 5: putting performance measurement into action, 166–167

Performance measurement system: five-step process to build, 154–167, 155*fig*; organizational role and cycle of, 152*fig*–153; report cards created from dashboard data, 167; Root Cause's unique, 150, 151–167

Performance measurements: accelerating social impact through, 167; assessing social impact through, 149–150; creating a system for, 149–167; dashboards built from, 161–166; gathering customer feedback for, 143; mission linked to, 154; tools used for, 159; what to consider before taking the, 153–154

Performance reviews, 164–165

Personal development guiding principle, 20*t*

Phone surveys, 159

Pikas, J., 22–23

Positively Outrageous Service (Gross), 119

Pouyat, S., 187, 199–200

Powell, C., 51

Predictable revenue sources: description of, 40; shifting revenue to, 40–41*fig*

Price point, 114

Pricing products/services: determining price point, 114; knowing the competition for, 114; setting appropriate, 120; taking into account costs of goods sold, 114

Produce in America, 170

Product development: Chrysalis Enterprises case study on, 89–91; connecting mission to, 87, 92–93, 94–96; leadership and scalability issues of, 96–97; structured process of business planning for, 91–97

Product development lessons: 1: determine if mission connects to earned-income strategy, 92–93; 2: consider stakeholder needs, 93–94; 3: find intersections between mission and stakeholders, 94–95; 4: identify potential ventures, 95; 5: select and plan the venture, 95–97

Products: appropriate pricing of, 114, 120; development process of, 87–97; venture closure and preservation/transfer of, 236–238

Profitability: leveraging mission to increase, 23–25; as mission-social venture fit criteria, 13; product/service development and acceptable margins of, 95; required for successful social venture, 18. *See also* Mission versus margin balance

Program performance indicators, 156

Program-level dashboards, 164

Program-Related Investment (PRI), 71

"Proof of concept" stage, 68

Pryce, J., 67, 84

Public perceptions: overcoming negative, 11–12; shaped through advocacy, 10–11

Public policy: guiding principles on, 20*t*; organizational capacity for, 42

Public Television's Business Connection and Motor Week, 100, 112

Pursuit of the Dream (documentary), 100, 112

PYD (Partners for Youth with Disabilities), 44

Q

Qualitative performance data, 157

Quantitative performance data, 157

R

Ratio performance data, 157

Rebuild Resources, 24, 180–181, 182

ReCompute, 204

Report cards, 167. *See also* Performance dashboards

Reputation: considering how social venture will impact, 14; TROSA's social venture impact on their, 10–12. *See also* Image

Resources: business planning to acquire, 28; nonfinancial, 40;

shifting revenue to predictable funding sources, 40–41*fig*

Responsible Minnesota Business, 25

Risk: lessons on governance to reduce, 192; minimized by due diligence of governance, 188; organizational capacity for mitigation of, 42–43

Risk mitigation, 42–43

"Road show": launching the, 43; planning the, 31–32

Robinson-Humphrey/Salomon Smith Barney, 15

Rocky Mountain Institute, 203

Roos, D., 171, 172, 174

Root Cause: business planning process used by, 30–43; founding of, 45, 168; ICE (InnerCity Entrepreneurs) initiative of, 151–152; mission of, 29; tracking social impact methodology of, 151–152

Root Cause How-to Guide: Business Planning for Enduring Social Impact, 45, 154, 168

S

Salesforce.com, 137

Sam L. Cohen Foundation, 29

Scalability: description of, 96–97; Lean social enterprise and, 181

Schorr, J., 213, 225

Schwartz, M., 99, 109, 111, 120–121

Service development: Chrysalis Enterprises case study on, 89–91; connecting mission to, 87, 92–93, 94–96; leadership and scalability issues of, 96–97; structured process of business planning for, 91–97. *See also* Customer service

Service development lessons: 1: determine if mission connects to earned-income strategy, 92–93; 2: consider stakeholder needs, 93–94; 3: find intersections between mission and stakeholders, 94–95; 4: identify potential ventures, 95; 5: select and plan the venture, 95–97

Service inquiries, 143

Services: appropriate pricing of, 114, 120; development process of, 87–97; venture closure and preservation/transfer of, 236–238

Seventh Generation, 23

Small Business Administration, 45, 65, 87, 151, 168

Social Enterprise Alliance, 15, 25, 65

Social enterprise champion: characteristics of, 60; staff-board alignment and role of, 58–60

Social enterprise stages: growth or expansion stage, 69, 70*fig*, 75–81; mature stage, 69, 70*fig*, 81–82; start-up or seed stage, 68, 70*fig*–73*fig*; survival or establishment stage, 68–69, 70*fig*, 74–75

Social enterprises: advocacy as vital to, 123–126, 132; allowing mission to drive the, 97; characteristics of, 169–170; definition of, 169; four stages of development, 68–82; image building by, 99–101, 108–109, 131; lean manufacturing by, 171–181; as mitigating vs. ending root causes of social problems, 124–126; spectrum of social capital market finance tools for, 73*fig*. *See also* Nonprofit sector; Social ventures

Social impact: accelerated by effective business planning, 44–45; business plans to create enduring, 27–29; guiding principle for, 20*t*; identifying indicators of, 36; indicators of, 156–157; ITN*America's* experience with creating enduring, 29; performance measurement system for assessing, 149–167; Root Cause case study on tracking, 151–152

Social impact measurement: business planning for, 28; organizational capacity for, 42

Social Impact Model: articulating the, 33–37; business planning for, 27–45; envisioning success to develop, 35–36; illustration of work process, 34*fig*; operating model component of, 36, 37; social impact strategies component of, 36–43

Social impact strategies: description of, 36–37; determining organizational capacity to implement, 38–43; development of, 37–43; set the time line for implementing, 37–38; shifting revenue to predictable funding sources, 40–41*fig*

Social problems: identifying ventures best suited to address, 95; mitigating versus ending root causes of, 124–126; need and opportunity analysis for defining, 35; steam shovel metaphor for growth of, 126

Social venture closure: lessons learned on shutdown/service transfer, 235–238; One Plus case study on, 228–233

Social venture failure lessons: 1: on internal governance, 233; 2: on organizational capacity and capability, 234;

3: commissioners and funders, 235

Social Venture Network, 25

Social venture success lessons: actionable advice, 238–239; business failure causes and warnings, 233–235; importance of champions, 58–60; importance of planning and preparation, 51–56; look for unexpected opportunities, 50–51; selling the sizzle, 61–63; on shutdown and service transfer, 235–238; using staff-led model, 56–58

Social ventures: aligning organizational mission to, 3–4; aligning staff and board around, 47–64; criteria for aligning mission with, 12–14; definition of, 4; explaining the "why" of, 55–56; mission and margin both required for successful, 18; product or service development for, 87–97; scaling back or shutting down the, 227–240; TROSA case study on creating and running, 4–12. *See also* Social enterprises

SS: description of, 177; process of using, 179

Staff: guiding principles on, 20*t*; performance measurement system role of, 153–154, 160;

performance reviews of, 164–165; product/service development and minimized displacement of, 95; social venture failures and, 237–238

Staff-board alignment: assessing organizational capacity for, 51–56; *Entrepreneurial Culture Pop Quiz* for engaging, 53, 54*e*–55*e*; looking for unexpected opportunities for, 50–51; marketing the idea of, 61–63; taking an adventurous approach to, 63–64

Stakeholders: leadership succession and communication with key, 223–224; product/service development and buy-in of, 91; product/service development tied to needs of, 93–94; social venture failures and, 237

Start-up/seed stage: challenges during, 70–71; description of, 68; equity capital sources during, 71–73; funding to financing continuum during, 70*fig*

Succession. *See* Leadership succession

Surveys: customer feedback, 143; performance, 159

Survival/establishment stage: capital needs and sources during, 74–75; challenges during the, 74; description of, 68–69; funding to financing continuum during, 70*fig*

Sweet Roots, Inc., 183

Swift, J., 48

T

Target beneficiary, 36

Target market, 114

Taylor, C., 107

Technology: GEFN (Good Enough, for Now) approach to using, 141, 145, 147; MissionFish's innovative use of, 135–147; organizational capacity for, 41–42; Web-based CRM (Customer Relationship Management), 137

Technology service lessons: 1: don't go it alone, 136–139; 2: make your service convenient and relevant, 39–140; 3: focus on "what" and not "how," 140–142; 4: ask your customers what they want, 142–144; 5: trust the data and make the change, 144–146

Tipping point, 107

Toyota Production System, 171, 174

Tracking spreadsheets, 159

Transforming Cities through Civic Entrepreneurs (Harvard University), 26, 182–183

TROSA (Triangle Residential Options for Substance Abusers) case study: background information on, 4–6, 16; double-edged sword of public perceptions during, 11–12; identifying what customers value the most during, 9; moving operations during, 7–8; public perception shaped by social venture during, 10–11; using TROSA Moving to build used furniture business during the, 8–9

Twin Cities Community Gospel Choir, 25

U

Under Armour, 107

U.S. Department of Housing and Urban Development, 83

U.S. News & World Report America's Best leaders list, 27

U.S. Small Business Administration, 45, 65, 87, 151, 168

Usability testing, 143

V

Value addition: board role in, 195–196; shared CEO-board leadership for, 196

Value-stream mapping: description of, 176; process of using, 177–178

Vehicles for Change (VFC): advantageous use of news media by, 104–105; advertising to generate car donations by, 102; building business on exemplary service, 112–118; creative marketing by, 105–107; donor base study (2005) by, 102–103; image created by, 100–101; important customer service lessons learned by, 118–120; optimum advertising campaign created by, 103–104; partnership in marketing approach by, 106–107. *See also* Freedom Wheels

Venture capital investors, 72, 96

Vision: of CEiS (Community Enterprise in Scotland), 241; of Goodwill Industries, 205; never compromise on, 208–209. *See also* Mission

W

Wages guiding principle, 20t

Wall Street Journal, 100

Walls, J., Jr., 17, 25–26, 169, 182

Waste not concept: as Lean manufacturing core principle, 172; seven kinds of waste to avoid, 174t

Web 3.0, 139

Web-based CRM (Customer
Relationship Management),
137
Web-based questionnaires, 159
Whole numbers performance
data, 157
"Widgets" buzzword, 142
Wolk, A., 27, 45, 149, 168
Womack, J. P., 171, 172, 174
Workforce development, 125–126
Working capital, 82

WWBIC (Wisconsin Women's
Business Initiative Corporation): background information
on, 48–49, 64, 65; moving
toward staff-led model, 56–58;
small business development
mission of, 52. *See also* CWAC
(Coffee With A Conscience)

Y
Yunus, M.; 27